NECK OR NOTHING

NECK OR NOTHING

The Extraordinary Life and Times of

BOB SIEVIER

༤༤༤

JOHN WELCOME

FABER AND FABER
London

First published in 1970
by Faber and Faber Limited
24 Russell Square London WC1
Printed in Great Britain by
Ebenezer Baylis & Son Limited,
The Trinity Press, Worcester, and London
All rights reserved

ISBN: 0 571 08466 4

To

D.G.

without whom it would not have been written.

Gratefully.

CONTENTS

8

ILLUSTRATIONS

Author's Note

I wish to express my sincere thanks to all those who so kindly gave me their assistance in the writing of this book, most particularly The Marquess of Ailesbury who guided me to the family history; The Earl of Rosebery who gave me the benefit of his unrivalled recollections of 'The Turf' especially as regards Sievier's reinstatement; The Earl of Birkenhead for giving me permission to use the story of his father and Sievier out hunting and to repeat his father's immortal farewell to the Bicester Hounds; Mr. J. A. Allen who suggested the whole thing and went on to give unstinted help in tracing references and suggesting lines of research; Mr. W. J. Collins to whom Mr. Allen introduced me and whose knowledge of the period and memory for research and references were invaluable; and Miss Rosine de Bounevialle who filled me in so fully on the final years.

I must also acknowledge my debt to the following who, seeing my advertisement in *The Times* or hearing otherwise of the preparation of the book, were kindness itself in answering letters or in supplying recollections or reminiscence: Mr. R. F. Chinnery; Mrs. C. M. Chappell; Miss Monica Deacon; Mrs. Dora Drew; Mr. Guy Deghy; Mrs. Dorothea Duff; Mr. Howard F. Fletcher; the late Mr. Geoffrey Gilbey; Mr. Michael Harrison; Mrs. L. Kathleen Hensley; Col. S. S. Hill-Dillon; Mr. H. L. Hobbs; Lady Howard; Mrs. Cecily E. Locock; Mr. W. Marsh; Mr. Paul E. Mason; Mr. Nigel Morland; Mr. James Morris; the late Major Dermot McCalmont; Mrs. G. R. Page; Dr. T. W. Phillips; Mr. Hew Renshaw; Mrs. Scarlett Sievier; Col. C. MacKenzie Smith; Captain J. H. P. Southby, c.b.e., r.n.; Mr. Maurice O. Springfield.

I must of course make it clear that none of the above are in any way responsible for or to be identified with any opinions I may have expressed or conclusions I may have drawn about the life and times of this remarkable and controversial man, his friends or his enemies.

If, in the above list, I have omitted the name of anyone who has helped it is through inadvertence not intention and I apologize in advance.

Finally I must thank once more Mrs. Saunders of the Writer's and Speaker's Research for her usual unfailing help, and the staff of the British Museum Newspaper Library at Colindale for their courtesy and assistance.

The quotations from Sir Patrick Hastings' *Cases in Court* on page 264 and page 265 are reproduced by the kind permission of Messrs. William Heinemann Ltd. to whom acknowledgment is made.

JOHN WELCOME

I

Born in a Hansom Cab

۶﷼ۻ﷼ۻ

'I was born in a hansom cab and have been going on ever since.'
It was not a bad way to begin an autobiography and that was how
Robert Standish Sievier began his, written at the age of forty-six when
little over half of his turbulent years had passed.

Whether or not he was in fact born in a hansom cab, for throughout
his life his regard for strict truth came second to his love of a striking
phrase or a good story, his childhood and early youth were every bit as
strange and dramatic as his supposed entry into this world.

He was not, however, as was freely said of him when he first made his
mark on the raffish society of mid-Victorian London, illegitimate,
and he took pains to scotch this rumour in the first pages of his
book.

He was born in the year 1860. His birth certificate gives the date as
the 30th May, the place as 10 Lloyd Square, Clerkenwell, and his
parents' names as Robert Moore Sievier and Alicia Maria Mary
Sievier, formerly Sutton. The only odd thing about the birth is that it
was not registered until six weeks after it occurred.

Very little is known of his father save that he qualified as a doctor
but did not practise. His occupation is given as 'Surgeon', and he died
at the early age of thirty-nine when Sievier was five. But the Sieviers
as a family were far from undistinguished. His grandfather, Robert
William Sievier, was a man of extraordinary talents. One of the leading
sculptors of his day, the gigantic crucifix at Alexandra Palace was his, as
were the sculptures outside the old Devonshire House and a statue of
Lord Harcourt in St. George's Chapel, Windsor. The Prince Consort
sat for him at Windsor Castle and he stayed with the Royal Family
while he worked there. Later in life he turned his attentions to science
and medicine and was made an F.R.S. He collaborated with Faraday
in his electrical discoveries and the improvement of telegraphy, invented a loom which the Bright Brothers developed, and discovered a

new method of smelting iron. The final years of his life were devoted to an attempt to find a cure for tuberculosis.

It was from his grandfather that Bob Sievier inherited his brains and his versatility. He also derived from him another less endearing characteristic which appears to have run right through the family—an uncontrollable temper so violent and all-consuming that at times it appeared to border upon brief insanity.

An earlier ancestor bequeathed to him his roving and adventurous nature. In the eighteenth century a Sievier emigrated to America. His son, John, changed his name to Sevier. John, in his youth, was a famous Indian fighter in Tennessee and explored then unknown country, pushing the frontier further west. At least one lake and river are named after him. Later he went into politics and became the Governor of Franklin, a state of the Union which had only a brief existence before being absorbed by Tennessee. The John Sevier Hotel in Johnson City, Tennessee, formerly the capital of Franklin, is named after him.

Sievier's mother was the daughter of Henry Sutton, a Captain in the Army. She was a hard, proud woman and horses and hunting were, at least in her youth, her only passions. In those days she hunted with Thomas Assheton Smith and that formidable man, who did not give praise lightly, called her his Diana.

Sievier, therefore, had solid grounds for his claim that he was at least as well born as many of those who later attempted to deny him the right to enter 'society' or to call himself a gentleman. The time of his youth, adolescence and early manhood was one of shifting social standards. New wealth was beginning to usurp power and to replace the privilege based on birth and tradition. Neither the old nor the new looked favourably on Sievier for he abided by none of their rules. Besides, he chose, when he wished, to run in appalling company and, when in that company, he did some frightening things. Always, and right through his long life, he was the rogue elephant, the joker in the pack, the archetype of the brilliant bad boy who never grew up and the explanation for much of this is to be found in his early upbringing or lack of it.

When Robert Moore Sievier died the family were left very badly off. His mother had some musical talent and she had to put this to what use she could by playing in public. She had little success and appears always to have been resentful at the decline in her fortunes. There were no near male relatives to take care of the boy and Sievier was left mostly in the charge of a series of maiden aunts who spoilt and cosseted him. Passed as it were from aunt to aunt and home to home his early childhood was spent sometimes in town and sometimes in the country. Always precocious, during the latter periods he quickly acquired proficiency in country pursuits. He inherited from his mother an instinctive knowledge of horses, a real love of them and an ability to handle them. This understanding of horses was, later on, to come into frequent conflict with the gambler's itch which possessed him almost from birth but it was there nevertheless despite what his detractors said about his management of his own and other horses entrusted to his care.

His precociousness came out, too, during his time in town. Looking much older than his actual years he was soon wandering off whenever he could into forbidden areas of mid-Victorian London. His mother, who seems never to have really liked or cared for him and to whom he yet remained loyal to the end of her life, thought that the Navy would be the best career for him. An old friend, Admiral Sir William King-Hall whom Queen Victoria favoured because he was a teetotaller, had some influence at Court and thought he could obtain for him an entry into Osborne. Young Sievier, who did not fancy 'staring at the horizon day after day' for the rest of his life, reacted violently to this suggestion as he was to do always to any suggestions which ran contrary to his impulses or desires, the aunts stepped in to rescue him, and it was eventually decided to send him to Doctor Harvey's School at The Château de Lyon at Boulogne. Another old friend, Sir Henry Thompson, came to the rescue when the school bills remained unpaid, but Sievier was a turbulent pupil and did not stay long at school. In later life he was to say that he was expelled, in the end, for making a book on the Derby. For whatever reason there is no doubt that he was soon back on his mother's and his aunts' hands.

Grown bigger now and a singularly handsome youth, his attraction for women already apparent, he was indeed something of a problem. None of the feminine households in which he passed his time had any control over him at all. One of the aunts lived near Ascot and when there he would slip away to race meetings, even then prepared to bet to the limit of whatever he had in his pockets. Back in London he roamed at will in the haunts he had discovered earlier and in others which catered better to a growing taste for sophisticated vice. There were plenty of them, for underneath a superficial veneer of respectability London still preserved or indeed in some instances improved upon and developed most of the trappings of Regency licence. The music halls saw him often as did the billiard parlours where he acquired a proficiency at the game which was to get him both out of and into trouble later on. Cremorne Gardens where the young swells took their fancy women was one of his favourite haunts. It was, in fact, a visit to Cremorne which led to his ultimate breach with the family and his departure abroad. A fancy dress ball was held there on the night of the University Boat Race. Sievier and a friend resolved to attend and Sievier chose to go as Hamlet. By his own account he was such a success with the ladies of the place that he did not notice time passing. Be that as it may eleven o'clock next morning saw a youthful Hamlet being driven down Piccadilly in a hansom cab. Never one to allow a dramatic situation to go past him he took good care that the passers-by appreciated the joke. This, as he remarked, was a part of the play which Sir Henry Irving had apparently cut but which he played with tremendous verve and abandon. This, at least, is one statement of his about his past which there seems no reason at all to doubt.

The exploit could not be kept quiet and a family conclave consisting of his mother and the aunts was assembled to decide what was to be done with him.

Young Sievier—he was only sixteen—had no intention of submitting tamely to the sentence about to be passed upon him. Two friends of his had just then decided to enlist in the Frontier Armed and Mounted Police of South Africa and to sail for that country. Going to see them he found that one of them, a youth called Bloxham, was already regretting his decision and that Bloxham's mother was trying tearfully to dissuade him from going. This was Sievier's opportunity. Impulsive as ever he made up his mind in an instant. Reassuring the weeping mother he told her that he would take her son's place.

The following morning with typical effrontery he went to the office of the agent and explained that he had earlier given a false name, Bloxham, but that he now wished to enrol under his correct name of Sievier. Whilst he was undergoing his medical examination, which he passed with ease, a fresh set of articles was prepared for him. He cheerfully set his hand to these and neither he nor the agent concerned themselves with ascertaining his exact age.

On September 22nd 1876 Trooper Robert Standish Sievier aged sixteen sailed on R.M.S. *Anglian* for the Cape of Good Hope. It was the same ship that had brought out Barney Barnato the founder of the fortunes of his arch-enemies the Joels only three years earlier.

The great adventure of his life had fairly begun.

2

Out and Away

$\twoheadrightarrow\twoheadrightarrow\twoheadrightarrow\twoheadrightarrow$

One who went out the year after Sievier to join the F.A.M.P. has left an account of the voyage in which he states that the recruits, having been given a free passage, were consigned to the steerage. He goes on to describe conditions in which food was so scarce that every meal-time saw free fights where the strongest prevailed and the weaker went hungry and to tell how the voyage took twenty-eight days and was one of the greatest discomfort, hardship and privation.

If Sievier suffered any of this he left no record of it. It seems almost certain, however, that he refused to submit to the restrictions confining recruits to the steerage and managed to penetrate those portions of the ship reserved for higher paying passengers, for he describes how he found opportunity to pay court to some of the prettier women on board and to take a leading part in the ship's concerts. On one occasion, indeed, he gave a solo rendering of *John Peel* and all in all his activities at these entertainments gave evidence already of his fondness for the stage and of the histrionic streak in his character which was never far from the surface. But most of all he played cards, gambling with a recklessness which rode him then as it was to do right up to the end of his long life. He said himself later that if there was nothing more important going on he would be tempted to bet on a match between two tame white mice and R.M.S. *Anglian* saw early evidence of that characteristic.

Napoleon or 'Nap' was the favoured game in the ship's saloon and by the time Sievier reached Capetown he had lost and pledged and lost again all his money, his luggage and possessions including his silver watch and a telescope which he had brought with him for use on the Veldt.

What he had not lost was his self-confidence. As soon as he stepped ashore in Capetown he made straightaway for the billiards room in the best hotel taking with him three other recruits who had been his boon companions on the voyage out. Their total capital amounted to four shillings and sixpence—and the skill of Sievier, aged sixteen, as a billiards player. He promptly entered a game of pool and backed himself to win. Such indeed was his skill that during the afternoon he increased the four and sixpence to six pounds. The following day he was back again with what was left of the six pounds after an evening's drinking. Confident now of his superiority over the other players he took on all comers and ended up with no less than eighty pounds in his pocket. It was the first if far from the last of his big coups and, like all the huge sums that were to follow it, the eighty pounds went straight through his fingers, blown away by a wild night on the town.

The F.A.M.P. in 1876 were a pretty tough lot. Their nominal strength was one thousand men but in fact their numbers rarely exceeded eight hundred. The authorities had some difficulty in keeping the roll up to that number which was why the recruiting drive had been mounted in England and free passages out offered to those who joined. According to one of their members it was the custom in the Colony to say that they 'were broken-down clerks, and young rackety men who had run through their money, and others who were unable to find employment at home'. If Sievier's history was typical it would seem to show that this description was not very far out. Moreover, even had they been at full strength, their numbers were insufficient to carry out the tasks allotted to them. There were in all nine separate posts, a depot and an artillery post, all of which were inadequately staffed and equipped. There were no beds in barracks, no tents for patrol, and no commissariat organisation. The officers, who were popularly supposed by the other ranks to falsify the strength returns in order to feather their own nests with rations drawn for non-existent troops, were frequently drunk on duty and no attempt at training or instruction was made at any time.

None of this was likely to worry Sievier very much, in fact a strictly applied discipline would have no doubt irked him a great deal more. His physical strength made him more than a match for any of his fellows and enabled him to stand up to the hardships of the life. His knowledge of horses stood him in good stead, too. Discipline being so lax the men were allowed to purchase their own horses and he was able to mount himself adequately where others failed and suffered for it.

At headquarters in King William's Town he soon passed through the riding school and was posted to Grey Town where he joined a unit and took part in the usual patrol duties. These were long and hard and the troopers carried on their horses everything they possessed including all their issued rations.

These things would not have bothered Sievier had there been any action, but there was none. The monotony of these long, uneventful patrols alternated with spells in uncomfortable, insanitary barracks with no compensating excitements by way of adventure on the field or romance and entertainment when in town became unendurable to his roving and restless nature. He had become friendly with a doctor at Dordrecht and through him he managed to obtain his discharge.

A spell as assistant to his doctor friend was ended when he compounded sulphate of zinc instead of sulphate of magnesia for a Boer baby. The mistake was only rectified by a hell-for-leather ride to the parents' farm where he arrived just in time to prevent the medicine being administered. This was followed by a short period teaching English to the two daughters of a Boer farmer. The younger of these was pretty and attractive and, to the end of his days, Sievier could not keep his hands off a pretty woman, nor, to be fair, could he keep women away from him. The outbreak of the Kaffir war put an end to this escapade and his seventeenth birthday saw him a sergeant in the Queenstown Volunteers.

Sievier has left a highly-coloured account of his exploits at the Battle of Ibeka, the first engagement of the war, and of his subsequent service. It is sufficient here to say that he ended the war with a reputation for personal bravery, was awarded the special service medal and that he found time in short leaves from the front to own, train and bet on a mare called Snowdrop in some scratch races got up by the troops at Dordrecht. She did not win but she whetted his appetite for owning racehorses and backing them when they ran.

The war over he drew four hundred pounds in back pay and sailed for home in the *Dunrobin Castle*. Near Robben Island the ship struck a reef, the boilers blew up and she sank in twenty minutes. Sievier was one of the survivors and he found himself on the island in the company of a handful of other passengers, male and female in varying stages of undress and nudity. He himself was clad only in a pair of trousers and a military helmet with a spike in it which he was bringing home as a souvenir. Of the four hundred pounds he had lost all but seventy.

The castaways were rescued and brought back to Capetown. Sievier took the next boat to England and arrived to find he had been reported as having been wounded in the jaw.

He was now nineteen years of age, virtually penniless, as hard as nails and with a better opinion of himself than most men. There was, however, the problem of what to do next. His mother was in no position to help. No one at all this time, unlike during his schooldays, appeared to be coming to the rescue financially. Of one thing he was quite determined—a steady run-of-the-mill job was not for him. His adventurous few years in Africa had, in any event, quite unsuited him for one. He resolved to try his luck on the stage.

There was at least one characteristic of Sievier's which was wholly admirable. He was never beaten. Time and again fortune or his enemies appeared to have him on the floor, wrecked, discredited, penniless, broken, with no hope but to sink into poverty-stricken obscurity. Always he fought back and right to the very end succeeded time after time in rehabilitating himself in one differing career or another.

He was a man of no industry whatsoever but of tremendous and versatile talents. His quick brain and ready wit appeared able to adapt themselves to almost any calling towards which his wayward fancy led him. He had been a soldier; now, at nineteen he proposed to turn himself into an actor. Needless to say he had no doubts at all that he could make a success of this new career.

Putting his name on the books of English and Blackmore, theatrical agents, he left his photograph with them and described himself to them as an actor who was 'disengaged'. As he was later to point out, since he had never had an engagement, this was true enough. He bought—without paying for it—as much of a wardrobe as he thought he would need and in a remarkably short time found himself a 'utility man' in the Theatre Royal, Dublin, at a salary of thirty-five shillings a week. Being a 'utility man' entailed playing walking-on parts of all sorts most of them without a line to deliver. This sort of obscurity never came easily to Sievier and he must have been something of a trial to his fellows as he sought to convert these silent parts into talking ones by inventing his own lines and creating opportunities to use them.

After the Dublin season ended there came short periods of work at Nottingham and Plymouth. During the time at Plymouth he made his first appearance in the witness box and had his first brush with the law. It was a minor triumph. He was far more successful in the box than in any of his appearances on the stage and it seems to have whetted his appetite for more.

Some members of the Company including Sievier and the prompter, Fitzroy, were taking what he describes as a stroll after the hotels were closed. Just what they were up to Sievier does not say but it is safe to assume that it was a great deal less innocent than he infers. At all events they encountered the police, whatever Fitzroy did it drew attention upon him, he was arrested and charged with obstruction and using language calculated to lead to a breach of the peace.

When the case came on the solicitor whom the company had instructed to defend Fitzroy was not at all anxious to allow Sievier to give evidence on behalf of his client. In this he shared the fears and apprehensions of many more distinguished advocates who were to follow him in acting for Sievier down the years. As a witness he was dangerous to a degree, to his case, his counsel, himself and anyone for whom he was appearing. He was unpredictable, he said too much, he was always anxious to score a point, he could not let a joke go past him and his temper was too ready to hand. In fact right to the end of his days he regarded a law court as a theatre—his theatre—and himself an actor playing a leading part, than which there is for a litigant no more dangerous delusion. Even at the age of nineteen these traits were apparent and the solicitor, who appears to have been a man of some experience and ability, had recognized them.

The case went badly from the beginning. Fitzroy's fellow members of the company were hazy in their recollection whereas the police were not. Feeling that he could not make matters worse and might just possibly make them better the solicitor decided to call Sievier.

This was exactly the sort of situation Sievier loved. Here was a challenge, a losing battle that might be won, a chance to excel, an opportunity to flaunt authority and to occupy the centre of the stage, all at the same time.

At the end of his evidence-in-chief which he gave comparatively quietly and which bore out what Fitzroy had said, the chairman of the magistrates leant towards him and asked him if he had heard any bad language used.

It was the moment for which Sievier had been waiting. 'Yes', he said.

The solicitor saw his worst fears realized and poor Fitzroy thought his friend had taken leave of his senses. But Sievier, as usual, was both acting and gambling. He knew the answer would cause a sensation and he gambled that another question would be asked which would give him the chance he wanted. It is a dangerous gamble to take in court but this time he was right.

'What did you hear?' asked the chairman.

'I heard that policeman over there call us a lot of bloody actors!'

That answer won the case. Unfortunately for Sievier it did more. It established in him a contempt for the law and lawyers which he never lost and which was to cost him dearly later on. 'The one witness who was originally not to be called,' he wrote when telling of this event, 'saved the situation. So much for the law.' But he had set himself a very dangerous precedent.

After a short engagement at the Haymarket Theatre he was offered the chance of going to India to play at the Gaiety Theatre, Bombay. He was still only nineteen and he jumped at it.

On the boat he ploughed a wide furrow through the strict rules of class and caste that prevailed in P & O liners. He made the most, too, of his opportunities with those wives who were returning to a life of boredom and emptiness on lonely hill stations. Once ashore he found that the chit system and the ready availability of credit and moneylenders allowed him, despite his lack of resources, to live a life of ease and luxury such as he had not dreamt of at home. He kept up an establishment, he went racing and gambling and enjoyed everything that credit could buy. This and the tendency, already strong in him, to make influential enemies, brought about his downfall.

Fancying himself slighted by Hewitt, the chief comedian of the company, who left him without a cue during a scene, he resolved to take his revenge. To do so he had to wait his opportunity but this he was prepared for. Time never mellowed Sievier's antagonisms. He was one of the few people of whom it could truly be said that he never forgot and never forgave. Real or fancied wrongs or insults were all totted up and stored in the recesses of a singularly retentive memory.

A few days later in another play he was due in his turn to cue the comedian. He did so and as Hewitt opened his mouth to speak Sievier went straight on into a speech of his own which he had prepared for the occasion. The comedian was left open-mouthed and stranded on the stage. It did not improve their relations nor Sievier's chances of getting parts. Finally his engagement and his credit ran out together.

His principal creditor pursued him to the steamer and even chartered a boat to chase the departing debtor down the bay. It was only the intervention of a friendly chief engineer who hid him, he says, in the propeller shaft which saved him from arrest. He was not quite twenty years of age.

3

Paying the Piper

꙳꙳꙳꙳꙳꙳꙳

Now there was the piper to pay. And there was precious little with which to do it. Indeed right to the end of his long life Sievier never did quite pay the piper, who was still standing waiting by his bedside when he died. He was extraordinarily naïve about money, another instance of the strain of perpetual adolescence which ran so strongly through his character. In all his numerous escapades and bankruptcies he tried to preserve a highly individual code of his own. This was that he would pay or do his best to pay and indeed mostly did pay those who had been kind to him, given him extended credit or avoided harrying him when times were bad. But let a tradesman or other creditor press him or dun him or serve him with a writ then they had—he said—forfeited his goodwill and were cast into outer darkness to recover their money as best they could. He always, also, believed in borrowing from Peter to pay Paul and as time went on his finances became so involved that no one, either in the bankruptcy court or elsewhere, ever succeeded in unravelling them. None of this at any time effected a reduction in his standard of living and much later he was to swear in evidence that from this year forward almost to the end of his life he never lived at a rate of less than £5000 a year and more often his expenditure was well over £10,000. The comparative figures in the present day would be at least £50,000 and £100,000.

On his return to London, again penniless and in debt, he took up bachelor quarters in the fashionable Week's Hotel in Dover Street and looked around for someone to succour him in his immediate financial difficulties. His uncle, a parson, to whom he had wired for help from the boat, had already turned him down. His mother's response, too, was cold. In any event she was in no position to pay his debts for her own circumstances were far from good. At last help came. The Vicar of Keswick, an old family friend, advanced him enough to clear off his Indian commitments. That done he settled down to enjoy life in London.

For anyone with a good appearance, a ready manner and the accents of a gentleman—and Sievier had all of these—credit in London then was easy and ample. Hatchett's coffee room just across the way was a sort of club for the *rastaquère* elements of the racecourse, the stage and the sporting life. Gentlemen riders, unemployed actors, younger sons, and those of the merchant princes who were racing men all frequented it. They soon accepted the young Sievier as a boon companion and he made free of their company.

Very shortly, too, he had some money at his disposal for one of the maiden aunts, who was horrified at the thought of his returning to the stage, decided to make him an allowance. By now his thoughts, prompted by his love of gambling and horses, were turning more and more towards the racecourse. An example of how naïve and inexperienced he still was behind the façade of youthful sophistication, is his losing £40 to the three-card-men on the train back from Sandown. This loss was to have an important effect on Sievier's future. At Esher he found he could not pay and things were looking ugly.

R. H. Fry, then one of the biggest if not the biggest bookmaker in England, was on the train. Fry, who had begun life in a humble way as a draper's assistant, at this time handled the accounts of the richest and greatest of the racing fraternity; he was on familiar and in some cases visiting terms with members of the aristocracy. He lived in style and mixed with the best. He was a kindly, unassuming, friendly man, open-handed and generous almost to a fault, and his books, had they been examined, would have shown losing accounts amounting to tens of thousands whose owners for one reason or another were never pressed.

Sievier went along the train to where Fry was sitting and got into his compartment. Without introduction or preamble he told him who he was and explained his predicament. Fry, apparently attracted by the youngster's presence and audacity, put his hand in his pocket and gave Sievier the forty pounds in notes. The gang was paid off and Sievier's nerve had once more rescued him from an awkward moment.

He never forgot Fry's kindly act. That was the way it was with him. He would pursue an enemy to the ends of the earth and carry personal vendettas beyond all and any bounds of reasonableness but he never deserted a friend or forgot a kindness. He was as quick to remember a good turn as he was slow to forget an injury. The years ahead and his unbroken association with Fry were to bear witness to that.

It was in that year, 1880, that his long love affair with the racecourse really began. It was then that he determined to make it his way of life

24

to master its lore and its details and to adopt it as a career. Two events influenced him in this. The first was Archer's victory on Bend Or in the Derby. Archer, with one arm strapped up as a result of an accident, out-jockeyed Rossiter on Robert The Devil and won a breathless race by a head. Sievier was bewitched by the feat and, indeed, by Archer's abilities and personality. The race impressed upon him the importance of jockeyship and he resolved when racing to keep a weather eye on anything ridden by Archer. He was to profit by this in the immediate future.

The second incident was rather more typical, personal and bizarre.

Fred Gretton was from the North of England; he was a partner in Bass's Brewery, one of the emerging merchant princes and a very rich man. He was also parsimonious, secretive and difficult. In 1873 he had parted company with Mat Dawson, who had up till then trained for him, and sent his horses to John Porter of Kingsclere. Porter at that time had been going through a lean period and for three years Gretton's horses had more or less kept the stable going. But the association between the two men was purely a business one. Porter saw that the horses won when they could, as he was bound to do. Gretton expressed no appreciation of what Porter did for him nor were the customary presents to a trainer ever made. Instead he demanded the strictest accounting when settling the stable bills.

In 1876 Porter bought for Gretton a small, tough colt by Sterling out of Isobella whom they christened Isonomy. The price was 360 guineas and Isonomy was one of the very great bloodstock bargains of the time. He might well have won the Derby as a three-year-old but Gretton, who backed his horses for tremendous sums when they were fancied and who worked his coups in the greatest secrecy, determined to keep him for the Cambridgeshire where he believed he could get the price he wanted. This he duly did, Isonomy won, and so well was the secret kept and the stable commission worked that he started at 40—1. This victory brought Gretton £40,000—or it should have done for the story which delighted the racing world at the time was that, so devious were his methods and such precautions did he take in covering his tracks when striking his main bet, when settling day came he had forgotten the name of the bookmaker with whom it had been made and failed to recover his money.

As a four-year-old Isonomy won four out of his six races but Gretton did not further endear himself to the racing public by scratching him from the Cambridgeshire that year because he considered the odds too cramped to carry his money.

Isonomy only ran twice in 1880. He was entered for the Manchester Cup and given 9st. 12lb to carry, a record weight for that event. As was natural with the previous history of horse and owner there was an immense amount of speculation as to whether he would run at all or, if he did, if he was fancied at that weight and would be backed. He was, in fact, ready to run for his life but no one except Gretton and Porter knew this and the secret, as usual where Gretton was concerned, was well guarded.

But Gretton kept a mistress. She was the barmaid of the Bath Hotel and the Bath Hotel was directly opposite Sievier's rooms. Sievier was accustomed to drop into the Bath for his morning drink and he soon noticed that Gretton, too, was a frequenter. From that it did not take much observation to ascertain that Gretton and the girl were more than mere acquaintances.

Gretton was old and Sievier was young. So was the barmaid. She was also a very pretty girl. Sievier had all the predatory attitude towards women of the lower-classes prevalent amongst men of his type and time. Moreover, as he was self-confident, breezy, humorous and handsome, women fell for him all too easily. Gretton was mean; Sievier was open-handed. He took the girl out to dinner and made love to her. There and then she whispered to him the information he wanted to learn. Mr. Gretton had backed Isonomy.

The next morning with all the money he could lay hands on, some of it in fivers and tenners effected by runners with off-the-course book-makers, Sievier backed Isonomy to win him £3000. When the news came through that Isonomy had won he was drinking in Hatchett's with a few cronies. Immediately he ran into the bar of the Bath. Finding himself alone he shouted 'Isonomy's won' vaulted the bar and roundly kissed the girl.

As always he was generous to those who had helped him. The girl received a handsome present from his winnings—£500—and he showered clothes and hats and gloves on her in profusion. The following Sunday he threw a princely party at Skindle's Hotel at Maidenhead— with the barmaid, decked out in her finery, as the principal guest.

Sievier, as usual, could keep nothing to himself. The story was too good not to be told. Everyone in sporting circles knew of his big win, his flamboyant gesture of the Skindle's party, who the principal guest was and why she was there. Gretton of course heard all about it. Sievier had made another influential enemy.

With the remains of the £3000 burning a hole in his pocket he went racing more enthusiastically than ever, and opened a credit account with R. H. Fry. But he was still very raw and inexperienced and the luck didn't last. He opposed Robert The Devil in the Cesarewitch and that finished him. He couldn't settle.

Fry as usual was sympathetic, but Sievier was determined to find enough money to repay his benefactor. He went to the aunt who had given him the allowance and confided his troubles to her. She paid his debts but she made it a term of this repayment that he should find some gainful employment. The only trade he knew anything of was that of an actor. It was the choice of two evils for his aunt, the racecourse or the stage and, of the two, the stage seemed the lesser one. She did not, however, think that being an ordinary actor was good enough for a Sievier and she actually went to the lengths of setting him up with his own repertory company. It didn't last as nothing lasted with Sievier when he had control of money. His standard of living was far too high for that of the manager of a set of strolling players. By the time the company reached Birmingham there was no money left to pay anyone. It folded and he was back on his uppers again, having lost all his aunt's money as well as his own.

Although he continued to live at Week's and to keep up appearances, breakfasting at Long's in Bond Street off 'a wet devilled sole and champagne cup served with silver mugs' in company which included the Duke of Hamilton and Lord Gerard, that winter was not an easy one. The only money came from a short spell acting at the Haymarket and what the generous and forgiving 'Aunty Minty' was still able to spare him.

Nevertheless May 30th 1881 saw him celebrating his 21st birthday with a champagne breakfast at Long's. Most of the guests were in one way or another connected with racing and, with no assets at all save more credit from the kindly Fry, he himself was soon back on the racecourse again.

He was young, he was brave, he was learning and luck went with him. Soon he had collected enough to repay his aunt and as usual with him when he felt under a personal obligation the debt was paid promptly and in full.

By the time Goodwood came round he was riding high on the tide of fortune. He engaged a personal servant and took rooms at the Old Ship Hotel in Brighton. From there he drove a tandem daily to the course where he entertained his friends to luncheon parties beneath the trees. Already he was becoming something of a figure in racing.

Young, spruce, spry, with a flower in his buttonhole, a ready laugh and a carrying voice, invariably in the company of handsome if flamboyant women and dashing men he was someone to be noticed and talked about. Also he was beginning to acquire the reputation of being a knowledgeable and fearless plunger. He loved it all for he always gloried in being the centre of the stage and at the beginning of this Goodwood meeting he was on the eve of his first big killing.

As has been said he had always a tremendous respect and admiration for Archer. That Goodwood Mat Dawson and Archer brought down a filly from Newmarket called Dutch Oven whom they thought to be a future champion. In the midst of a long luncheon under the trees Sievier recalled having made up his mind to back her. Sending a messenger to R. H. Fry he had £200 each way with him on the filly in the Richmond Stakes. She came home at 6—1 and brought him in £1500. Watching the manner in which she won her race from St. Marguerite, Sievier came to the conclusion that Archer had had a considerable amount in hand. Later in the meeting she ran again in the Rous Memorial, this time set to give St. Marguerite 3 lb. Remembering his reading of the earlier race Sievier reckoned she could do it and backed her once more, this time having £500 on at 3—1. He was right; she won by three lengths. From these two victories he went on betting and winning. In Brighton after the meeting Fry, who never kept to strict settling days, handed him a cheque for £6,000. But this was far from the full extent of his winnings. There was more money from cash investments, too. All in all that meeting must have brought him in close on £10,000. He stayed on for the 'Sussex fortnight' going to the Brighton and Lewes meetings and playing up his winnings. When it was all over he had cleared, it is said, more than £20,000. And he was just twenty-one years of age!

It could not last and it didn't. The luck turned and the fortune he had made went as quickly as it had come. After Doncaster where nothing had gone right he decided to try his luck as a bookmaker. This was his first but far from his last attempt at making a book. None of them save for a few years in Australia later on was anything other than a disaster. He had neither the temperament nor the mathematical ability to make a successful book. He was not a calculating machine. He was a plunger and a gambler. Foxhall, who won both the Cesarewitch and the Cambridgeshire that year, the Royal Welch Fusiliers who backed him to a man, and his own inability to lay-off broke him and his book together. Another long winter stretched ahead.

He weathered it as he weathered most things and he kept his ear to the ground with the result that he obtained information about Paulet, the Lincolnshire winner of 1882, which he backed at a long price. But once again the money thus won did not last. Thinking that England could well do without him for a time he set out for Monte Carlo and Naples. When he saw a liner lying in the Bay of Naples he asked what she was and whither she was bound. Hearing that she was the *Liguria* on her way to Australia he made his mind up in an instant, booked a passage and boarded her. He was off on another adventure.

4

Down Under

The Australia where Sievier landed on his twenty-second birthday May 30th, 1882, was far removed from the prosperous, independent and forward looking country of today. It was then a remote colony, its cities were still in the early stages of their development and many of their principal streets bore a strong resemblance to those of the American west. There was no rail link between Sydney and Melbourne, communication being by road or sea. Federation did not come until the Act of 1900 and there were still customs barriers between Victoria and New South Wales.

It was a rough and ready society. Remittance men and cast-off scions of rich or noble families abounded as, amidst many that were respectable and hard-working, did scallywags of all sorts. The days of Orton, the Tichborne claimant, when surnames could be and were borrowed, assumed or cast away at will had not long passed, if indeed they had passed at all for Sievier very shortly was to adopt another name for his own purposes with consequences which were to follow him for the next forty years.

It was a society with an all-absorbing and engrossing passion—horse racing. Dick Luckman, who was later to become the 'Scout' of the *Daily Express* and who arrived in Australia a year or two before Sievier, has described his astonishment at the open way in which racing was discussed amongst his religious relatives and bets struck by persons such as bank clerks. In the hypocritical atmosphere of Victorian respectability back in England these were people who would have been horrified to talk of racehorses or who might well have lost their jobs had they been seen having a bet.

It was a society which suited Sievier down to the ground. He called no man his master and expected no one to call him such. He had no airs or graces himself and looked for none in the company he kept. The Australians took him for what he was and he took them as he found them. But he had no money, for he had, of course, gone through on the boat what little he had brought with him. Quickly appreciating the universal interest in racing he decided to set himself up as a course bookmaker and to make a book. It was a rash decision indeed in a strange country with unknown horses but he had for once learnt something from his former failure.

A visit to a meeting had shown him that Australian bookmakers would only take bets 'on this and the next', that is to say the punter had to name the winner of not one race but two. Moreover odds were never called but the bookmakers walked about striking bets which they noted down and no cash settlement was made on the course. Thus, even if he won, the punter had to wait for the following day before drawing his money. Sievier saw that if he were to introduce English methods of one bet one win and immediate cash settlement this should give him an enormous advantage in at least attracting a flow of ready money.

For reasons known only to himself but perhaps because he knew the risks he was running and wished to try out his revolutionary methods under a *nom de course* he adopted his mother's name, Sutton, for his first venture. Pronunciation, too, may have had something to do with it. His name was pronounced 'Siveyer' not 'Seevyer' and he may readily have appreciated that he would have some difficulty in conveying this delicate difference to the tough Australian crowd. Once his mind was made up he engaged a clerk and drove out to Morpethville, the Adelaide racecourse. He had virtually no cash resources at all and was setting out to challenge methods of betting hallowed by years of operation in a country where he was unknown. If things did not go right he might well be not only penniless and under a burden of debt but also in some considerable physical danger before the day was out.

All this served only to spur him on. Taking up his stand by the rails he waited until the enclosures were full and then, in his stentorian voice which carried to the farthest corners of the race-course, he announced that he had just arrived from England, that he would bet 'one race, one win' and pay in cash as soon as the winner had weighed in.

People stopped to listen. Having heard, they came to look. Then the more eager began to bet. As they did so others followed. When the news of immediate cash settlement spread, punters swarmed to make their wagers with this curious Englishman who offered such attractive terms. He ended the day winning £1,500.

But the papers got hold of it. He was a true racing sensation. The next day not only did the Adelaide dailies have full reports of his dealings but his name and activities were given wide publicity in all the other states as well. Sutton, it was said, a prominent English bookmaker, had come to Adelaide and revolutionized the ring. Thenceforward he was stuck with the name of Sutton whether he wanted it or not and there were many in Australia, even including the law reporters later on, who were never quite sure which was his correct name, Sutton or Sievier. 'Sutton was the bookmaker and Sievier the gentleman,' was how he blandly explained it all later on.

Following this success he went on to Flemington Racecourse at Melbourne and there Luckman, who had heard of the sensation he had created at Adelaide, saw him 'very well-dressed in new light English tweeds which were our envy, calling the odds fearlessly and taking in a bunch of ready money.'

Luckman had had a series of bad days. He betted with Sievier and his luck turned for he backed three winners in a row. 'When are you going to back a loser?' Sievier asked him as he paid him over the third, and the two men became friendly. A young man called James Duke, who had left Eton in a hurry at the age of seventeen and was spending some time in the colonies for his own good, also had Sievier pointed out to him at this meeting.

A relative of his mother's, a Captain Standish whose father was Sievier's godfather, proposed him for the Victorian Club, the equivalent of the Victoria Club in London. He was seconded by the Hon. William Pearson, the vice-chairman of the Victoria Racing Club and elected without a ballot. He attracted, Luckman noted, a big volume of business and this did not go unremarked or un-envied by the other bookmakers. Nor was it his habit to spare others in success. His dismayed competitors heard from him at the top of his voice and resented it.

Money in great quantities was coming his way now. He was lucky at other forms of hazard, too, and took £500 from a gambler called Lammerse playing dice on the coach going up to Warrambul Races. And when in that golden time the odd bad streak came, his courage saw him through. One day at Randwick he was cleaned out after the third race. He could not refuse to continue betting or he would be for ever discredited and made into a laughing stock by his enemies and the other members of the ring. He turned to the crowd about his pitch and told them bluntly that there could be no cash settlement by him that day but that if they liked he would take their bets and pay the following afternoon. The sporting Australian crowd delighted in his frankness and accepted his terms. He won seven hundred pounds on the next three races and settled in full the next day.

His success in Australia was founded on three things, his instinctive knowledge of horses and an almost uncanny ability to sum up their characteristics in an instant, his study of form and his skill in reading a race. As a bookmaker and a manipulator of figures he was quite hopeless. But in that year and the few that followed when things were running right for him those three qualities mentioned above, coupled with his courage, were enough to see him through.

Known everywhere as 'the Englishman' he collected a large following wherever he went. His great voice, cheery presence and unfailing nerve made him a personality to be admired or feared on racecourses all over Australia. Despite everything they could do, and in some instances this even came to physical violence, the other bookmakers could not stop him. But in the middle of all this tremendous success he committed one dreadful error—he married.

Marriage was never made for Sievier nor Sievier for marriage. It is said that some people who care greatly for animals and have an affinity with them—and Sievier had—are incapable of being good to a woman. Certainly Sievier treated his wives disgracefully and his mistresses not much better. Yet he could and did charm women time and time again. The mighty voice could be modulated to terms of tenderness; his extraordinary eyes, full of expression, which in his tempers shot out what almost seemed to be sparks of living rage, could be turned when he wished to softness, sympathy and true kindness. He was a lover of women but not of one woman.

At all events, going with a friend to a charity bazaar held—of all things—to raise funds for the building of a new wing to a church he saw and was captivated by one of the young ladies behind a stall. She was the daughter of an official in the Government Mining Department at Melbourne and they were married shortly afterwards. He was twenty-two and she a year younger.

By reason of Sievier's occupation it was difficult for the young couple to set up any sort of permanent home. They moved around from furnished lodging to furnished lodging in St. Kilda, Adelaide, Melbourne and Mordialloc. But even so Sievier does not appear to have had any true intention of settling down. With £70,000 in his pocket after his first full season bookmaking in Australia he was enjoying life too much for that. Whether she tried too hard to cage the wild thing she had caught will never be known. Perhaps her parents, too, interfered. There seems to be at least some slight evidence that they did and Sievier was never one to brook interference in his affairs from wherever it came.

The marriage appears to have been a failure almost from the start. In March 1884 she left him and went to her parents' home. There was a short reconciliation and then, on the last day of 1884, they finally parted.

She may have been in love with him. The fact that she came back to him more than once would seem to show that she was. For there were, too, flagrant infidelities. One of these that was well-known and cited in the divorce petition was in 1883 from which a daughter was born in May 1884, the first documented member of Sievier's many illegitimate families.

But apart from his marriage his luck held and for four years he was a prosperous and prominent member of the Turf in Australia. During that time he sent home money to settle his racing and other debts in England and to wipe the slate clean. And although most of the other members of the ring were forced into adopting his methods and hated him for it, and his wife's 'respectable' friends disapproved of what they described as his disreputable activities, it must not be thought that he made only enemies.

The proprieties and those who observed them were always targets for Sievier's scorn. But he was ever ready to help a friend down on his luck or a lame dog. When he had money he was lavish in his assistance to those who he thought needed it or had calls on his bounty. Many a broken-down gambler, jockey or racing man then as afterwards had cause to thank him, and these were loans which were never called in. It was the rich and greedy, then and always, with whom he fought, not the poor and needy. Both classes knew it and loved and hated him accordingly.

In 1886 he resolved to return home for a holiday. Hardly had he landed than he was served with a petition for divorce on the grounds of 'cruelty, desertion and adultery'. He allowed the suit to go undefended. No doubt he wanted his freedom and he says himself that it had been arranged that his wife should divorce him during his absence and that he would not defend the action. This may be so but the wife's affidavit grounding the petition contained some singularly unpleasant charges which were hardly likely to have been included had the divorce been a friendly one, and the fact that he did not answer them was another thing which was to lay up trouble for him later on. In Victorian England to be the guilty party in an undefended divorce action was a social crime to be reckoned with.

Despite the slow communications of those days news of his successes in Australia had come home before him. The young man who had brought English betting methods to the Antipodes and made a fortune from them was something of a celebrity in a small way. He was elected to Boodles' and General Owen Williams, that enigmatic and slightly sinister member of the Marlborough House set who lurks somewhere in the shadows of almost all the great Victorian scandals, made him a member of Sandown Park.

As usual he found himself in the middle of the fastest and gayest of company and the huge sum which he had brought with him from Australia began to slip through his fingers like quicksilver. Newmarket was bad, Epsom was worse, and Goodwood finally finished him. He had taken a house for the meeting and entertained there in his customary style. After dinner each evening they played baccarat, the latest society craze, for high stakes. Not only was he a loser at racing but by the end of the week thousands had gone to his guests across the card table.

The holiday was over and it had not lasted as long as he had hoped. There was nothing for it but to return to Australia and to try to re-make his fortune. He had to borrow £300 from a friend in the K.D.G.'s to pay for his passage out.

But the luck had changed and the golden years had gone. By now, too, the fame he had won was beginning to turn into notoriety. He lost heavily at cards, £5000, for instance, went in one evening at hazard after racing at Flemington. His enemies and those on whose corns he had trodden in the days of his prosperity began to sense that he was not invincible and that he might be brought down.

There was at that time a smashing good horse in Australia called Malua whom Sievier, in recalling the best of those he had known in that country, placed second only to Carbine. Malua was owned by a J. O. Inglis who was an amateur rider and a good one. But the form displayed by Inglis' horses was sometimes erratic to say the least, a fact which affected Sievier's bookmaking transactions and upon which he had commented with some truculence. Malua was in the Adelaide Cup and set to carry a welter weight. There was considerable speculation whether Inglis was going to try with him or not.

Some days before the race, greatly to his surprise, Sievier was approached by Inglis' brother and asked to back Malua for the stable.

This he did and then began to back the horse himself winding up by standing to win £10,000. But he was by no means happy about the affair for he could not understand why he, of all people, had been singled out to put the stable money on. He was less happy still when one of his many informants came to him with the news that the regular stable commissioner was laying against the horse and that Malua was drifting steadily out in the betting.

But it was difficult indeed to get the better of Sievier in a race-course trick. His wits were very much about him and a challenge sharpened them. In Australia in those days jockeys were not forbidden to bet. Sievier knew Ivemy, Malua's rider. He made it his business, naturally enough, to know every horse and jockey in the country. Ivemy liked a gamble, he liked winning and he wanted money.

On the day of the race Sievier did not go to Adelaide but stayed in Melbourne where he was then operating. Instead he wired a trusted friend *Lay Ivemy 2000 to nothing for me against Malua today* thus securing considerable financial benefit to the jockey if Malua won. Win he did, easily at 100—7 beating the 3—1 favourite Conjecture by three-quarters of a length. Ivemy never rode for Inglis again nor was Sievier again asked to do the stable commission.

He crossed swords, too, with his fellows in the Victorian Club when he discovered by accidentally reading a wire in the post office that Nordenfelt, the raging favourite for the Champion Stakes, was unlikely to run owing to a leg injury at work. He kept the information to himself and in the Club backed Matchlock, who was in the same ownership as Nordenfelt, to win him a fortune. In addition he laid heavily against Nordenfelt with the other bookmakers who thought him mad and said so. Two days before the race Nordenfelt was taken out and Matchlock won it. He collected enough at least temporarily to restore his fortunes but his remarks as he did so did not further endear him to his colleagues.

He was living as hard as ever. No day was too long for him. His wonderful constitution saw to that. He trained a few horses for himself with moderate success, went coursing, pursued his occupation as a bookmaker at every sort of meeting including wild up-country places such as Wagga Wagga, and he found time to ride in and win an extra-ordinary steeplechase near Mordialloc which might have come straight from the pages of Banjo Paterson.

His private life was lurid and chaotic and it was during this time that the incident occurred of a man being found dead under the balcony of his house after a riotous card party in which high words had passed between the dead man and Sievier. This incident has never been satisfactorily explained. Sievier in his recollections says the man was not dead at all but asleep. Something serious did, however, happen, and although nothing was ever brought home to any member of the party the incident was used to blacken Sievier in a slander action years afterwards.

By this time he had become disenchanted with Australia and resolved to return home. He had in fact booked his passage when there occurred his first open clash with the Establishment, his row with Lord Deerhurst.

5

Sutton v. Deerhurst

George William, Viscount Deerhurst, was the son and heir of the Earl of Coventry, the Victorian nobleman who gained prominence on the Turf by owning Emblem and Emblematic, full sisters and winners of the Grand National in successive years. Coventry was a kindly, charming man and was generally held to be the epitome of the English country gentleman of the time. The son, however, did not take after the father. Spoilt, arrogant and something of a ne'er-do-well he had failed his Sandhurst entrance and narrowly escaped being sent down from Cambridge. Then he had been packed off to Germany and finally went out to Victoria to cool his heels and to act as A.D.C. to the Governor.

Deerhurst landed in Australia on October 25th 1886 and one of his first official duties was to accompany the Governor to the Melbourne Cup Meeting at the beginning of November. Sievier was at the meeting under the name and guise, of course, of Sutton, the Englishman and leading bookmaker. Since he was a prominent figure on the Turf it may be taken as certain that he was pointed out to Deerhurst who may even have backed with him.

Whether Deerhurst and Sievier met then or not they certainly later on became acquainted and one day a month or so afterwards they were both on the Hurlingham pigeon-shooting ground at Melbourne. Betting ran high on pigeon-shooting at the Melbourne Hurlingham Club in those days. Deerhurst lost the sum of £281 to Sievier and others, and at the end of the day he could not settle. The rules of the club were strict on this point and required cash settlement after each day's shooting. Deerhurst therefore was in an awkward position. Sievier rescued him by settling the amount Deerhurst owed the others in cash himself and allowing his own debt to stand over.

The days passed and he was not repaid. Sievier settled his own debts of honour and expected others to pay him his, or at least to acknowledge them. As no cheque arrived his anger grew. Deerhurst went racing on

New Year's Day and saw Sievier there but made no attempt to settle. Rumours were rife as to Deerhurst's gambling and high play which rumours came, of course, to Sievier's ears. He tried to seek the young man out to effect a settlement, and it soon became apparent that he was being deliberately avoided. Deerhurst spent much of his time at the Melbourne Club of which Sievier was not a member. On enquiring for him there he found that Deerhurst had gone to the lengths of instructing the hall porter not to reveal his presence on the premises. Eventually Sievier put a watch on the Club and, on finding that Deerhurst was indeed there, sent in a note peremptorily demanding settlement. As a result Deerhurst made an appointment to meet him at nine o'clock that evening when, so he said, he would pay his debt. But Deerhurst, having defaulted in paying, failed also to keep the appointment.

By now Sievier was furious; once more he ran Deerhurst to ground in the Club. Cornered, Deerhurst asked for time. Not unreasonably Sievier suggested that he be given a post-dated cheque. This suggestion was answered with the scarcely original excuse that Deerhurst had not got his cheque book with him. Sievier then said that a cheque form could easily be obtained in the Club. Thereupon Deerhurst lost his temper, high words ensued and Sievier left. The next morning he received the following letter:

> Melbourne Club. Sir,—I shall be in a position to pay you before Friday 12 noon. In the meantime post me, and be damned.—DEERHURST

It would appear that Viscount Deerhurst put his own liberal interpretation upon the rules for payment of debts of honour.

For Sievier this letter was the last straw. Not only was his money being denied to him but the young sprig of the nobility had the temerity to insult him as well. He immediately resolved to get his money come what might and to avenge himself for the gratuitous insult contained in the latter portion of the letter.

His first step was to report Deerhurst to the Secretary of the Victorian Club of which Deerhurst was an honorary member. This may not have been a very wise move for the majority of the members of the Victorian Club were also members of the ring, whom Sievier had treated with scant respect ever since his arrival in Australia and from whom he had taken several fortunes. Moreover the Ivemy and Nordenfelt affairs and his outspoken retailing of them still rankled. Also, lords were lords in those days and Deerhurst was, besides, A.D.C. to the Governor. The Secretary replied asking him to give Deerhurst more time.

By then Sievier had already written to Deerhurst as follows:

> Sir,—I am in receipt of your letter. I shall be pleased to receive the amount you are in my debt for settling your account at Hurlingham and will answer the latter portion of your letter when I meet you in person.—Yours, etc.

Deerhurst now began to become frightened. He sent a message to say that he would telegraph home for the money. In fact he borrowed it from a friend and paid up.

But Sievier had not done with him yet. The insult of telling him to 'post and be damned' still rankled. And with Sievier when insults rankled action sooner or later invariably followed.

Things came to a head on February 19th 1897. Deerhurst and Patrick Agnew, the secretary of the Club who aped his betters by wearing an eye-glass and affecting the manners of a swell, had dined at the club and gone on to the theatre to see a performance of *Siberia*. From the theatre they repaired to the private bar of Gallagher's Family Hotel in Bourke Street. This was then a favourite rendezvous of sporting and racing men. They were alone in the bar for a little time and then Sievier and two others came in.

Exactly what brought Sievier there that evening is in dispute. It was stated later on in the appeal that Deerhurst had told Sievier to meet him there and had invited friends along 'to see the fun he was going to have with Sutton'. Deerhurst and his faction, on the other hand, contended that Sievier had discovered that he was in Gallagher's and had come determined to pick a fight. From whatever reason a confrontation took place.

Sievier asked Deerhurst if he could speak to him privately and received the contemptuous reply that whatever he had to say could be said then and there.

'Very well, my lord,' Sievier answered. 'If you wish it publicly, publicly you shall have it.' He then asked him, why, when owing him money, Deerhurst had told him to go and be damned for it.

Deerhurst replied; 'I said it, and I'll say it again.'

'Very well, you will either have to withdraw that or to leave the bar,' Sievier told him.

Deerhurst then did something quite extraordinary. So extraordinary was it that it does at least give some appearance of being premeditated.

He raised his right hand, whether he actually clapped Sievier on the shoulder was subsequently in dispute, but his words were not. 'I am a captain in Her Majesty's Police Force,' he said, 'and I place you under arrest.' He was not, in fact, a captain in any police force and had no powers of arrest, and when his own counsel at the subsequent hearing referred to him as 'an impetuous, foolish young fellow who had played a very curious and foolish part,' he was making a considerable understatement.

Sievier did not even bother to hit him. He slapped his face.

Deerhurst then said, and the words can stand without comment to testify to the sort of man he was: 'Remember you are hitting not only a gentleman but an officer,' and, turning to Agnew who had not been making matters any better by standing about twirling his eyeglass and making contemptuous remarks about Sievier such as 'What's all this about? You have got your money, haven't you?' Deerhurst went on; 'If Mr. Sutton was a gentleman I would give him a hiding'.

At this, so Deerhurst said, Sievier rushed at him and took him by the throat. One of Sievier's friends pulled him off and averted further damage. Deerhurst then left the room 'rather more quietly' as Sievier described it, 'than I should have done.' If Deerhurst had indeed set a trap for Sievier he had found that he had caught a tartar, as others who sought to trap Sievier were also to find in the years to come.

The matter was trivial enough and should have been left there. Unfortunately Deerhurst, smarting under hurt pride, could not let it rest. The young Earl of Dudley in the course of a tour round the world in the steam yacht *Marchesa* was then visiting Australia. To him Deerhurst took his troubles and laid his version of the facts before him. It is significant that he did not at any time consult the Governor. He could hardly have chosen a worse counsellor than Dudley.

William Humble Ward, second Earl of Dudley, was later to attain some prominence as Lord-Lieutenant of Ireland and Governor-General of Australia though he never, perhaps, was big enough for the greatness thrust upon him. At this time he was twenty years of age. He had raced a bit under the *nom de course* of 'Mr. E. Wardour'. The reasons for his adopting this pseudonym were never disclosed but they may have been to conceal his activities on the Turf from his father. There was a history of reluctance to settle in the family and considerable pressure had had to be applied to compel the first Earl to pay his debts in the year of Kisber's Derby. Sievier himself described Dudley pretty accurately when he said of him that he was, 'an autocrat by inclination but scarcely a sahib by attainment.'

On hearing Deerhurst's sorry tale Dudley appears immediately to have decided that the peerage must close its ranks and that privilege must be protected by any means within his power. It did not seem to matter to him that Deerhurst had sought to evade payment of a debt of honour. He was a peer and, as such, above the obligations of ordinary men. Instead of telling him to forget the whole matter Dudley advised Deerhurst to report Sievier to the committee of the Victorian Club. Deerhurst made his complaint and, although the conduct of which he accused Sievier had nothing to do with betting, the committee expelled him without a hearing.

Dudley and Deerhurst must then have thought that that finished the matter and Sievier too. They had procured his dismissal from the bookmakers' club with all its attendant rights and powers so far as making a book, laying-off and settling were concerned. No longer could he use the club for the conduct of his business, the adjusting of his book and the finalizing of his bets, nor could he avail himself of its services. By and large they had to all intents and purposes stripped him of his livelihood. And it had all been done by others for them without exposing themselves to any publicity, by a mere exercise of pressure behind the scenes. They reckoned without their man. Sievier, as always, struck back. He caused a summons for assault to be served on Deerhurst. The process server caught up with Deerhurst on the racecourse, as no doubt Sievier hoped he would, thus ensuring that the matter would receive the maximum publicity. Forced into the open at last, Deerhurst issued a cross summons, also alleging assault.

The case came on for hearing on March 10th 1887 in the Melbourne District Court. In the interval Sievier did not further endear himself to Government House circles by proclaiming loudly and in public that what he should have done was to have put the A.D.C. over his knee and spanked him.

To realize just what Sievier had done and was about to do in taking on Deerhurst and the assembled ranks of privilege behind him it is necessary to cast oneself back into the social climate of the eighties. This is not an easy task nowadays when the aristocracy has long been stripped of the exercise of power.

In 1887 England and her Empire, which was rapidly approaching its apogee, were under the rule of a hierarchical oligarchy. Britain ruled the world and the aristocracy ruled Britain. The House of Lords then possessed power that was both real and absolute and was to continue to do so until deprived of it by Lloyd George in the early years of the following century. Not only did it possess power but it exercised it, ruthlessly, and in some cases—that of Irish Home Rule, for instance—in the personal and particular interests of its members and against the will of the nation as expressed by its elected representatives in the Lower House. Most of the ruling caste still lived in semi-feudal pomp on great estates presiding despotically over enormous retinues of servants and dependants. Dismissal from one of these establishments without a reference— and such dismissals or the threat of them were arbitrarily employed, often for selfish or sexual ends, for *droit de seigneur* or something very like it was still far from unknown—meant literal ruin for those who suffered it. Without prospect of further employment they sank quickly into the scum which lay close beneath the glittering surface of Victorian high life.

The bearer of a noble name had a passport given him at birth to arrogance and privilege exercised at will and without responsibility. Often amongst the better-natured these qualities were latent and unconscious and put to use more by thoughtlessness than with deliberate intent but they ran right through the whole aristocratic concept of society, sometimes accompanied by a broad streak of cruelty inherited from Regency times. All this was then given unquestioning acceptance by the many varying inferior classes and strata that made up the nation. An aristocrat was a man apart, subject to his own rules, born to deference and entitled to respect, and he who challenged these tenets did so at his peril. The conduct of Deerhurst and Dudley throughout the events leading up to this case, Deerhurst's behaviour during and after it, and the influence Dudley was to exert against Sievier later on, bear striking testimony to all this.

The court, as might be expected, was crowded on that mild day in March. Almost every magistrate who could sit on the bench— twenty in all under the chairmanship of a Mr. Panton—had turned up to hear the case. More important however to its conduct and ultimate decision was the fact that the Earl of Dudley, Deerhurst's confidant and adviser, also arrived and was promptly accommodated with a seat beside the magistrates, a fact which did not go unnoticed by Sievier's counsel. Sievier was represented by a Mr. Duffy and Deerhurst by no less than two counsel, Mr. Purves and Mr. Stawell. Since he could not afford to pay his gaming debts one rather wonders who discharged their fees. It is of interest, too, that Sievier was referred to as Sutton throughout and that is the name under which the case is reported.

It became immediately apparent when Sievier was cross-examined, that the object of Deerhurst and his advisers was not so much to question the facts but to discredit Sievier in any manner they could.

'Are you divorced?' Mr. Purves asked him and, when he was answered that this was the case, went on: 'Are you living with any woman at present?'

Mr. Duffy rightly objected to this but Mr. Panton, the Chairman, over-ruled him, and the following extraordinary series of questions in a case which dealt only with a common assault were allowed:

'Are you living with any unfortunate woman at the present time?'

'No.'

'Did you bring an unfortunate woman here from Tasmania and afterwards send her to England? Did you take or accompany any unmarried woman to England?'

'No.'

'Then you don't know of any woman whom you seduced in Australia and brought to Melbourne, and whom you subsequently took to England with you?'

'No, I do not.'

'Have you had a woman of respectable connections in your house in Melbourne and subsequently degraded her to the position of your mistress.'

'Certainly not.'

'You don't know another young lady in Melbourne whom you caused to fall and whom you afterwards sent to San Francisco?'

'It is utterly untrue.'

There were more questions in the same vein, which were denied, and no attempt was made afterwards to support these wild allegations. As far as the actual assault was concerned very little of the cross-examination was taken up with it. Sievier did, however, assert and maintained under questioning that Deerhurst had struck him on the shoulder when making his ineffective and illegal 'arrest'.

'Did you,' Mr. Duffy asked Deerhurst when he in turn was being cross-examined, 'instruct your counsel to ask questions of Sutton in regard to his relations with women?'

'I may have. I did not mean that he should be insulted.'

'Did you or did you not?'

'I instructed Mr. Purves to bring out Sutton's character as much as possible.'

Deerhurst's further cross-examination well displays what manner of man he was—a silly, spoilt, vain and arrogant youth.

'Is Mr. Patrick Agnew your mentor in matters of morals?'

'What is that?'

'Have you any idea what the word mentor means?'

'No, I have not.'

'Were you in mortal terror of Sutton?'

'No, certainly not.'

'And you thought you would inform him of the fact that you were a captain of police in the colony. You did not know whether you were a police officer or not?'

'No. I thought I was at the time.'

'You said "I arrest you". Now what was in your mind when you said that?'

'I wanted to get out of the house and in order to do that I had to do something to make Sutton frightened.'

'But surely Mr. Agnew would take care of you. He would not let you be smacked?'

'I don't know. There were three of them.'

'What did you think there was sacred about a policeman?'

'You go and hit a policeman and you will see.'

Eventually the bench of magistrates retired. Twenty-five minutes later they returned and Mr. Panton delivered their verdict. There had been a difference of opinion, he said, but by a majority they had agreed to dismiss the case of Sutton v. Deerhurst and to convict Sutton on the other count. They admitted the evidence of provocation but nevertheless sentenced Sutton to fourteen days imprisonment. It was a severe sentence indeed for a simple assault. The Establishment was certainly demanding—and getting—its pound of flesh. Sievier immediately appealed.

General opinion on the case is well enough summed up by a quotation from *The Australian* the following day:

> It is beyond question that Mr. Robert Sutton committed an egregious blunder when he summoned a real live lord to the Police Court for an assault. If his accuser had not been a lord it is doubtful if he would have been expelled from the Victorian Club . . . they fed fat the ancient grudge they bore him for other rumoured escapades. The whole affair bore a very fishlike smell. Sutton was naturally incensed at not receiving the money he had won from

Deerhurst. . . . Everybody is at a loss to know why the British lord didn't show fight when struck. The 'officer and gentleman' excuse is much too thin. Lord Deerhurst will do well to remember that in sporting circles in Australia lords are expected to observe the usages of society in the same manner as ordinary mortals even though we have a Justice Shallow or two who may think differently.*

Deerhurst, although the victor, had come out of the whole business far from well. But he then proceeded to make matters much worse for his own good name in Australia. When the appeal came on a few weeks later he failed to appear, nor was he legally represented. He had decamped. Either he had been told to go or else took fright, for it came out during the hearing that he had left the country. As Mr. Duffy commented during his address: 'Lord Deerhurst apparently thinks he is safer out of court. "He who fights and runs away may live to fight another day". Lord Deerhurst no doubt has heard of this ancient and apposite motto.' And that was how it was read throughout Australia.

At all events Sievier, in racing parlance, enjoyed a walkover. The conviction was quashed and the decision reversed. There was a squabble over costs which went to the Supreme Court. Eventually Sievier was awarded £52 10s. 0d. costs which he subsequently, and after great difficulty, recovered from Deerhurst in England.

* The cartoon from *Melbourne Life* showing Dudley and Deerhurst mounted on a kangaroo whose head is a portrait of Mr. Panton which is reproduced on plate 3a further shows the Australian view of the affair.

6

Ups and Downs

꙳꙳꙳꙳꙳

With victory over Deerhurst safely under his belt Sievier sailed for home. There was a Mrs. Armstrong on board the P & O liner together with her husband, and small son. She was the best-looking woman on the ship. She bewitched him by her rendering of Tosti's *Good-bye*, and they engaged in a whirlwind courtship. Later, that Mrs. Armstrong became famous as Madame Melba.

Once landed he took a Flat at No. 1 Burlington Gardens. Next door, in Cork Street, and very conveniently as he remarked, was Sam Lewis, the money-lender. Lewis was to money-lending what R. H. Fry was to book-making. He was at the head of his profession, money-lender to the nobility and gentry of Britain, liked, trusted and respected by his many clients. A small, bald man with a merry eye and an instant readiness in repartee it was said of him that he knew more secrets than any man in London. His office at times resembled a club with young sprigs who had nothing else to do dropping in on him to learn all the gossip of the town. Like Fry he was renowned for his honesty and straight dealing. No man ever had cause to complain of the treatment he received at the hands of Sam Lewis and, again like Fry, if he thought the man or the occasion required it he could and did exhibit forbearance and kindness. Sievier came to know him well and, needless to say, to avail himself of his services.

At once he plunged into the pleasures of the town. In June, notwithstanding that he had made a book in Australia and was a divorcé, with sublime effrontery he had himself presented at court. Unfortunately for him Lord Dudley was at the levée where the presentation took place. The Earl of Dudley was horrified and scandalized to see before his eyes Sutton, the Australian bookmaker, make his bow to the Prince of Wales under the name and guise of Robert Standish Sievier. Here at a royal levée and being received by the heir apparent was the very man who had dared to lay hands upon a peer of the Realm and then challenge him in

47

court. Not only that but Sutton or Sievier had refused to accept the prejudiced verdict carefully secured. He had appealed and won and in so doing had caused caustic remarks about the aristocracy to appear in Australian newspapers. It wouldn't do at all. Lord Dudley, like Sievier, was a good hater. He promptly set to work to have the presentation cancelled.

Meanwhile the bad luck in betting which had attended Sievier in Australia had followed him home.

Soon, once more, he had to face the fact that he could not settle.

The Ring, led by R. H. Fry, refused to hound him. In fact it was a bookmaker who rescued him. Bob Howett operated from Nottingham. He had made a huge fortune and lived in style on an estate called Woodborough Manor. It was there that he provided winter quarters for Sievier. Whether he also paid for the string of hunters that Sievier took with him is undisclosed but he certainly housed and fed them along with their owner. With all the hospitality of Woodborough Manor at his disposal Sievier spent a pleasant winter hunting three days a week and filling the rest of it with country pursuits. In the spring he won a race at the South Notts point-to-point on an Irish horse of his own called Kilworth, and this victory enabled him to get a good price for the horse at Tattersalls when the season ended.

All this somewhat offset the set-back he had received when, on the 24th February 1888 a letter came from The Heralds' College informing him that certain people had come forward and testified that he had been *engaged on the Turf in Australia as a bookmaker, and that in such trans-actions you bore the name of Sutton.* As a result, the letter went on to say, his presentation had been cancelled.

Dudley and Deerhurst were having their revenge upon him in places where their words carried weight. And Dudley, at least, was not done with him yet.

But the Epsom Spring Meeting of 1888 saw him back racing again and ready to have a go at restoring his fortunes. Owing to his failure to settle he could only back in ready money but this he had from the sale of his horse. He began in, for him, a very small way. At the end of the first day he had won £110.

The City and Suburban was then run on the second day of the meeting. By backing the winners of the two races run before it he had turned the £110 into £2100.

Sir George Chetwynd ran Fullerton in the City and Suburban that year. Sir George was by far the cleverest man on the Turf at that time

48

and, although a member of the Jockey Club and a former steward, one of the sharpest. Sir George's son Guy, who, like many another son of a clever father, was following in his parent's footsteps without the ability to fill them, was one of Sievier's boon companions on the racecourse and across the card table.

Fullerton's running the year before had been the subject of some scrutiny and comment. When Lord Durham had made the Gimcrack speech of 1887 it had contained certain scorching remarks widely believed to relate to the methods employed by Sir George to ensure that his horses won races at prices most beneficial to him. Subsequently Lord Durham had gone further and had written a letter to the Senior Steward of the Jockey Club which named Sir George and contained a blunt accusation of cheating with his horses. Sir George had promptly issued proceedings for libel and slander against Durham. The defence to these proceedings, which had only just then been filed, stated flatly that the accusations were true. And the horse about which most of these accusations were concerned was Fullerton.

Naturally the racecourse was ringing with the scandal. Racing men were taking sides, new friendships were being formed and old ones broken, all over Sir George, Durham and the running of Fullerton.

On his previous form no one could say whether or not Fullerton should win this City and Suburban. Sir George, tall, handsome, reserved and appearing unconcerned by the whole affair, was, naturally enough, not disposed to offer any assistance to those who enquired about the chances and well-being of his horse.

Merry Hampton, George Abingdon Baird's Derby Winner of the year before, was made favourite. Fullerton was at prices varying from 6—1 to 8—1. Sir George, in his memoirs, says that he did not really fancy Fullerton. His trainer had not been able to give him enough work, nor had they tried him and, as a result, he only had a very small bet on him. Be that as it may there was someone else who did fancy him and had a very large bet on him, all of £1000 in fact.

Sievier did not pretend to be in Sir George's confidence. It would have been a rash man who had done so for it was never suggested that anyone, save possibly his jockey, Wood, knew the workings of Sir George's mind or the movement of his money.

But Guy Chetwynd was close to his father and the stable and sometimes worked part of the commission. Sievier and Guy Chetwynd were, as has been said, close friends. It is not altogether fanciful to suppose that young Chetwynd dropped a hint to Sievier and that that hint was enough. At all events he started off by taking 7—1 to £300 in cash, then he got £800—£100 and Bob Howett, who was with him, had another £300 on for him at 8—1.

When he saw the horses cantering down, his eye, his knowledge and his intuition told him that Fullerton was fit and ready to run for his life. He went back into the ring and had another £300 on thus making up his total bet of £1000.

Merry Hampton broke down and Fullerton won without being troubled. Sir George's comment was that Fullerton was not a true stayer and 'only the easy nature of the course' enabled him to get the extra half mile. But it must be remembered that Sir George was writing after the law case had gone against him and was attempting to put the record right as regards the running of his horses and his transactions.

For whatever reason he won, win Fullerton did and Sievier netted almost £8000. On the next race he cleared £4000 and he ended the meeting with £16,000 in his pocket. He had started the previous day with £110 in cash.

The following Monday he settled in full with the Ring and was back betting in credit and in comfort once more. It is perhaps of some irony and interest to note that Fullerton was sold shortly afterwards for a high price to Lord Dudley for whom he proved an expensive and hopeless failure, a fact which must have given Sievier some considerable satisfaction.

This time the luck held a little longer than usual. As a result he began to contemplate owning and running horses himself and on a considerable scale, but before doing so he determined that he must really master the art of training and managing them. Up to now he had been an amateur amongst professionals. From here on he made up his mind to know as much about the Turf as any man and to be accepted as an expert by the inner circle of racing men. Thenceforward horses, racing and the Turf were to be his whole life and they were the things to which he remained true throughout all his turbulent career. Whatever else he may have done, when he came to own and manage horses, those horses always ran openly and ran to win. He was never once in trouble over a horse owned or trained by him nor was the form, fitness or performance on a racecourse of any one of them ever questioned by the stewards in any country.

Off the Turf Sievier may have done, and indeed did do, desperate things that no ordinary man would have for one instant contemplated; on it he was a tower of rectitude. It was this which won him the respect of men in many walks of life from members of the Jockey Club (though he had his enemies there, too, as will be seen) to the poorest punter and to racecourse thieves. 'Good Old Bob' was not an empty cry when it came to be made. It was a title he had earned and, as he deserved it, so he kept it.

He was enjoying then one of his periods of comparative respectability which were to alternate throughout his life with bouts of *nostalgie de la boue* in which he kept the most appalling company and during which his behaviour rivalled or outdid that of his companions. He was to be seen at Newmarket day after day, quietly dressed, his great voice still, his flamboyance curbed. Usually he was alone, studying, watching, learning, casting an eye that grew ever more knowledgeable over the various strings. It was then that he learnt to appreciate the importance of conformation and action and to match that knowledge with what he saw, to divine in an instant when a horse was coming to himself and when his condition was beginning to fall away. He studied and analysed form and kept an accurate betting book. No longer was racing an amusing and exciting diversion; it was a way of life. He made friends amongst the real racing men and most of these friendships endured. One of them was with William Allison, the outspoken Special Commissioner of *The Sportsman*.

Allison, an exhibitioner of Balliol and a barrister, had from his early youth a passion for horses and racing. Being bored by the law he had bought shares in the Cobham Stud where the Derby winner Blair Atholl stood, subsequently acquiring a controlling interest in it. The company failed and went into liquidation and Allison drifted into sporting and political journalism. He was a literate man and a graceful, if prejudiced, writer. Soon he had made a name for himself and achieved a position of power and influence on the Turf. Sievier was fortunate to have acquired this friendship which proved a lasting one.

But he was being dunned by certain persistent creditors for purchases made—mostly presents for women friends—years ago. This he considered an impertinence, and here he was far from exceptional amongst his fellows. By and large in Victorian London anyone who aspired to the ranks of the swells lived on credit and to settle one's bills with any degree of promptitude was thought to be a mark of the middle-classes.

Tradesmen, of course, had to live and so they over-charged accordingly. Astounding bills would ultimately be presented at great houses or to millionaires like Baird. Then, at length, they would be paid in full for if it was considered common to pay promptly it was thought even worse to haggle with a tradesman when final settlement came to be made. When 'Ducks' Ailesbury was dying in a Brighton lodging house he was asked by a friend how he had come to aquire such enormous debts. 'I paid two prices for everything,' he said sadly. It was not the whole truth or anything like it but it had a grain of truth in it.

Whether the hounding of Sievier by high-class tradesmen at this time was inspired or not we shall never know. At least it can be said that it was unusual for someone of his standard of living to be pursued for comparatively small sums. At all events in September of 1888 Asprey of Bond Street put him into bankruptcy. He was furious. 'I have no sympathy with petitioning creditors,' he declared in the witness box in his examination and this was indeed so, as he was to show. Other creditors came along to prove in the bankruptcy, including wine merchants, a Bond Street jeweller and various purveyors of high-class goods. Certainly of Sievier it could never be said that he spared himself anything at the expense of his creditors. This time, however, he paid them all in full except, apparently, Messrs. Asprey who must nevertheless have been satisfied in some way, for he secured his discharge six months later. And he continued to spend lavishly on credit in Asprey's in the years to come.

He also became engaged once more to a rich and well-born girl, but this engagement was broken off owing, he thought, to further interference from his noble enemies and certainly the cancellation of his presentation and the circumstances which led up to it received well-promoted publicity and may indeed have had something to do with it.

After all this he decided to spend his winter re-visiting Australia and returning by way of Monte Carlo. In Australia he saw Carbine win the Melbourne Cup carrying 10st. 5 lb and noted him down as one of the best he had seen. The Duke of Portland heard of Carbine's prowess and subsequently paid 15,000 guineas for him. Carbine was brought back to stand at Welbeck and Sievier was to profit by his recollection of him when backing his progeny.

In Monte Carlo where he intended to see out the rest of the winter he had a disastrous time at roulette. Nothing would go right for him. He loved the life, the mild climate, the scenery, the cosmopolitan society, the long late nights whose effects he walked off climbing up the old Corniche road 'against the collar' from Mentone to La Turbie. His constitution, as always, was up to any demands which he put upon it but his pocket was not. The day came when he found himself 'stone-broke', sitting on the shore looking at the sun dancing on the sea.

There seemed no way at all of raising even enough money to pay for his journey home. Then this extraordinary man, ruminating on his circumstances and how to get out of them, suddenly decided to make use of his immediate experiences by writing a play. He returned to his hotel, took pen in hand and wrote the title *Stone Broke* across a sheet of hotel writing paper.

It turned out to be a farce, and a short one, to be used as a curtain raiser. Seen in retrospect and set down in cold blood the plot concerning the efforts of two young men who find themselves 'stone-broke' to circumvent the efforts of their landlady to collect her rent seems silly enough. But curtain raisers were popular then and writers with the skill to fit fun and farce into a small compass and combine them with theatrical effectiveness, few and far between. Armed with the manuscript Sievier raised the money to return home and immediately sold his maiden effort for £50. Later on it was produced at the Grand Theatre Islington with success and then all over the provinces bringing in a steady income for a few years. It did not, however, bring Sievier any luck for it was the indirect means of his making a new and powerful enemy and causing an unsuccessful skirmish with the law.

7

Libel—and another Marriage

$\maltese\maltese\maltese\maltese\maltese\maltese$

Back in England and through the kind assistance of Sam Lewis and R. H. Fry he took up fashionable quarters and went racing once more. He soon showed he had not lost his flair for picking a likely horse.

In May of 1891 he noticed a filly called Comedy winning a Maiden Plate at Kempton and decided to follow her career. The next time out it was obvious to him that she was not trying. Knowing everyone on the racecourse from the highest to the lowest he made enquiries about her connections and found she was owned by an Irishman called Fulton who had, to use his own expression, 'a very jovial idea of the rules of racing.'

Deciding that she was being kept for something he watched the weights for the big handicaps and when those for the Cambridgeshire were published found she was in with 7st. 3lb. Keeping his ears open he made discreet enquiries both on the course and in places like Romano's where knowing men gathered. Fulton planned his coups in great secrecy and this time there was no pretty barmaid to give the game away.

At length a chance conversation with someone who had been lucky or clever enough to watch Fulton's string at work told him she was being trained for the Cambridgeshire distance. Keeping the knowledge thus acquired to himself he began to back Comedy and went on backing her right up to the start of the race. She won comfortably by half-a-length.

That night he celebrated in Romano's. Prominent amongst his guests was the Marquess of Ailesbury, one of the reigning princes of the restaurant and a tatterdemalion swell who was rivalled only by George Abingdon Baird in ruffianly behaviour, unruly conduct, bad manners and profligacy.

George William Thomas Brudenell-Bruce, fourth Marquess of Ailesbury, was known to the fancy as 'Ducks' or 'Billy Stomachache' and to his family as 'Dear Willie'. The Brudenell-Bruces had for centuries been the hereditary wardens of Savernake Forest. Over the years they had taken their task seriously and discharged it with thoroughness and care, not aspiring to or displaying distinction in any walk of life but serving the forest and their sovereign and gradually acquiring grandeur and titles as generation succeeded generation.

With 'Dear Willie's' father, however, a raffish streak came in from somewhere. He died in his twenties, dissipated and alone in Corsica where he had gone in the hope of repairing the damage he had done to his constitution by his reckless way of life. Willie and Mabel, his sister, were brought up by doting grand-parents, allowed to run wild, spoilt and cosseted, their every whim pandered to.

Willie was expelled from Eton. After that for a very short time he hunted a pack of hounds from Savernake. Then he turned his attentions to the Turf. Like Sievier he would bet on anything—he once lost a big sum through his inability to recite the Lord's Prayer without making a mistake. Certainly he and Deerhurst were scarcely good advertisements for the education the Eton of those days provided. His boon companions were racegoers of the roughest sort, who sponged on him mercilessly; the trainers he chose for his horses were those most suspect by the authorities. By the time he was twenty-one his debts amounted to £175,000 and the Ailesbury estates in Yorkshire had to be sold to meet them. In 1888 he and his trainer were warned off the Turf together over the running of a horse of his called Everitti. He married an actress called Dolly Tester who was held by everyone, including his family, to be too good for him. He dressed like a broken-down stable lad, studded his conversation with four-letter oaths and surrounded himself, as did George Abingdon Baird, with a bodyguard of bruisers to protect him in the brawls his drunken habits frequently brought upon him.

Baird, who had one time been a first-class gentleman rider on the flat and who had modelled his style on that of Fred Archer, had by now all but given up riding and was spending his days and nights in senseless debauchery, some of the nights being spent with Dolly Tester without apparently the Marquess missing her. Both vied with each other in ridiculous spending and at times the bizarre spectacle could be seen of these two young men with their private armies of bruisers, roaming the West End, beating up bystanders, buying off prosecutions and pursuing, each in his own way, a heedless path to a squalid grave.

Yet, as Sir Claude de Crespigny who knew them both points out, as with Baird, somewhere in 'Dear Willie' was a better, kinder, side.

It was the snobbery of his superiors which had twisted Baird. With 'Dear Willie' it was his heedless upbringing and the command of too great resources far too soon. He was a weak, shy man. His lonely, spoilt childhood had made him ill at ease with those of his own station in life. He felt unsure of himself with them and could only receive the deference needed to bolster his security from the raffish crowd in Romano's and on the racecourse. He was generous—far too generous—and, at the beginning of his career, gay and fun-loving and fond of company. Unfortunately, as de Crespigny says, it was wrong company that he ultimately found congenial.

At all events Sievier was neither afraid of his bruisers nor his bad name. He had no cause to be fond of the Establishment himself, and they soon became friends. Sievier used to stay and make merry with 'Ducks' at Savernake. During those times Lady Mabel, 'Ducks' sister, was also there. She, too, was proud and wilful, but she was also hand-some, moderately rich in her own right, interested in the Turf for she had a string of horses in training with Sherwood at Epsom, and high-spirited. In addition, at that time she was engaged to another.

Whether the lure of forbidden fruit had anything to do with it cannot be known but Sievier laid siege to her affections and won them.

His courtship was not looked on with favour by the rest of the family. The grand-parents were horrified at the thought of this rascal becoming one of them, this extraordinary adventurer and gambler who had no visible means of support, who had been, so they were told, a bookmaker no less, in Australia, and whose presentation in Court had been cancelled because of it. 'Dear Willie' was bad enough but to have another of that ilk marrying his sister surpassed their worst fears.

Even more disturbed by his suit was the staid and stately Lord Frederick Brudenell-Bruce, 'poor unfortunate Willie's' uncle and trustee. Especially was he concerned because Lady Mabel's fortune was not tied up in any way but was at her disposal. She had received £50,000 when she came of age but she had something of her brother's prodigal habits and had already gone through £16,000 of this. There was thus £34,000 left, a tidy sum—and Sievier had just gone bankrupt again. This time there was only one petitioning creditor, a man called Freece who dunned Sievier over a stock-exchange transaction and who re-ceived Sievier's usual treatment in such cases. The sum, in fact, was not a large one, about £800.

As well as going bankrupt, however, other troubles were besetting Sievier and bringing him into a prominence which both he and the staider members of the Brudenell-Bruce family can scarcely have welcomed.

Early in March *Stone Broke* was produced and, as has been said, enjoyed a fair success with both critics and public. This was, of course, very satisfactory but its immediate sequel was not.

There was then in London a fashion for flimsy and short-lived papers containing society tittle-tattle, most of it scandalous and much of it libellous. One of these papers was called *The Bat*. It was owned and conducted by a certain Jimmy Davis who was at times an impresario, an author of musical comedies and a dramatic critic with a particularly virulent pen. Davis lived in some style in Curzon Street where he entertained all Bohemia in great splendour. Young sprigs of the nobility, hangers on, penniless scribblers, and ladies from the chorus of his theatrical productions thronged his house and partook of his bountiful hospitality. They also, in their more relaxed moments, provided material for his pen.

One of the writers who frequented Curzon Street was George Moore, lately of Moore Hall in Ireland. Moore was some years afterwards to achieve fame with the publication of *Esther Waters* the story of a servant girl in Victorian England set against a racing background which was one of the first 'realistic' novels written in English. But at this time he was very poor indeed. He brought to Davis pieces of information gleaned from hanging about where those on the fringes of high places mixed and existed on whatever Davis gave him for these and for 'spicing up' scandalous paragraphs prepared from reports sent in by others.

As Davis' expenses increased *The Bat* sailed ever closer to the wind. There is, in fact, a whiff of discreet blackmail about the whole operation for Davis' apparent income seemed far from sufficient to sustain the style in which he lived though nothing definite in this regard was ever proved against him. Finally, however, he went too far. He chose the wrong man to libel when he published a scurrilous article about the Earl of Durham. A writ of criminal libel was immediately applied for by Durham and Davis decamped for Paris to avoid its consequences. Moore and his brother Augustus who, known as 'Masher' Moore, had recently joined the staff were left with no means of support whatever.

There was however still plenty of material left in the offices of *The Bat* for use in subsequent issues. Moore and his brother resolved to change its name to *The Hawk* and to continue publication in the same manner as before with Augustus Moore as the nominal proprietor. The issue of March 29th 1892 contained the following paragraph:

The latest dramatic author is Mr. R. Standish Sievier, who has written and has had produced a play called *Stone Broke*. Readers of this paper may remember Mr. R. Standish Sievier. Some years ago R. Standish Sievier, *alias* Sutton, managed to get presented at The Prince of Wales' Levée. When the true character of this person was discovered the presentation was cancelled publicly in the *Gazette*. Sutton, or Sievier, had been an actor, and after some curious card transactions with the officers of a well-known regiment he went to Australia, where he turned bookmaker. A brutal assault on Lord Deerhurst led to his being condemned to imprisonment and his true character being made public. He had been divorced by his wife for cruelty, desertion, and adultery with a well-known lady in Australia, whom he induced to leave her home, and he was 'warned off' for using disgusting language. He managed by his plausibility and misrepresentations to get engaged to a charming young lady of some fortune in this country, but the Lord Chamberlain's officials having induced her parents to see me, and I having secured them an introduction to Mr. George Lewis, whom I supplied with the facts, the engagement was broken off. Sutton, or Sievier, is a good-looking, plausible scoundrel, who hoodwinked one of the officials of The Heralds' College into getting him presented to the Prince of Wales, and, among other lies, Sievier actually stated he had held a commission and obtained a medal for bravery in action. He was asked as to what regiment he had belonged. He boldly declared the Connaught Rangers. This was a little unfortunate, as this happens to be my brother's regiment. Sievier, or Sutton, was actually photographed in uniform, boldly displaying the medal on his breast.

When this was brought to his attention Sievier, not unnaturally, was furious. He determined to take an action for libel against the paper. With this in view he consulted Messrs. Wontner, the well-known West End solicitors. Messrs. Wontner sent a case to advise to C. F. Gill who was then with determination and single-mindedness climbing the ladder of success at the bar.

Gill had first come to the attention of the public when he had been briefed to oppose the great Sir Charles Russell Prosecuting on behalf of Harry Marks, editor of the *Financial News*, in one of the then fashionable cases of criminal libel. Consumed with ambition and avid for fame Gill had seen that if he could secure an acquittal against such formidable opposition his name would be made. 'This case,' he confided to a friend, 'will either make me or break me,' for he had determined to fight it with all the scurrilous methods at his command. He was by turns, Ashley, Horace Avory's clerk, records, 'aggressive, insinuating, provocative and irrelevant.' Ashley and others castigated his conduct by branding this line of defence as 'street corner tactics'. Sir Charles Russell refused to speak to him for years and a bitter enmity sprang up between them. But he won his case and achieved the fame—or notoriety—he desired. Clients with controversial cases beat a path to his door.

In an age of great advocates, however, Gill never quite achieved the foremost rank. Though he was to match his wits against and sometimes even to prevail over such as Clarke, Carson, Isaacs and F. E. Smith, he himself would hardly have claimed to be their equal. A dour, reserved, methodical man, he had immense reserves of industry and application. Educated at the Royal School, Dungannon, he had neither social nor family contacts to help him make his way at the Bar. But he had an enormous capacity for hard and unremitting paper work. His cases were prepared with the most infinite pains even, it is said, to the extent of working out every possible answer a witness might make to each question of his cross-examination. No flash of genius ever illuminated the actions he fought, but hard work, care, conscientiousness and a sort of plodding ruthlessness brought him in the end a fine practice, position, wealth and standing. In his private life, such of it as is known, he was conservative, blameless and both prudish and censorious by nature. He was scarcely a man to appeal to Sievier nor Sievier to him. He appears also, somewhere beneath the dour exterior, to have possessed a singular streak of vindictiveness which well-matched Sievier's own vengeful disposition. 'Gill had a weakness for saying nasty things in a nasty way,' Ashley said of him and this may be one of the clues to the strange character concealed inside his burly frame.

Gill advised Sievier against proceeding with the case on the grounds that having been just adjudged a bankrupt and having had his presentation cancelled he was unlikely to recover damages. Sievier refused to accept this advice and a series of conferences which appear to have been stormy, then took place. While these conferences were going on Augustus Moore himself went bankrupt. This, as Gill took pains to point out, made civil proceedings quite unrealistic since no damages could be recovered from a bankrupt. His blood now thoroughly aroused, Sievier demanded the issue of criminal proceedings against Moore on the grounds that the publication was a criminal libel and likely to cause a breach of the peace. He also told Messrs. Wontner that he was quite unimpressed and dissatisfied with Gill's handling of his case so far. He conveyed this opinion to Gill also and in no uncertain terms.

It is evident that the two men quarrelled and, remembering Sievier's impulsiveness, his quick temper and biting tongue it is not unreasonable to suppose that he upbraided Gill in terms which Gill regarded as unforgivable. Whatever happened there is no doubt that Gill thenceforward was to be and remain a bitter, vengeful and unremitting enemy. Sievier did in fact issue proceedings and then dropped them. He never explained why.

While all this was going on another incident took place which did Sievier no good either then or afterwards. He was staying in the Hotel Metropole in Brighton in a suite of rooms. The fact that he was an undischarged bankrupt did not make the least difference to his mode of living. On the last night of his stay he sat in on a card game with an acquaintance, Renton, and a man called Kavanagh. Renton lost £2000 to Sievier and there was some unpleasantness with the management about gambling on licensed premises. Renton could not settle then and there but he promised to meet Sievier at the Hotel Victoria in London the following Monday and to pay him then. Before Monday arrived it came to Renton's ears that Kavanagh was a well-known card-sharper. He kept the appointment on Monday in the company of his solicitor and refused to pay on the grounds that Kavanagh was a sharper, but at this time made no charge against Sievier personally.

There was a glass door to the room in which Sievier, Renton and the solicitor were talking. Suddenly, in the midst of the conversation, the head and shoulders of Kavanagh appeared in the upper portion of this 'like a picture in a frame' as Sievier put it afterwards. This appearance of Kavanagh made Renton even more suspicious, hot words ensued in which Sievier was, apparently, called a cheat and once more Sievier, not this time advised by Gill, called in the law to protect his reputation and issued proceedings for slander. Renton later apologized and the proceedings were discontinued, but the story of Kavanagh appearing 'like a picture in a frame' was so well worth repeating that Sievier could not refrain from telling it to his friends in Romano's and elsewhere. The tale went abroad and lost nothing in the telling. It did not help his standing with the elder and more respectable members of the Brudenell-Bruce family nor in the higher reaches of society. Why Sievier on the one hand was so careless of his good name and on the other so ready to rush to law to protect it is one of the mysteries of his singularly complex character.

Despite all these things or perhaps because of them, for 'Ducks' and his sister were scarcely likely to be deterred from caring for a man by reason of libels in *The Hawk* or disputes over cards, his suit prospered. Neither the grandparents' protests nor Lord Frederick's firm hand were of any avail. It was all too clear that Lady Mabel favoured him. To try to separate them she was sent to her step-mother, Lady Evelyn Riddell, in Northamptonshire.

During this visit Lady Evelyn left for a short stay with friends. A day or so after she had left Lady Mabel asked her step-father to drive her to Willoughby station as she had arranged—she said—to go to London to see an aunt. This, all unsuspecting, 'Puggy' Riddell did. The next thing he, or anyone else in the family knew, Lady Mabel and Sievier were married. It was October 1893. Sievier's present to the bride was a gold-fitted dressing-case (this remained throughout his life a favourite and stable present to his lady-friends) which cost almost £2000. It was not a bad present for a bankrupt to give and it took some skilful arranging by one of his friends to manage it. Lady Mabel had as part of her patrimony a residence at Shanklin in the Isle of Wight. This was a bit out of the way for both of them so they set up house together in Lowndes Square.

The runaway match was to prove, like Sievier's first marriage, a hopeless failure. Both had strong characters and violent tempers and they were, as it turned out, quite incompatible. From the beginning their personalities clashed. On the rare occasions when they were alone Lady Mabel used to play patience endlessly, game after game, without speaking and without intermission. Sievier found this infuriating and, as was his way, he told her so. In return he was told that it was a habit he would be well advised to acquire for himself. One night he asked her to teach him with the result that he discovered the fascination of it. Thereafter to the end of his days when alone he would bring out his cards and play Canfield, betting with himself on the result, using it to determine whether or not he should go racing or stay at home, whether the next day's racing would be a good one for gambling or not. Once on the course he forgot all about it.

Lady Mabel's horses were not of any great account being mostly handicappers and selling-platers but in their own sphere there were one or two sure of winning races. Sievier had appreciated this when he went to look over the string. Not being entirely satisfied with the way in which

Sherwood was handling them he moved the lot to Vic Sanders at Epsom.

This proved a wise step and Sanders promptly began to win races with them. They were run under Sievier's supervision and one or two, notably Odour and Boaz, were more than useful in their own class. It was owing to Sievier's cleverness and opportunism that they were successfully exploited.

But merely supervising the running of a string of second-class race-horses was hardly likely to satisfy him or to provide whole time employ-ment for a restless nature such as his. From Lady Mabel he secured £5000 of the sum she had brought with her into marriage and with this he determined to set himself up once more as a bookmaker. It was a most ill-advised venture. Not only, as has been said, was he tempera-mentally totally unsuited to carry on a bookmaking business but he was still an undischarged bankrupt.

The latter fact, whilst it did not deter him, made it essential that he should operate in the name of another. With this in view he called in the assistance of his two cousins, Edward Harcourt Sievier and Herbert Percival Sievier who was known as 'Punch' Sievier.

The business name of 'Punch & Co.' was adopted and a staff engaged. Amongst those employed was a junior shorthand writer called Thomas Henry Dey. Looking very much younger even than his years—he was in his late teens—Dey gave the appearance of being innocent and naïve. In fact he was neither of these things. Knowing nothing at all of the business at the outset he soon proved to have a brilliant head for figures and quickly mastered the mechanics of it.

Dey's mind was the very opposite of Sievier's. His was a cold, calculating nature. He was fascinated by the actual mathematics of making a book to show a profit. Save when he was convinced that the odds and the chances fully worked out were in his favour he did not gamble himself. In no time at all the brains behind the business were entirely Dey's and the control of it, in so far as control was ever exercised, had slipped out of Sievier's careless hands into those of the youthful Dey.

Sievier was determined to make the business a fashionable one catering for 'the swells'. Although so far as the Establishment at least were concerned the brand of the adventurer was now indelibly upon him, he was enabled to do this because he was known to everyone in racing and liked by most. News of his exploits in Australia had filtered through. The Deerhurst affair was not held against him in places other than those where the writ of the Establishment ran. Deerhurst on his return from Australia had gone on to the stock exchange where he became somehow involved in the Baring crisis. As a result of this he followed Sievier's footsteps in emigrating to South Africa with the intention of joining the British South African Police. That Force, however, failed to find a vacancy for him with the result that at the very moment when Sievier was setting up as a bookmaker Deerhurst was taking over a butcher's business and tending shop in Salisbury, Southern Rhodesia.

Dudley's fortunes had lain in rather more prosperous paths. Indeed, with the immense wealth his family had acquired from finding coal beneath their lands, they could scarcely fail to have done. In 1891 he had married with great pomp, and in the presence of the Prince of Wales, Rachel, daughter of Charles Henry Gurney of Keswick Hall, Norfolk. Through the influence of his young wife he had begun to attempt to carve out for himself a political career. In this he was not noticeably successful despite his wealth and power. On the Turf where he was also anxious to make a name for himself both as a rider and owner he was an almost complete failure. Harding Cox, one of the outstanding amateur riders on the flat of his day, sold him one of his favourite and most successful horses for a big price with the object of giving Dudley 'an armchair winning ride'. But Dudley failed to win on him, and subsequently disposed of him to The Marquess of Cholmondeley as a covert hack. He was a heavy gambler and a bad judge of his own and other people's horses. He sold Cloister, one of the best of all the great Grand National winners, when on his running it was clear that he must have had an outstanding chance of taking that race; he gave Marsh, who trained for him, a bad time with his injudicious betting, and at one time his name—or so Sievier declared—actually appeared in the forfeit list. He was not one of the best loved of the patrons of the Turf and shortly after his marriage he retired from it. But his enmity towards Sievier for the ridicule to which he had been held up in Australia remained with him for the rest of his life.

Dudley did not like losing, whereas Sievier's huge betting coups, his equally staggering losses and his ready acceptance of them gained him admiration and liking at least amongst the masses.

One story widely told at the time is typical of him and shows how his resilient and ebullient nature gained him popularity with the crowd. Leaving one day after a particularly disastrous meeting he was accosted by Old Kate the racecard seller who had suffered similarly. 'Give me something for me supper, Mr. Sievier,' she said. 'I'm cleaned out'.

'We're in the same boat, Kate' he told her. Then he put his hand into his pocket and, after searching for a bit, came up with two sovereigns. 'It's all I've left,' he said. 'Let's split it.' Handing her one he laughed and walked on.

It was essential for the fashionable type of business contemplated by Punch & Co. that the premises be in an area frequented by smart people. A set of chambers in 4 Bennett Street, St. James's, were therefore rented. The next problem was the furnishing and pictures. These must be of the sort that would make the smart clientele feel at home for a fashionable bookmaker's office in those days was, as well, a sort of club where the swells could forgather, smoke their cigars and exchange gossip of the girls and the halls as well as information and news from the racecourse.

Sievier solved the problem of obtaining such embellishments with typical ingenuity and effrontery. Going down to Savernake with 'Ducks' Ailesbury, now his brother-in-law, they removed from the mansion heirlooms, pictures, carpets and other articles sufficient to furnish Punch & Co. on a truly magnificent scale. They were not too careful in setting about their work or perhaps they had dined too well before they started, with the result that they irretrievably damaged some ancient ormolu in the billiard room by pulling it too hastily away, and one family picture still bears their knife marks where they attempted to cut it out of its frame.

Thus when Punch & Co. opened its doors the staid Brudenell-Bruce relatives were scandalized to hear that portraits of their ancestors were gazing down at the frequenters of a bookmaker's office in St. James's Street, and that priceless furniture and heirlooms from Savernake were being used to adorn the premises and attract custom. There was, however, very little that they could do about it since 'Dear Willie' was the owner of the life estate and it had all been removed with his permission. There were, as it happened, worse worries in store for them.

Willie was by now so deep into the moneylenders' pockets that he was desperate. His debts at this time amounted to the staggering figure of £230,000. Casting about for a method of satisfying the moneylenders' demands which grew more pressing day by day he decided to sell the whole of the Savernake estate, lock, stock and barrel. Technically, as tenant for life, he had power to do this. Having made this decision he looked around for a buyer and soon found one.

Sir Edward Guinness of the Dublin brewing firm was searching for an English estate to go with his great wealth and his hopes of a peerage.

1b. Herbert Randall

1a. 'Ducks' Ailesbury

2. 'Gogo' Sievier jumping a wall out hunting

Savernake was recommended to him by none other than the Prince of Wales and he was willing to pay £750,000 for it.

Willie was delighted. Not only would his debts be paid but he might once more get hold of some ready cash as well. But the relatives were neither amused nor pleased; nor were they prepared to let Savernake go without a fight. Lord Frederick, the trustee, and Lord Henry, the heir, were horrified at the thought of 'a mere upstart merchant, a *nouveau-riche* Irishman' succeeding to the estates which had been in the family for eight hundred years without sale or interruption. They set about contesting the proposed purchase with every weapon at their command. Ultimately they took the matter to the House of Lords and Sir Edward looked elsewhere for an estate of sufficient grandeur to go with his millions.

Willie, meanwhile, was banished to furnished lodgings at Brixton and given an allowance of £40 a week which he did not consider sufficient—nor was it—for one of his tastes and habits. The creditors continued to harass him, not unnaturally, considering the huge sums he owed and the rate at which he continued to spend, for he was quite incapable of grasping the realities of this situation or of any other.

In Willie's difficulties Sievier did not desert him. He staved off the creditors, or tried to, paid something to the more pressing and brought money and gifts to Willie in his lodgings. Willie's health was now failing. Dolly Tester had long since gone. None of his old so-called friends on whom he had squandered his birthright remembered him or stood by him. It was left to Sievier alone to provide sustenance and help. This, freely given to Willie dying deserted in Brixton, went unregarded by the family. They appeared to hold him in some way responsible for the latest disaster 'Dear Willie' had brought upon them and he certainly did not help matters by tendering some gratuitous advice to the trustees on how best to deal with the proposed sale of Savernake. 'A very able, dangerous scoundrel' was how the sixth Marquess described him in a note left amongst his papers when he died. In fact 'Dear Willie' was set on collision course with catastrophe long before Sievier met him and it was only Sievier's kindness and generosity which did anything to lighten his last days and to soften his squalid end.

Punch & Co. was a success from the start and should have continued as such. Young Dey supplied the balance and the business brains; Sievier and his cousins brought in the customers. Sportsmen of all sorts thronged the place. But it had grievous handicaps, chief amongst them being the feckless character and gambling instincts of its proprietor and the fact that he was an undischarged bankrupt.

Sievier simply could not stop betting. When he had been there a little time and had begun to master the business young Dey saw that Sievier's reckless gambling, almost all of which was done with the funds of the firm, must sooner or later lead to disaster. He went to his employer and implored him to stop, pointing out that if he would only confine himself to laying horses they had the foundation of a splendid business and a good living for them all. 'I know you mean well,' Sievier told him. 'But I can't help it. It's a disease. I shall back horses to my dying day.' Which, in fact, is exactly what he did.

At that time Sanders was doing quite well with Lady Mabel's string. Fred Allsopp, then a leading jockey, was retained by the stable. He rode them a considerable number of winners, but he used to bet himself and would wire his fancies on all sorts of horses to Punch & Co. Though his knowledge of racing told him it was madness, Sievier could not stop himself following the jockey's tips. Always optimistic and open with any information he had, he would pass these tips on to the office staff. The result of this was that almost all the employees caught the disease and began betting for themselves with Punch & Co. He did nothing to stop this. Sometimes, when one of their own horses was fancied, he would put the whole lot of them on to the odds to a sovereign. Since Lady Mabel was also betting heavily it was obvious that although money was pouring in and Sanders was really working wonders with the material at his disposal a crash was bound to come. Added to all this Sievier was often absent from the office for months at a time on jaunts to Paris or Monte Carlo or just away racing and enjoying himself too much to come in. His personal expenditure was enormous, for the best was barely good enough for him, and the family that year was increased by the birth of a daughter.

But, as always with Sievier, it was fun while it lasted. 'My tastes' he was to write a few years later in the *Winning Post* when giving a puff to a famous Piccadilly firm 'have always been *à la carte* as opposed to *table d'hôte*, and I have dealt with Fortnum & Mason since I was twenty-one —on the nod of course!' He was nothing if not frank about his sins, and those were the days when he was young enough to enjoy them to the full. Writing about that time after thirty-five years Dey could still remember the stratagems and games they got up to in order to keep Punch & Co. alive. 'The Principal is out of town but a cheque will be sent to you immediately on his return,' was an excuse he used so often it came almost automatically to his lips. As he said, too, it was usually true. On one occasion he drew all his own savings which amounted to £100 from the bank and used them to keep the firm alive on settling day. At another time of crisis Sievier was for once on the premises when an irate creditor called. The sum was £20 and there was no money to meet even that amount. When Dey asked what should be done Sievier pulled some sovereigns from one of his pockets. 'Throw those into a drawer in your desk and offer to pay him out of the petty cash,' he said. This Dey did with a lordly air and the client, impressed with his surroundings and the munificent carelessness over the petty cash, went away impressed and delighted.

No one can now nor ever will unravel the tangled finances of Punch & Co. The fact of Sievier's bankruptcy cast all its affairs into confusion from the start. He was constantly trying to obtain his discharge and failing; since he could not operate a bank account and large sums were passing through his hands, notes and bills of exchange went flying round London and on these he was sometimes sued either alone or jointly with his wife.

In 1894 Willie Ailesbury died and his successor promptly issued proceedings to recover the furniture and fittings removed from Savernake. About this time Sievier decided that London was becoming too hot to hold him and that he would follow the example of Davis and others and take up residence in Paris. Comfortable quarters were secured in the Rue de la Parosse and here he and his family went. Soon after their arrival a second child, a son, christened Robert Brudenell-Bruce Sievier, was born.

Before he left, the business, along with Dey, was transferred to Bob Howett's son but Sievier retained some interest in it. He was constantly back and forth from the Continent and the horses were still running in Lady Mabel's name. Somehow he found time to write a book called *A Generation** which, he says, was published by Downey & Co. and sold 7000 copies. It ran, he records, to 480 pages and how in the midst of all the hurly-burly of his life at that time he managed to complete it remains a mystery, as does the book.

For a few years more Sievier appears to have continued some sort of loose association with the business which was subsequently called the Field Syndicate. Ultimately, Dey having left to found a firm of his own in which he went from success to success, it was sold to Charles Clark. Clark was a man of much the same calibre as R. H. Fry and he was to prove a lifelong friend and benefactor to Sievier.

*No record of this work appears in the British Museum catalogue.

Despite the fact that two children had been born to them in successive years the marriage was not prospering. Except in their extravagances and their mutual love of racing they had little or nothing in common, save for their almost ungovernable tempers. The acts of physical violence to her which Lady Mabel liked to recount in after years, if they occurred at all, may well have been the result of unendurable provocation. Apart from her temper she was a cold, hard woman and utterly unforgiving. It was about this time that she began to behave to him, in the words of one who knew her, 'as if she hated his guts'.

Whether the physical violence took place or not she had other excuses. For, as always, there were infidelities. Sievier was made for mistresses and not for marriage. In this, as in his gambling, he remained forever the adolescent. He was born to be a bachelor and a hunter. He loved sex for itself as many men do; he was a sexual expert and an athlete; he could make women happy in bed if nowhere else. At this time several liaisons or associations were going on, two of which were to prove significant. One led to the founding of a family and the other paved the way to the happiest and most brilliant period of his life.

Another association began at that time, too. Sanders' successes with the moderate string at his disposal were beginning to run out. Casting his eye around for a trainer who might do better for them Sievier decided on Charles Morton of Wantage, then just at the commencement of a career which was to bring him undying fame on the Turf.

One day Morton was strolling in a paddock at Wantage when he saw a man leading a horse into his yard. Approaching him he asked what he thought he was doing. Morton did not take lightly to strangers hanging about the premises, especially when they were accompanied by horses of whom he knew nothing. The reply he received was that this was one of Lady Mabel Sievier's horses and that Mr. Bob Sievier presented his compliments and would Mr. Morton be kind enough to train it for them.

'This was the first I had heard of such a thing,' Morton wrote afterwards, as indeed it was, for Sievier, typically, had neither written nor spoken to Morton about it but just sent along the horse in the brazen assurance that it would be accepted. His judgment of Morton was accurate for, hearing the message, the trainer laughed. 'I knew him well enough, of course,' he went on, 'who didn't? I accepted the compliment in the spirit in which it was offered.'

Thus, in a small way, began the association between Sievier and Morton which was to lead to several seasons of splendour and success on the Turf and finally to end in circumstances which made Sievier the greatest and most powerful of all his many enemies.

He was, during this time, nominally at least based on the Rue de la Parosse where Lady Mabel and the children also were. In January 1895 they resolved to see out the last of the winter on the Riviera. Leaving the children with a nannie they travelled to Monte Carlo where they engaged a suite of rooms in the Hotel Metropole.

Sievier had with him a manservant called Froome and Lady Mabel brought her maid, but both were desperately short of money. A chance meeting and a bet on a game of billiards appeared to offer a way, as it had done long ago and several times since, of recouping their finances. But this particular victory at the billiard table, as it turned out, was to prove a costly one.

8

'Drinking' Horn

There were at that time circulating in the lower reaches of Bohemian London two brothers called Horn. They lived on their wits, their skill at play, such as it was, and sponged on their friends. The sons of a solicitor who practised in partnership with a man called Francis under the name and style of Horn & Francis, this firm acted for them in the troubles which their way of life brought frequently upon them and they appear to have had some sort of loose association with it in the way of bringing in business, touting for clients and other extra-legal activities. When Horn senior died Francis carried on alone until he was struck off the rolls and sent to prison for professional misconduct and malpractice.

Known respectively as 'Hunting' Horn and 'Drinking' Horn they were a thoroughly undesirable pair and enjoyed a reputation, even in the circle where rules of settling were not strictly kept, for avoiding their obligations. They didn't mind betting but didn't like paying, one who knew them has said of them, and 'Drinking' Horn had been expelled from The Badminton Club for this very cause.

'Hunting' Horn was so called because at the least excuse he was quick to describe his last 'twenty minutes over the grass without a check', whereas it was well known that he seldom sat on a horse and never jumped a fence. 'Drinking' Horn had earned his sobriquet for obvious reasons. 'Always staggering and swaggering' was Sievier's own description of him and it appears to have been a fair one. He was, however, far from being the naïve and innocent young man he was later portrayed to be nor was he the helpless alcoholic described to two different juries by two different sets of learned counsel. In the year 1895 he was fifty-six years of age and was considered by himself and others to be a skilled billiards player.

In the nineties the billiard-room at the Hotel Metropole was the rendezvous for the smart and sporting set after the Casino closed at midnight. One evening Sievier dropped in there after play had finished and found it thronged with people. Ernest 'Drinking' Horn was among them. No doubt he had had his fair measure of drink but subsequent events would seem to show that he was neither drugged nor helpless as was later sought to be proved. There is no doubt that drink infected both the Horns with braggadoccio. Seeing Sievier enter, Horn promptly challenged him to a match at billiards for a substantial sum. The exact amount of this initial sum has never been made clear.

Never one to refuse a challenge especially at a game in which he, too, held a high opinion of his own proficiency, Sievier agreed to the match and the terms.

Since Sievier did everything at the top of his voice and the top of his voice was tremendous, attention was immediately focussed on the pair. Both men were skilled players who thought well of themselves. It had all the makings of an amusing and interesting event. Chairs were set around the table to supplement the usual billiard-room benches, the game on the second table was abandoned. Onlookers gathered about and side bets were struck on the result.

After discussion it was agreed that Horn should be given a start. Even with this handicap Sievier beat him with a certain amount of ease. Horn who, as has been said, did not like being beaten and disliked paying up even more, suggested a return match. There was some discussion about whether this should be for double or quits but in the end the stake appears to have been settled at £700. Horn asked for and got a further start based on the result of the first match. At the beginning everything went right for him. He reached ninety-eight when Sievier was seventy. Horn was in play and had the winning of the game and the saving of his money at the end of his cue. But his nerve was not up to it. He made the shot that should have allowed him to run out, and he missed.

This, of course, was just the situation in which Sievier revelled. All his life he was an actor manqué. Always with him there was an audience seen or unseen. Here it was all around him, comprised of friends, acquaintances and, no doubt, enemies for there were always enemies wherever Sievier was. All was at stake; he would be indeed hard pressed to pay if he lost; he badly needed the money a win meant to him. The odds too were against him; if he failed to make the necessary break Horn was unlikely to fluff his shot again. These were the sort of circumstances he loved and which brought out the best in him.

He took his cue, chalked it, looked around him, paused, lined up his shot—and ran out.

It is not hard to imagine the subsequent scene—Sievier's triumphant whoop, Horn's disconsolate face, the back-slapping and congratulations, 'Well done, Bob, you pulled that one out of the fire!', for the victor; the commiserations for the vanquished. Then there was the standing of drinks, the settling of bets, the general chatter after tension amidst the haze of cigar-smoke and the fumes of brandy and soda.

But if the game had brought out the best in Sievier subsequent events showed him at his worst, or very nearly so. He was always ruthless in pursuing his winnings if he was in want or if he thought the loser was likely to refuse to pay. Both of these things were present in this situation —he needed the money and he knew Horn's reputation for evading payment.

The game, which had started at a late hour, had taken some time. By now the small hours of the morning were well advanced. So—or this is what was suggested by Sievier's enemies—was Horn's drunkenness. Drunk or not he showed no inclination to pay and Sievier did not intend to part from him until he did. Dawn came and went, the rest of the company had gone to bed, still no payment had been made and still the two men were together.

At length, and whether it was in the hall of the hotel or the sitting-room of Sievier's suite was never determined and does not greatly matter, Horn produced his cheque book. With typical swagger he handed it to Sievier. He then told him to make out two cheques, one for £100 which would be paid immediately and the other for £600 which could be collected in due course. This is how Sievier relates it and it must at least be said that his evidence cannot nor could not be contradicted for Horn maintained that throughout the interview he was too drunk to remember anything nor to know what he was doing. Sievier then wrote out the cheques and he wrote them in Lady Mabel's name. He later in evidence and very foolishly gave at least three different reasons for making out the cheques in his wife's name. There was one perfectly good explanation and it was, of course, the true one, and that was that he had no bank account since he was an undischarged bankrupt but his wife's account was still open and in operation. Why he chose to make a mystery out of it is something only he himself knew but it does illustrate one of the many factors in his character which made him the despair of those who sought to conduct his cases for him. He appears always to have had the conception of the law as a sort of extraordinary game in which those who made the cleverest and most confusing replies ultimately triumphed. It is hardly necessary to remark that he was not unduly troubled by the sanctity of the oath.

The fact that Sievier himself wrote out the cheques may not be so much to his discredit as at first appears—and certainly appeared or was made to appear to certain eminent barristers and judges—for in the set to which he and Horn belonged it was, and, indeed, sometimes is, quite customary for one man to hand a cheque book to another with the request that he make out the cheque for the payer to sign. But again, in evidence, Sievier refused to stick to one explanation as to why he had done this and gave several differing ones including making the wildly improbable suggestion that Horn had tried to deceive him by making the words out for one amount and the figures for another.

The whole matter is even further complicated by the fact that Sievier's valet, Froome, gave certain damaging evidence as to what he found in the sitting-room the following morning. Froome swore that lying on Sievier's desk were several torn up cheques made out in Sievier's handwriting which bore defective signatures beginning with the letters A.E., Horn's initials. The implication was that Horn had been so drunk that Sievier had had to try several times before he could obtain a legible signature.

Too much credence should not however be placed on this evidence for Sievier subsequently discharged Froome for impertinence. Froome appears to have had difficulty in obtaining another position as a result of this and there is no doubt that every word he uttered in court in evidence in the case of Sievier v Wootton twenty-four years later drips with the stored-up malice of an embittered man. It may also be questioned just what Froome was doing examining his employer's desk and piecing together torn up papers he found there. Sievier, too, may well have been fully justified in discharging him for it is a fact that he was almost always well-liked by his servants.

But then, after obtaining his own cheques, Sievier did something which he could never explain away and which was the most damaging incident in the whole affair. There was also staying in the hotel a gentleman who went under the name and style of 'Tricky' Williams. Nothing whatsoever is known of 'Tricky' Williams save that he had earned the sobriquet conferred on him, that he had been one of the onlookers at the billiards match and that, so Sievier said, Horn owed him £700. When Sievier had obtained the two cheques for Lady Mabel he then wrote out a third for Williams which Horn also signed. His explanation of why he did this was that Horn had asked him to. It was not very convincing.

The two men then parted and Sievier went to his wife's bedroom.

'Mabel, I have some good news for you,' he said and told her of his winnings. After that he rang for Froome, gave him the cheque for £100, told him to go down to Smiths' Bank and cash it. Then he prepared himself for bed after what was, for him, only a mildly strenuous night.

On the way to the bank the valet examined the cheque and subsequently said that the signature might have been made 'with a stick or a pen'. Be that as it may the cheque was cashed without query, and the valet's efforts in evidence later on to establish that this was only done because the clerk was young and inexperienced read even more unconvincingly than any evidence of Sievier's.

When Froome returned he was met by Sievier, he says, in his dressing gown and Sievier told him to go to Williams' bedroom, to get Horn's cheque from Williams, take it to the bank, cash it and bring back the money to Sievier. If this is true it does, of course, show that some extraordinary swindle was being worked on Horn but again it rests entirely on Froome's evidence and Sievier, who acted on his own behalf in the case of Sievier v Wootton, made a complete hash of his cross-examination of Froome. Moreover, reckless though he undoubtedly was, it would seem to be extending recklessness towards the point of insanity to make a servant with whom one was already on bad terms party to such an obvious trick.

At all events when Horn woke up sometime during that day he was immediately in sufficient command of his faculties to realize that he had lost a great deal of money the night before. He took steps straight away to repair his position as best he could. It is significant that he did not at any time confront Sievier. Instead he sent to the bank to stop all the cheques. His £100 had been cashed and lost but he did succeed in stopping the other two, the one for £700 having in fact been queried and held as it was doubted by the bank that there were sufficient funds in his account to meet it. Then, to justify his actions, Horn raised a hullabaloo in the hotel, making wild accusations that he had been both drunk and drugged though just who drugged him and how it had been done he omitted to explain.

These accusations grew wilder and wilder and flew around Monte Carlo. Lady Mabel intensely disliked the notoriety which had been thrust upon them. She telegraphed the British Ambassador in Paris, Lord Dufferin, who was a relation of hers, to see if anything could be done to silence Horn and stop the scandal. Dufferin sent Sir James Harris, the British consul at Nice, along to investigate. Harris appears to have held some sort of impromptu court of enquiry as a result of which Horn was banished from Monte Carlo never to return. Harris appears also to have suggested that the whole thing was so embarrassing to the Sieviers that they might like to leave also. Wisely, from his point of view, Sievier refused to hear of this and they remained on until the season ended in March.

But relations between husband and wife were steadily getting worse. What money Sievier had or had won all went at the Casino. He didn't care. The thrill of the risk, as he said himself, was worth more than the certainty of possession. But she did. His reckless gambling frightened even her. Eventually she succeeded in extracting from him a promise that he would stay out of the Casino. For some time he loyally kept it and when the day of departure came they were able to settle the hotel bill (to Sievier's intense indignation this was not, on this occasion, allowed to remain on a running account) and pay the train fare, though precious little else was left.

And then, at the station, she missed him. She had a fair idea where he was and she was right. The lure of the last fling had caught him again.

He had only a few minutes before the train left. In that time he had two maximums on twenty-nine and another on zero. They all came up. Then, borrowing a tablecloth from an attendant, he swept his winnings into it, slung it over his shoulder and ran out to a waiting carriage. He bundled himself and his tablecloth into their *compartiment de luxe* on the Paris train just as it was pulling out from the platform. Spilling the notes out of the cloth on to the seats and the floor he counted them. He had won the equivalent of £7000 in French money.

She would not speak to him. All through the journey she remained cold, hostile and unforgiving while he spent his winnings lavishly on champagne and dinners and tips. Back in Paris, leaving her in the Rue de la Parosse, he was off again; playing up his winnings. 'Increasing my stake has always been my forte when winning.' Sometimes it worked and sometimes it went. But this time he was in one of his lucky streaks and once more, for a while, there was money to spend and burn.

His restless nature would not allow him to remain still. Although he was based in France and did most of his racing there in a comparatively small way he was constantly to and fro to London and back, for he still had some sort of an interest in the bookmaking concerns operated by his cousins and by Dey.

75

And nothing could prevent him getting into and out of escapades of all sorts of descriptions. On one occasion, returning from London to Paris he fell in with Fred Rickaby, Jack Watts and other leading jockeys who were going over to ride at Longchamps. He had made the journey so often that he thought he knew exactly where the cross-channel packet was berthed. Telling his manservant—he never moved without one, but Froome had gone and been replaced—to escort the jockeys to the boat, he stayed late on the train in other congenial company. Then, hurrying in the darkness, he made his way to the steps where he had embarked a day or two before. So sure was he that the boat would be there that he kept no look out for it. The result was that at the end of the steps he walked into empty air. The boat had been moved to another berth an Sievier went into the sea.

Splashing about he roared and shouted for help. Attracted by the commotion a French sailor came to the quayside and peered down at him. Since a fair sea was running and he was besides in some danger of being pulled under by the mackintosh he was wearing Sievier's position was one of some peril. This did not deter him as much as the wetness and discomfort.

'Qu'est que vous faites là, M'sieu?' the sailor asked him. The reply he received was couched in such basic Anglo-Saxon that he understood it without any trouble. A rope was fetched and Sievier was pulled on to the quay. The incident did not affect his spirits in the slightest and he made all he could of it. When he got on board his entrance to the saloon in his sodden clothes, declaiming details of his adventure, was worthy of the theatre. He emptied the contents of his bowler hat over those who laughed at him and enjoyed every minute of the sensation he caused. Then Jack Watts tipped him a winner on the way across and all was indeed well.

There was also another and far less pleasant encounter. This time it was with Gill, the barrister who had advised, or, as he held, mis-advised him in the *Hawk* case. They met in the Café de Paris. It was not perhaps the place where one would have expected to meet a prominent Presbyterian and pillar of rectitude such as Gill. This Sievier commented on, as usual at the top of his voice. No doubt he said unforgivable and inexcusable things. Words ensued and Sievier flew into one of his wild rages. A scuffle of some sort took place and Gill ended up on the pavement.

Gill had recently prospered exceedingly. Dignity tinged with pomposity was beginning to sit markedly upon him. The incident was humiliating in the extreme. His loathing of Sievier and animosity towards him were proportionately increased. It was a mutual dislike which became more bitter as both men grew older.

But during those years the most exciting and important thing which was to happen to Sievier was the beginning and then the burgeoning of his association with Eleanor Master.

9

Toddington

❧❧❧❧❧❧

Eleanor Master was tall and blonde and beautiful; she was also a thoroughly nice woman. A fairy tale princess, she truly loved Sievier and if he ever loved any woman it was she. To the end of his days a full length picture of her in Edwardian dress went with him to all his many houses.

A niece of a Governor of the Bank of England, she had been presented at Court and was married to a country gentleman called Hoskin Master. But once she met Sievier no other man existed for her. Being rich in her own right she took a house at 16 Walton Place, Pont Street, and lived there during the early days of their association.

Sievier always longed for a country life and what he wanted she wished him to have. They looked around for a suitable property in which to set up house and, some time in 1897, they found one. This was Park House, Toddington, or, as it later became known during Sievier's occupancy, Toddington Park, Bedfordshire.

At this time, Sievier, try though he might, had not yet succeeded in obtaining his discharge from bankrupty. As negotiations for the lease of Park House were proceeding he went before the Registrar to try once more for his discharge, but the best he could do was to have it suspended for two years. He was, however, far from being without means for his gambling was going well. A banking account was opened in the name of 'R. Sawyer' into which his winnings were paid. An 'R. Sawyer' or someone like him does appear to have existed but he must have been a man of straw, for the signature 'R. Sawyer' bore such a remarkable resemblance to Sievier's own that the bank requested him to change it to 'Robt. Sawyer'. A little later Mrs. Master was given the name of 'Mrs. Sawyer' and an authority to draw on this account so that she could use it to pay for some plumbing at Walton Place. Later the account was transferred to the name of Major Arthur Charles Silverthorne a well-known amateur cricketer and a friend of Sievier, but 'Robt. Sawyer' continued to sign the cheques. In two years no less than £47,000 passed through this account. That was not all. There had been a reconciliation with his mother and an account was opened for her in the Dunstable Branch of Barclays Bank. Sievier had authority to draw on this account and did so. In the same two years £34,929 11s. 6d. passed through it. It was sarcastically remarked by counsel when Sievier was being examined as to these and other matters in the perjury trial that if this account really belonged to Mrs. Alicia Sievier she was a lady who took a great interest in racing matters for almost all the cheques paid in or out were either to or from bookmakers or other racing men. There can be little or no doubt that these two accounts were Sievier's own and £75,000 is not a bad sum for an undischarged bankrupt to have had at his command during two years.

His position made the negotiations for Park House a matter of some delicacy. Mr. Cowper Cooper, its owner, wanted an assurance that the rent was secure. The solution arrived at was that Mr. Daunay, Sievier's solicitor, took the lease in his own name with a proviso that he could assign it whenever Sievier obtained his discharge. Cooper, however, demanded a guarantee for payment of the rent. Mrs. Master agreed to give this and wrote the following letter to Daunay which, quite incidentally, shows also her feelings for Sievier at the time:

Dear Mr. Daunay—With regard to the house at Toddington I have, since seeing you, discussed the matter with Mr. Sievier and his mother again. It will be, as I said, an opportunity for a country home for myself and my children, so you can accept my guarantee that I will pay the rent and see that you are not in any way out of pocket if you will take up the lease. It can be passed over to Mr. Sievier should he, at some later period, be in a better financial position. This will suit me admirably since I would do anything for Mr. Sievier and his children, even to paying the Jews, but he says he will do that himself some day. Yours truly, ELEANOR MASTER.

It was Sievier himself, however, who conducted the correspondence with Mr. Cowper Cooper's agents and it contained such typical Sievierana as 'I do not want to be treated as a cipher by such omnipotent dictatorship', and 'Turn that idea into smoke by the accompanying boxes', there being a dozen match boxes included in the packet with the letter.

At last however, the business was completed. The lease of Park House,

Toddington, with about three thousand acres of shooting and eighty acres of meadow was signed. The rent was £475 a year.

The marriages of both Mrs. Master and Sievier were now irretrievably wrecked. Mrs. Master left her husband and was cut off by his relatives and friends, and in 1898, just after the birth of their third child, Mabel, Sievier and Lady Mabel parted. A deed of separation—there was no divorce—was drawn up, by which Sievier covenanted to pay his wife £40 a week for life. This covenant, it may be added, was dutifully kept. He took the two older children, Gogo and Bruce, and brought them with him to Toddington Park. The youngest child remained with her mother.

Now Sievier had the companionship of a beautiful woman whom he loved and who loved him; he had, too, a country estate where he could live in the style and state he had always wanted, fill his stables with hunters, give cricket and shooting parties and entertain with a regal hand.

At once he set about improving and adding to the property. The sum of two thousand five hundred pounds was spent on a billiards room, more bathrooms and other additions. Mrs. Master thought the coach-houses not big enough for the carriages they required and they were enlarged. Work began immediately on the levelling of a small hill on the estate and the construction there of a superlative cricket ground which commanded views over much of the counties of Bedfordshire and Cambridgeshire. Gardeners, gamekeepers, grooms, a chef, a butler and a full household staff were all engaged. The cellars were filled with champagne and other fine wines. Soon Bob Sievier's friends were to know that if in adversity he demanded money, in affluence he dispensed it with a ready and lavish hand.

At first, during settling in, things were moderately quiet. He went hunting with the Oakley; it was not to be expected that he would be anything other than a thruster and all his life he went most gallantly to hounds. As soon as they were old enough the children were mounted on the best, turned out by the most expensive tailors and expected to go as well as they looked. From their very early days he treated them almost as equals. They were brought up to behave in a manner far in advance of their years and Gogo who was both pretty and precocious certainly suffered from this. As a parent Sievier was careless and unpredictable. Once when he complained about something Bobbie had done he was asked if he had ever taken any steps to teach him manners or discipline. 'I sent him off the cricket field for being rude to an umpire,' he replied after deep thought.

WHAT IS IT?

(Dedicated without his kind permission to Mr. Panton.)

EARL DUDLEY (Showman): "Ladies and gentlemen, you doubtless supposed that this was a genuine honest Australian Kangaroo. You were mistaken, however; it was merely a Toady. But it is one no longer; for, as you perceive, I have made an Ass of it!"

(From *Melbourne Life*; reproduced in *The Winning Post*, 1905)

3a. What Is It?

ME AND MY MENAGERIE.

THE STAFF OF THE "WINNING POST."

3b. Me and My Menagerie

4. *Rex v. Sievier.* The Scene in Court

A groundsman from Lords was employed to lay the pitch on the cricket ground but by the time summer came it was not yet ready for the kind of cricket Sievier wanted played there. Nets were, however, put up up and they were made available to anyone in the village who wanted to practise. He himself was an enthusiastic if not very effective bat and much of his time that summer when he was not racing was spent on the cricket ground. Even on racing days often he would rise early and be out at the nets at six o'clock having arranged with H. L. Hobbs, a useful bowler from the village, to meet him there and give him a knock. Other times he would place half crowns on the stumps and anyone from the village could have a go at bowling him out and collecting the money. In this way he began to form a shrewd idea of the capabilities of the various players, for already he was thinking and talking about forming a Toddington team.

So that first summer at Toddington with Eleanor Master and the children slid by. Now, with her resources at his command and such money from his betting as was still in his bank accounts, he was anxious to get back into real racing again and to set himself up as an owner. He had tasted the interest and enjoyment of managing a string, albeit a minor one, when he had had Lady Mabel's horses under his control and he had not forgotten it.

October came and with it the final order discharging him from bankruptcy. The lease of Toddington Park was forthwith assigned to him, 'Sawyer' was killed off and Mrs. Sievier's account closed. He was not to see the inside of the bankruptcy court again for over thirty years.

Straightaway, in November, he began to buy horses and arranged with Charles Morton to train them for him. His first acquisition was a little horse called Crarae which he bought out of a seller in Manchester for 560 guineas. Morton did not care for his purchase and said so for Morton could rival Sievier himself in outspokenness. Sievier wanted Crarae to run in a race for which he was entered the following day. Crarae was to prove that Sievier had lost neither his eye nor his flair for picking horses but this was not to be the occasion. Without telling his owner, Morton sent him home with his other horses and settled down to a game of cards with Sievier and a well-known commission agent called Charles Mills.

A large, thick-set man, Mills was a betting commissioner and a heavy gambler. A number of important stables employed him to work their betting commissions for them so as to get the best odds available. He was a heavy gambler himself but a shrewder one than most for much of his gains he kept. A curious set of circumstances had given him his start. As a youth he had been a bookmaker's runner for the Birmingham firm of Morey and James. There he had made the acquaintance of a well-known commissioner who liked him and sometimes took him along to teach him the lore of his specialized trade. This commissioner was accustomed to take a house at Goodwood with a trainer and two of his owners for whom at the meeting he would work whatever commissions were necessary. Just before the meeting he was taken ill and suggested young Mills as his replacement. Mills successfully carried through a difficult betting coup and from then never looked back though it was on a filly called Winkfield's Pride a year or two later that he really founded his fortune. This filly was owned by an Irish solicitor. She was trained by W. T. Robinson with the Cambridgeshire in view. Given 6st. 10lb Robinson and his connections knew that she was something of a racing certainty. Mills was brought in, sworn to secrecy and told to work the commission. He started backing Winkfield's Pride at 100—1 against and ended when she was 9—2. She won in a canter and Mills himself cleared £25,000. With some of this he bought a large house on Wimbledon Common which he called Winkfield Lodge. There he lived quietly and very few of the inhabitants of Wimbledon knew who he was or what he did for a living. As the years went by he acquired richer and more powerful clients one of them being Solly Joel.

The card-game continued all night. When morning came Morton, knowing he had no runner that day, went off to get some sleep. Hardly had he undressed when Sievier, apparently as fresh as when the game started, came to his room and asked him in no uncertain terms what he was doing preparing for bed when he should be getting ready to saddle Crarae. 'Crarae will win today,' he said.

'He won't because I've sent him home with the rest,' was Morton's reply. 'Now go away, I want to get some sleep.'

'You're a nice bloody trainer,' Sievier told him, slammed the door behind him and went off in a rage.

But in racing matters knowledge and common sense usually prevailed over his outbursts of temper and temperament. Crarae, as he quickly realized when he thought about it, was better put by. Morton had been right and money wagered on the horse would have been thrown away. His ruffled feelings were further assuaged when he saw that Tod Sloan was to ride Proclamation in the Manchester November Handicap and that the price offered was the astounding one of 25—1.

It was of course Tod Sloan 'the monkey up the stick' who made it certain that in future all jockeys would ride leaning forward over their horses' withers and with their leathers pulled up. He was not, however, as is often thought, the originator of this style in England. A negro called Simms had come over a few seasons earlier and had tried it out. But Simms was a very bad jockey; he had been a hopeless failure and had returned to America with his name and his style discredited. This was one of the reasons which led to the catcalls and derision that greeted Sloan on his appearance on English racecourses.

Up to his time races in England had been run slowly and in snatches. Sloan changed all this. He shot away from the start, rode his race all the way and was often past the post before his bemused opponents had decided where to commence their finishing run. After Sloan not only the seat of the jockey but the whole art of riding races had to be changed. When one adds that he was also the possessor of wonderful hands and was a superb judge of pace it is not surprising that to many of the English jockeys he appeared to be a competitor who had dropped in amongst them from another world. They didn't like it and there was considerable hostility to this bewildering newcomer.

It was Lord William Beresford who was Sloan's foster father in English racing. He was in partnership with Pierre Lorillard the American tobacco millionaire and together they brought him over to England and backed him. This was powerful patronage; too powerful for Sloan's best interests. For Sloan if a genius on a horse was a fool on his feet. Cocky, brash, over-confident and over-indulgent he made enemies almost as easily as did Sievier himself. Lord William treated him as a valuable plaything, never checking his excesses and laughing at his follies. Puffing a large cigar in the paddock and parade ring, exhaling its aroma over the great, telling them in the unabashed accents of Indiana just what he thought of their horses and the way they were trained, enjoying to the full his position as a clockwork toy of the *haut ton* Sloan did not realize that once the hands that wound the spring were withdrawn he would be broken, and he was. That time had not come yet. He was then at the height of his fame and prowess.

Sievier had appreciated Sloan's genius from the first. He put everything he had or could raise on Proclamation in the big race and was rewarded by seeing Sloan get him home by a neck from Invincible II ridden in the old style by Otto Madden, the then champion jockey. His winter keep was well provided for. He went back to Toddington a rich and happy man.

The outbreak of the Boer War in October 1899 was not taken with any seriousness by the classes in England from which wealth and power were drawn. It was looked upon as just another small war of Empire against a semi-barbarous nation, a few Boer farmers, who would be quickly quelled by the might of Empire and the show of force. The lessons of Majuba Hill and the Jameson Raid had not been learnt. England was still in the mental climate of hubris engendered by the great Jubilee of 1897. It was very quickly dispersed.

Black Week in December of that year saw the humiliating defeats of Magersfontein, Stormberg and Colenso. Morale at home came down with a crash. Suddenly it was seen that the Empire was not invulnerable, and its arms very far indeed from being invincible even when pitted against Boer farmers armed with rifles and a few German quick-firing guns. Moreover the army in the field was not of sufficient size to meet the tasks which now faced it. More men were needed and called for. Sievier had experience of South Africa and of campaigning there which was more than could be said for the vast majority of officers already at the seat of the war. The opportunity of seeing active service once again appealed immediately to his adventurous nature. Straightaway he volunteered and was accepted.

Early in the new year a scheme was put forward and approved to provide for the raising of bodies of Yeomanry which, recruited from countrymen who could ride and shoot, would provide the type of mounted infantry that it was at last being realized were badly needed to fight this sort of war. Sievier decided that he would set about raising a troop of South Bedfordshire Yeomanry to take its place in the proposed Yeomanry corps. In order to do this he applied for and received the approval of Lord Valentia who was then head of all Yeomanry affairs and of Lord Cowper who commanded the South Bedfordshire district.

With typical energy he threw himself wholeheartedly into this new task, campaigning for funds, and personally supervising the riding and musketry tests for each man. Remembering his previous experiences on the veldt he knew just what requirements his men should fulfil. The examination he put them through was thorough and severe, with the result that a high proportion of the proposed recruits failed to come up to his exacting standards and were turned down. He himself possessed many if not all of the qualities required of a leader of irregular cavalry—courage (no man ever dared deny him that), dash, experience, an eye for ground and the ability to inspire the men he led with his own unbounded confidence. He might well have made a name for himself in yet another field had he been allowed to do so.

For quite suddenly difficulties began to be put in his way. The Imperial Yeomanry Committee summoned him before them and asked him if he was prepared to step down from his proposed command and to serve under a regular officer. This was not an unreasonable request, especially in the military climate of the day which demanded strict observance of seniority and precedence, and he accepted it. But the cold reception given him by the committee, so unlike the enthusiasm with which his first proposals had been received, raised in him suspicions that backstairs influence was somewhere at work against him. In this he was right for he soon met further obstruction and opposition, and petty restrictions were applied to him and the men in his command. His letters went unanswered, equipment was held up, barrack accommodation refused. His suspicions hardened into certainty.

He had a fair idea who it was that was exercising this influence. He made it his business to see if he was right and soon did so for there were many who liked him, approved of his project and were willing to help. The man behind it all was none other than Dudley, his old enemy from Australian days and elsewhere.

Dudley, the failure on the racecourse and the Turf, had seen his influence at Court and in Parliament steadily grow under the skilful guidance and persuasiveness of his wife. One would have thought he might well have forgotten Sievier or at least allowed him to pursue his life, which touched Dudley's nowhere, unimpeded and unhindered by him. Apparently he could not. Perhaps he was afraid of him for it has been hinted that Sievier knew of certain youthful indiscretions committed by Dudley in Australia, and Dudley and his wife had great ambitions.

Dudley did not confront Sievier personally; that was not his way. He went to Lord Valentia and told him that Sievier was not a fit person to be entrusted with Her Majesty's commission nor should he be permitted to command troops in her army and in the field.

Sievier heard of what Dudley had done while he was still awaiting a reply to the last of his urgent letters requesting instructions concerning the enrolment of himself and his men. He was told, and he knew it to be true, that it was of no avail pursuing his military career any further. Official notice to that effect was on its way and would arrive in a matter of days.

He resolved to forestall it and to go out with a gesture which would bring the matter before the public and do something to satisfy the wrong done to him. Letting the press know what he was doing he held a parade of his men at Luton. There he addressed them, telling them of how he had been denied the pleasure and honour of leading them into action and that they must re-enlist separately in other corps. Then he took off his hat and roared out suddenly in his great voice: 'In the Queen's name I disband you!' As he had hoped and indeed arranged, the incident received considerable attention in the public prints throughout the country.

Dudley himself later went out to the war but, as Sievier took considerable pleasure in pointing out, he played no very glorious part in it for he occupied a desk in the Adjutant-General's office and the greater part of his military career was spent in comfort in Capetown.

But Sievier was also accustomed to add when telling the story that Dudley really did him a service in preventing him from going to South Africa, for the year was 1900 and had he gone he would never have bought, owned and raced a mare called Sceptre.

IO

Annus Mirabilis

✜✜✜✜✜✜✜

After his disappointment over the Yeomanry affair Sievier went back
to Toddington and finished his season's hunting. Then he took his
mother and the two children off to Monte Carlo for a few weeks in
the sun before returning to England and devoting himself to the serious
business of racing. Prior to his departure for the Riviera he had been to
Newmarket to watch the various strings at work. He wanted to pick the
winner of the Lincoln if he could. A horse called Sir Geoffrey who was
in the race with 8st. 6lb impressed him in his work. After studying the
handicap he backed him to win a big stake. On the opening day of the
flat, fresh from the Riviera sun, he arrived back at Dover to be handed a
telegram from his commissioner telling him that Sir Geoffrey had won
the Lincoln. The starting price was 100—12 but Sievier had of course
obtained far better odds and had won £9000. It was a good way to
start the season.

Following his usual practice he played up these winnings at Liverpool,
Derby and Newmarket. Now he had resources in plenty at his disposal
and he used much of them in buying horses, all of which he sent along
to Morton's yard. Then he and Morton decided to make a trip to Ireland
to see if they could find something that would win them better races
than those Sievier's horses had been running in up to now. In this they
failed but Sievier made the acquaintance of Mr. Kennedy of Straffan a
substantial breeder whose methods of producing yearlings he studied
and admired and of Mr. F. H. Peard the well-known veterinary surgeon.
While they were there they heard that the late Duke of Westminster's
yearlings were to be put up for sale at Newmarket in July.

Coming back on the mailboat Sievier remarked that this sale offered
a wonderful opportunity of obtaining something likely to win a classic.
Morton agreed but added with typical pessimism that he didn't think
there was the slightest hope of doing so. John Porter of Kingsclere, he
pointed out, would be there. He had trained for the late Duke, he would

know exactly what the potentialities of the yearlings were and it was most unlikely that he would let anything worthwhile escape him for he would be buying in for the young Duke who was then in South Africa. Sievier refused to be discouraged. He said that he would study the catalogue and that he would consult Mr. Peard whose knowledge and abilities had impressed him, and would attend and bid for those lots they both picked out. This conversation well illustrates the difference between the characters of the two men. Both were heavy gamblers but that is where any similarity ends. Sievier was ebullient, breezy and optimistic; Morton gloomy, cautious and ever more pessimistic as the day of a race or the decision to bid for a horse approached. Where Sievier was appreciative, Morton was critical. Both were quick-witted and outspoken and during their association a constant verbal battle was waged between them.

It has often been said that had Sceptre remained in Morton's care during Sievier's ownership she might never have been beaten. What is overlooked is the fact that had she remained with Morton she almost certainly would not have run in all five classics. Morton would have preferred to have made sure of winning one. Sievier, as always, played for the highest stakes. He gambled for immortal fame and the possibility of sweeping the board.

But that is to anticipate. When they returned to England the question of bidding at the July sales was put aside for the moment for the Epsom Spring Meeting was coming along. In those days the City and Suburban was still one of the most important races in the calendar, the best horses were run in it and there was a strong ante-post market. That year the Australian trainer J. E. Brewer had two horses entered, The Grafter and Syurla, both of which appeared to be well-fancied. One of Sievier's informants told him that it was probable that Syurla would start at the shorter price of the two but that the coup would be worked with The Grafter.

Resolving to find out what he could for himself Sievier went down to Epsom where Brewer trained. There he put up at the King's Head and left an early call. On the Downs just after dawn he rode his hack quietly towards where he had been told Brewer worked his horses. He was quite alone; there was no one else about at all. But he was in the right place. Soon he saw four horses coming towards him. It was a trial of Brewer's two for The City and Suburban.

Quickly concealing himself behind a convenient bush Sievier watched and noted all the details of the trial. The Grafter was a big, ponderous rough-looking horse, long in the back and with little about him immediately to take the eye. But he had won the Melbourne Cup and Sievier knew something of the worth of Melbourne Cup winners. The way The Grafter went in that trial convinced him that here was the winner of the big race. He backed him to win £35,000, and had a saver on Mr. John Miller's Insurance.

From his box at Epsom, Sievier and his friends saw The Grafter, ridden by Mornington Cannon, win comfortably from Insurance. He had brought off yet another huge gamble. Then he went to Newmarket for the Guineas and backed The Prince of Wales's horse Diamond Jubilee to win him £5000. There, too, he took a fancy to a huge two-year-old called Toddington which he backed to win him a big sum in The May Plate. Toddington obliged and Sievier cleared £20,000 at the meeting. After that he saw Crarae justify his purchase and Morton's judgment by winning the Earl of Chester's Welter Handicap, having backed him to win £10,000, and went on to Kempton Park to increase his winnings by a further £7000 on another horse of his called Gamecrip trained by Morton and ridden by Sam Loates.

All the time he was looking around for better class horses to improve his string. Toddington had caught his eye and he resolved to have him. Toddington was the property of a Mr. James Musker who owned and controlled The Home & Colonial Stores and who was one of the many merchant princes who were then moving into racing and thus into the society which the Prince of Wales was opening to the plutocrats. Sievier sent a friend of his, Tom Vigors, who was the Irish Racing correspondent of *The Sportsman* and also a bloodstock dealer, to see if Musker would sell. Musker would not part but similarly Sievier would not take no for an answer. He instructed Vigors to go back and not to leave Musker until at least a price had been named. In order to get rid of Vigors, Musker asked for 10,000 guineas which he thought would end the matter and put off any possible purchaser.

'I'll give it to him!' Sievier said when Vigors returned with the news. 'He's mine!' And he went off straight away to Musker with the money in his pockets, in cash, twenty-one £500 notes, no less, and handed them over. Then, to round off the deal he somehow persuaded or compelled the totally reluctant Musker to give one of the £500 notes to Vigors as commission for securing such a magnificent price!

When Morton heard of all this he was horrified. He was even more worried about the whole deal when Sievier took him to inspect the horse. 'Never have I seen such an enormous two-year-old,' he wrote afterwards. 'Although very early in the season—it was then May—he stood fully 16.3 hands. I could only just reach the top of him.' He turned to Sievier and said, 'He's all right now but what is he going to be this time next year? The chances are that he'll turn out to be a roarer.'

'That's right,' Sievier said. 'I knew you'd crab him!'

Sievier insisted on running Toddington in the Woodcote at Epsom but before that they tried him with Crarae. Toddington was receiving 3lb from handicapper Crarae. They both knew that Crarae could go more than a bit and he had won the Chester race comfortably. Sam Loates who rode Toddington in the trial gave away some ground through not being aware of the exact lay-out of the gallop on the Downs. Crarae won it by a neck but taking all the circumstances into account they both knew that the Woodcote was theirs.

It proved to be so and Sievier once more played up his winnings, backing Diamond Jubilee to win him £30,000 in the Derby. Having collected that, he ran Toddington again in a £1000 race at Kempton Park which he won. His winnings that week were £53,000. When, a year or so later, his bank account was produced in court it was shewn that no less than £262,000 had passed through it between December 1899 and November 1901. At this time, indeed, it has been said that in terms of ready cash he was one of the richest men in England and there is little reason to doubt it.

Now all racing England was ringing with his name. He was already something of a popular idol with the crowd. There were reasons for this. He embodied in many ways the damn-your-eyes attitude the ordinary staid Englishman has always secretly envied. He did the things nearly all of them in their hearts wished they could do—kept mistresses, drank champagne at all hours of the day and night, gambled for enormous stakes, and lived in style in the country or in the South of France surrounded by servants and beautiful women. Always well turned out— to the end of his life he favoured light coloured ties and grey Homburg hats—accompanied by some 'lovely woman' or other, unabashed by any man or any misfortune, forever ready to have a tilt at the nobs and to sympathize with the underdog or to fling a fiver to someone in need, he was indeed a flamboyant figure who brought brightness and fun into drab ordinary lives at the turn of the century. And then, too, his horses were always run openly and straight. Then and ever afterwards he was completely frank about their form and their chances. Anyone who cared to ask was told if one of his runners was fancied. Often those who didn't would hear of it anyway for his great voice could carry clear across a racecourse. 'So and so will win today! Help yourself!' was what he would shout out right and left if he had a fancied runner. There was never anything secretive about Sievier as to either his virtues or his vices. The actor in him compelled him to live all his life out in the fullest glare of publicity. Some gamblers conceal their winnings. He blazoned them forth. And they were followed by entertainment to all and sundry on the most lavish scale. Champagne flowed for everyone, sovereigns were scattered like the wind. No wonder the crowd loved him. No wonder the proprieties were scandalized.

Just then there were two minor set-backs, two checks in the triumphant progress. In winning at Kempton, Toddington appeared to break down. Sievier sent to Ireland for Mr. Peard who diagnosed a split pastern. Toddington never ran again and Sievier, ever the optimist about his own possessions, mourned the loss of next year's Derby winner. But William Allison, now a close friend and confidant, succeeded in selling the colt abroad for a good price. And there was plenty of money, in any event, to replace him.

The other incident was perhaps more serious in its consequences. A filly called Kaffir Queen had won a seller at Newmarket and Sievier wanted her. He bid 1100 guineas and she was knocked down to him. When it came to payment he offered Mr. Weatherby a cheque. Weatherby refused to accept it nor would he allow Sievier to take possession of the filly until payment was made in cash or the cheque guaranteed. Since Sievier had over £100,000 in his account at Lloyds Bank at the time and the insult was given in circumstances in which it would receive the maximum publicity he had every reason to feel aggrieved.

It was, however, very difficult to get the better of Sievier in social warfare of this sort. When he had at his command the sort of resources he now had he was accustomed to carry with him large sums of money, mostly in the form of £500 notes, to be used for cash betting and other purposes as and when required.

Feeling in his pockets he now produced three of these notes and handed them to Weatherby. He then asked for change.

Weatherby's were then and still are bankers to the Jockey Club. He was offered one of their cheques for the change due to him. This was a singularly stupid thing for Weatherby to do; it gave Sievier an opening which he was unlikely to ignore. Nor did he. Bitingly he informed Weatherby that since he had been asked for cash he wanted cash for his change and he declined in his turn to take the proffered cheque unless, of course, as he courteously added, it in its turn was guaranteed by a reliable source. Since Weatherby had not with him cash to the required amount he found the tables neatly turned upon him and that it was he who was now in a singularly embarrassing position. Moreover, Sievier's voice had not been modulated and a crowd was gathering to see the fun. Nor was Sievier slow to press home his advantage. He graciously told Weatherby that he would be happy to extend to him and his firm, as stakeholders to the Jockey Club, a certain due time to pay. Then he left him.

The story merited repeating. Soon the whole of Newmarket heard of it. But Weatherby's dignity suffered as a result. Another important enemy had been made and a feud developed which was conducted with animosity and which continued to the end of Sievier's life.

The trouble was, as usual, that he would never let an insult die. All this time as he collected friends so he made enemies too. He was convinced, with some justification, that Dudley had activated the whole of the racing and social establishment against him. This made him look around for real or imaginary slights or snubs from anyone whom he fancied to be on the side of authority. If he found any such, his riposte was immediate, deadly and hurtful.

Sir Blundell Maple, the furnishing magnate, was then a man of some importance on the Turf. He spent lavishly on bloodstock and up to that year held the record for having paid the highest prices in England for a racehorse and a yearling, the sums being 15,000 guineas for Common, the Derby winner of 1891 and 6000 guineas for Childwick as a yearling. His money came from his stores in Tottenham Court Road where he provided every essential article for the home. One could go into Maple's Stores, such was the boast of its proprietor, and not leave it until your newly purchased house had been furnished down to the last and most intimate detail. His money had brought him a knighthood, a position in the fluctuating society of the day and prominence on the Turf which was eventually to lead, just before his death, to his election to the Jockey Club. He was a man of immense self-importance and pomposity.

It was not to be expected that a man such as Blundell Maple would look upon Sievier's successes with a favourable eye. 'Can nobody stop this fellow?' he enquired in booming and pompous tones on the race-course in the hearing of many, one of whom, of course, conveyed the remark to Sievier.

Sievier's reply was swift. He remembered, he told the informant, a similar remark of Maple's made to Sam Lewis, the moneylender. (He may have remembered it; he may also have invented it). Maple—he said—met Lewis one day in Bond Street. Bending towards the money-lender, he enquired in his sublimest and most patronizing manner (Sievier called it 'veneered' hauteur!) 'Good afternoon, Lewis. How is money in Cork Street?' 'All right,' was the immediate reply. 'How is bedroom china in Tottenham Court Road?'

The story, as Sievier well knew, was far too good not to be repeated far and wide and he had collected another prominent enemy. But with the tide of fortune running so strongly for him that year nothing much mattered. Certainly the hostility of such a one as Maple whom he despised as a *nouveau riche* upstart (and said so) did not. But after all these excitements he relaxed from racing for the time being to concentrate on cricket.

There was a move on foot then to start a Bedfordshire County side. He gave a subscription of £100 and was elected vice-president. The Toddington ground had now been completed to his satisfaction. Selecting a village team he fitted them out in caps and belts made up of his racing colours of black, gold and red. After that he set about organizing the first of his famous cricket weeks. In this he was helped by the same Major Arthur Charles Silverthorne who had proved such a convenient ally in the matter of the Robert Sawyer bank account and by Archie Maclaren, another friend, captain of Lancashire and England and a great gambler. Maclaren had been a client of Punch & Co. during its brief and colourful life and was now betting with T. H. Dey.

With the assistance of these two a truly formidable side was gathered to play the village and take part in other matches. It included Lockwood the Surrey fast bowler, Hayward of Surrey and England, W. L. Murdoch who had captained Australia, and A. O. Jones the captain of Nottinghamshire.

But by far the biggest catch of all was W. G. Grace, the famous 'W.G.' the greatest cricketer of his time and one of the immortals of the game.

Grace was a huge man with a great spade beard. Until J. B. Hobbs beat it in 1926 he held the record for the number of centuries scored in first class cricket; he was also a useful bowler and a magnificent field. But he was something more than just a great cricketer. He was a character and a personality in his own right. An exponent of 'gamesmanship' decades before the name was invented he was a ruthless opponent either on the cricket field or across the billiards table. His appetites, too, matched his gargantuan frame and Sievier loved to tell how during these weeks he would drink champagne by the magnum out of a soda water tumbler and liqueur brandy out of a wine glass without any noticeable interference with the quickness of his eye or his wits.

Bellamy, the poulterer from Jermyn Street, sent down grouse for the cricketing luncheons, there was a butler to serve the champagne at dinner, the Yquem with the dessert and to place the port on the table afterwards. Later on in the new billiards room there were card tables set out for those who wished to play and a grand piano was provided for others who might want music with their fun. When the cricket weeks and later in the year the shooting parties became even more popular and the hospitality more extravagant it became necessary to build a bungalow in the grounds to accommodate the overflow of guests.

During these revels Mrs. Master was a gracious and lovely hostess. Other 'charming ladies' were there to enhance the evening's entertainment. They played the piano, sang or sometimes took a hand at cards or a cue at the billiards table. Sievier was now not just living like a lord; he was living like a rajah.

At times he entertained the company himself, holding them spellbound with tales of his early days in South Africa and Australia. He was tremendously good company then and always, especially when things were going well for him, witty, breezy, inventive, inexhaustible apparently both in mind and body. His was not a cruel wit unless he was wounded or thought he was and wanted to strike back. Then he did so with the speed and savagery of a tiger and much the same deadliness.

He was in demand, too, in those days at country occasions, village functions and suchlike, for in his formal after-dinner speaking he was as witty and amusing as he was during the revels at Toddington Park. It was during one of those after-dinner speeches that he made the oft-quoted remark concerning the reference to him as 'a gambler pure and simple'. 'Pure I may be,' he said. 'But I'm damned if I'm simple!'

There were revels indeed that summer at Toddington. There was money in waggon loads to be spent and life was to be lived for twenty-four hours in every day. No wonder invitations were sought after. The village loved him, the Bohemians adored him; but still the County did not call and the aristocracy stayed away.

This he resented; it was a burning wound that was always with him. He knew he was far more acceptable by birth and breeding than upstarts like Blundell Maple, Musker, or Sir James Duke with whom he

94

was soon to be in real trouble, or their offspring. It was true that he would truckle to no man and the English aristocracy demanded sycophancy or some mark of subservience before accepting either new wealth or old eccentricity. He was curiously blind and remained so all his life to the fact that he had wilfully flouted all the conventions and outraged every one of society's sacred cows. Here he was at the age of forty with two marriages behind him—and a token retention, at least, of the marriage bond was all important in the hypocritical society of the day—living with a well-connected woman who was not his wife whom he had filched from her rightful husband. And if that were not enough he had been bankrupt three times, struck off the roll of those permitted to attend court, been involved in heaven knew how many gambling scandals and was still likely to seduce your wife or run away with your daughter at the drop of a hat.

Sievier's sins were never forgotten or forgiven, but then he did parade them so. He never observed any of the commandments, but the eleventh least of all. Discretion had no place or part in his make up, but this he could not see or, if he saw it, he would not acknowledge it.

Unquestionably the urge to show the aristocrats and the rulers of racing that he could take them on at their own game and beat them in their best races was a prime motive in his determination to secure the best of the Eaton blood at the sale of the Duke of Westminster's yearlings which was now approaching.

Purchase of Sceptre—and Others

❧❧❧❧❧

When the catalogue for the Eaton sale arrived at Toddington Sievier read it carefully and marked the lots which appealed to him. This was his opportunity and he was determined not to let it pass. He had boundless confidence in his own judgment but the occasion was so important that for once he decided to reinforce it. The day before the Sale he, Charles Morton and F. H. Peard spent hours going through the catalogue and the pedigrees again and then in inspecting the colts and fillies themselves.

Morton was, as usual, dour and pessimistic, predicting once more that the whole thing was a waste of time. Who were they, he said, to pit their resources against those of the Duke of Westminster, the richest man in England and perhaps the world? Peard was Irish and more sanguine by nature. Moreover there was very little about buying yearlings that he did not know. It was he who purchased for the great gambling stable run by Mr. Purefoy at Druid's Lodge when its occupants operated huge and successful coups in conditions of such secrecy that they were known as 'The Hermits of Salisbury Plain'. The basis of the great success of Druid's Lodge was Mr. Peard's knowledge and flair as Sievier well knew. Certainly when he did decide to take advice he took the best.

The last time Sievier had bid for a horse had been the occasion of his encounter with Mr. Weatherby over Kaffir Queen. He had not forgotten the occasion and was determined not to expose himself to further insult, this time from Somerville Tattersall who would be conducting the Sale on behalf of his firm. Tattersall, like Weatherby, lived at the whim of the Establishment. In Sievier's eyes he was just such another lackey of theirs who might well be expected to refuse to take his bids on a trumped up and unconvincing excuse. Accordingly he armed himself with a large stock of his favourite £500 bank notes amounting in all to over £20,000. With these in his pockets he went round to see Somerville Tattersall at The Rutland Arms. It was, as he well knew, after closing time for the banks and there can be no doubt that he planned the whole thing and took immense pleasure in the scene that followed.

Using all the charm of which he was capable which was considerable he commenced by courteously introducing himself to Tattersall. He then told him that, since he seldom was a bidder at auctions, he must be quite unknown, from a business point of view at least, to the firm of Tattersall. Thereupon he produced the £20,000 in notes and handed them to the astonished auctioneer. He intended, he said, to make certain purchases the following day and the money was an earnest of his ability to pay for what he bought.

Tattersall, who was of a nervous and excitable disposition, was horrified at accepting responsibility for the huge sum so suddenly thrust upon him. He protested that he was quite satisfied to accept Sievier's bids without any such deposit. The production of it, he said, was quite sufficient to convince him beyond all doubt of the other's bona fides. Sievier, however, was not to be put off. He had been humiliated once by the authorities. Tattersalls and Weatherby's were in close liaison. Nothing resembling what had happened at Newmarket was going to occur again, of that he was utterly determined. He was also enjoying every moment of Tattersall's obvious nervous perturbation. The money, he insisted, must remain in Tattersall's possession.

'But where shall I put it?' enquired the anxious auctioneer. In short Anglo-Saxon words Sievier made the classic answer thus causing the prim and proper Mr. Tattersall even more embarrassment. After that Sievier bowed politely and left the room.

In the end Tattersall hid the notes on the top of his wardrobe and spent an anxious night watching them. The next morning he scurried down to Barclays' Bank, arriving as its doors were opening. There he deposited the money to the firm's account and went off to prepare for the great sale.

It was indeed a tremendous occasion. These were the most important lots of bloodstock to come under the hammer in England since Lord Falmouth's dispersal sale sixteen years before.

The ring was thronged with the rich, the great and the knowing of racing England. There was, however, one notable absentee. Hugh Richard Arthur, called by his intimates and known to his friends as Bend Or after the family's famous Derby winner, aged twenty-one and having only recently succeeded to the dukedom, was in South Africa on active service.

The young Duke owed his absence to those very sources of power and privilege which had prevented Sievier from taking his Yeomanry abroad and ensured his presence at the Sale.

George Wyndham, Her Majesty's Under-Secretary of State for War, had become step-father to the future Duke of Westminster by his marriage to Lady Grosvenor in 1884. A few months before the old Duke died Wyndham, who was anxious to push his step-son forward along the corridors of power, secured Bend Or's appointment as A.D.C. to Lord Milner, the Governor-General and Commander-in-Chief, Cape of Good Hope, and a coming star to whom ambitious youth was well advised to fix its waggon. In February 1900 Bend Or sailed to take up this appointment. On arrival he was almost immediately sent to the seat of the war as A.D.C. to Lord Roberts who had just taken over supreme command. Along with many another of England's *jeunesse dorée* who went to that war with their butlers, their valets and their cooks he knew less than nothing about soldiering and would have been the first to admit it. There is irony indeed in the fact that family influence and privilege brought about his military service whilst those same things prevented Sievier, the experienced soldier, from taking the field and enabled him to purchase the best racehorse even the great family of Westminster, with all their wealth and power, were ever likely to own.

As Morton had anticipated, the young Duke had, however, left instructions with Cecil Parker, his agent, and John Porter of Kingsclere, who trained for him, to buy in anything likely to turn out well. But, after the manner of those accustomed as of right to the enjoyment and employment of huge sums of money, he had not been specific as to price nor had he nor anyone else anticipated that the date of the sale would coincide with a time when a gambler such as Sievier was in the position of commanding and making full use of immense cash resources.

Despite all the interest aroused by it the sale started quietly enough. Sievier, however, soon showed that he was not going to allow the Duke's agents to have it all their own way. He bought a colt by Orme—Console for 700 guineas and another by Orme—Gantlet, later to be called Duke of Westminster, for 5,600 guineas.

Interest quickened when a colt by Orme—Kissing Cup, was led into the ring. Morton warned Sievier that by the look of him this one might be difficult to handle and could well turn out a rogue. He was however, an uncommonly handsome colt and Sievier determined to take a chance with him if he could get him. But Porter wanted him too. They commenced to bid against each other. Sir Blundell Maple's record of 6,000 guineas for Childwick was quickly passed. On they went until

Sievier bid 9,000 guineas. Porter capped it with another 100. At that, on Morton's advice, Sievier let the colt go and did not increase the bid. He was led out of the ring amid a murmur of astonishment and admiration, handsomely the holder of the record price for a yearling in England. It was not a record he was to keep for long.

Two lots later the filly everyone was waiting for was brought in. She was bay in colour, she was by Persimmon out of Ornament and she was later to be christened Sceptre. Her breeding could not be faulted for Persimmon was, of course, the Derby winner of 1896 in the Prince of Wales's colours and Ornament was a full sister to the mighty Ormonde. She had a great look of her sire especially round the muzzle. Peard told Sievier not to let her go.

It had been well said of Sievier that no one ever loved a good horse better. He himself has said that he fell in love with the filly from the moment he first saw her. There is no doubt that to those with eyes to see she had about her that 'look of eagles' which knowledgeable men will say they are lucky to come upon once in a lifetime. Her pictures scarcely do Sceptre justice. Above all she had presence, that indefinable something which, along with high quality, stamp a horse with greatness. 'There she stood,' Sievier wrote in his recollections, 'What I can only describe as a mass of perfection even to the merest tyro or captious critic—such a mare as perhaps for many years would not be offered for sale again or could be matched the world throughout . . . the value of money was lost in admiration. . . . She was at once a racehorse and a machine.'

But he was not alone in wanting her. John Porter knew her qualities and prospects better than any man and he had the Grosvenor millions behind him. When Sievier opened the affair with the monumental bid of 5,000 guineas Porter told Parker to add one hundred. Parker, the man instructed to do the actual bidding on the young Duke's behalf and responsible to him for the money spent, nodded his increase.

Sievier immediately made the bid six thousand. Parker added another hundred and Sievier, without hesitation, went to seven thousand.

A rustle of excitement ran around the ring. Here indeed was a clash of Titans, the millionaire Duke and the greatest gambler of his time locked in combat for a filly they both desperately wanted.

Parker added another hundred and Sievier went up to eight thousand. He exuded determination and confidence. Once more he was in a situation every moment of which he could savour and enjoy. He was the centre of attraction and all of racing England, its wealth, beauty, power, was watching him and hanging on his lips. And, even better, of them all only the agent of the richest, greatest, and most powerful dared enter the contest against him.

The story is told though it is almost certainly apocryphal that he had reclaimed his notes from Tattersall before this lot was offered. Then, to vouch each bid as he made it, he laid the £500 notes in front of him as a man does who deals cards. And as he laid them down he looked insolently each time across the ring to the place where Weatherby sat watching the bidding. Apocryphal though it may be it is certainly in character.

Another bid of a hundred came from Parker and another nine hundred from Sievier to make the money an even nine thousand guineas.

Both Porter and the agent were showing signs of strain. Porter had already advised Parker to spend over 18,000 guineas of the Duke's money and now he was being asked to beat a record he had just a few minutes ago made to secure a filly whose racing potential was, like that of any other untried stock, highly problematical. He was a cautious man and no one knew better than he how badly great sums spent on yearlings could prove to have been invested. Also, the young Duke was an unknown quantity. No one could tell what sort of a master he would turn out to be or how long he would stay in racing.

But they had defeated Sievier and won the Orme colt with one bid over 9,000. After consulting together they decided to equal this price and Parker nodded his bid to the rostrum.

Without a moment's thought or hesitation Sievier went to ten thousand guineas.

A gasp of astonishment ran around the ring. Porter hastily sent Parker off to find Captain Machell and to ask his advice. Machell was the man who, along with Sir George Chetwynd, knew more of horses, racing and bloodstock than anyone in England. Starting from a captaincy in an obscure marching regiment in Ireland, his knowledge, perspicacity, skill and fearless gambling had raised him to the ranks of the great. But Machell, a highly strung man who lived on his nerves, had lived on them perhaps too long. He was ageing prematurely and was to die in two years' time. The lure of the great risk no longer tempted him. Never one to mince words, when asked his advice, he said to Parker that a fool and his money were easily parted and that Sievier should be allowed to keep the filly.

So they let Sceptre go. Sievier had won. The filly was knocked down to him at ten thousand guineas.—'Dirt cheap as it happened,' was

William Allison's comment—and the price stood as a record until 1919 when Lord Glanely purchased a colt by Swynford out of Blue Tit for 11,500 guineas.

Not content with this Sievier bought the next lot, a filly by Trenton-Sandiway for 5500 guineas. He had now spent no less than 21,800 guineas. Later that day he also purchased a colt called Lavengro which had belonged to Lord Rosebery. The price was the moderate one of 700 guineas but it made his total expenditure up to 22,500 guineas, a fair sum for a recently discharged bankrupt.

It was Sievier who named the record-breaking filly Sceptre and he always took considerable pride in the aptness of his choice, explaining that, Persimmon being in royal ownership, he had chosen the name of a royal ornament. Then he set about arranging with Morton to take these yearlings to Letcombe Regis and prepare them for their entry into racing the following year. He anticipated that he would receive some caustic comment from Morton when he cast his eyes on Lavengro for this purchase had been an unorthodox one. Like Toddington, Lavengro was a truly enormous colt and he also possessed a pair of sickle hocks. He decided to prepare Morton in advance and to try to placate him by writing a letter saying that he was well aware that Lavengro's looks would not please everyone. In reply he received a telegram saying: *Lavengro arrived. This is not a brewery.—Morton.* Sievier had to admit that the colt did bear a certain resemblance to a dray horse, but he believed in his eye and his judgment and, as it happened, he was right.

He was constantly at Letcombe Regis during this time watching the progress of these expensive youngsters and waging verbal warfare with Morton about them. At the Doncaster sales he had made more purchases and now calculated that he had about £70,000 of horseflesh in Morton's care. He was especially pleased with the way Lavengro was turning out. 'He threw himself in the air in his stride,' he wrote afterwards, 'And reminded me more of Ormonde than any horse I have seen since his unbeaten career.' He took care to point this out to Morton but the trainer remained unimpressed. Morton, in fact, had his own worries, for Sceptre was proving a handful to break. She was full of fire and spirit and at first resisted the breaking-tackle and all attempts to back her. Then, when they started to work her, several times she unshipped her rider and went galloping loose across the Downs giving her trainer and his assistants long spells of the acutest anxiety until she was recaptured unharmed.

But when eventually they did have her cantering quietly with the string Morton became as near to lyrical as he ever permitted himself to be about her action. Although he tried to restrain Sievier's exuberance and enthusiasm both men in their differing ways knew in their hearts that in her they had a future champion.

But however well things were going for Sievier, he was never at peace. It has been truly said of him that a peaceful public or private life was the last thing he wanted. Always the warrior, he looked for battle of one sort or another; he longed for strife and he thrived on it. That season he was matching his wits and his money against the Americans.

12

The American Invasion

✿✿✿✿✿✿

Sloan's success on English tracks had not gone unheeded in America. Certain big operators there soon realized that he had created a situation well worth exploiting. The first of these to cross the Atlantic in his wake was a plunger of almost lunatic proportions called Charles Riley Grannan. Grannan had started life as a bell boy in an hotel in Lexington, Kentucky, and was to blaze his way like a short-lived comet across the race tracks of England and America, following his luck, buying information and betting in thousands. Grannan, however, soon transferred his attentions and his money from Sloan to the mounts of two other jockeys who had followed Sloan from America, whose dedication to the task in hand was far more absolute than his, and whose private lives did not attract the blaze of publicity which attended Sloan wherever he went. These were two brothers called Johnny and Lester Reiff.

When they arrived in England they were dressed in Eton collars and boys' suits. Both the Reiffs looked young and innocent. Johnny always wore knickerbockers hence earning the name of 'Knickerbocker' Reiff. With his air of childish purity he made himself the adored of the racing ladies in the paddock and was cherished and petted by them on the racecourse and elsewhere. In actual fact, to paraphrase Sievier's words about himself, childish the Reiffs may have been, innocent they certainly were not. Brilliant and accomplished jockeys both, they were unscrupulous in their methods of riding when on the course and in securing the most advantageous prices for their mounts when off it.

The Reiffs were controlled by an American trainer called Wishard who, in his turn, was financed by a Chicago hotel magnate, John Drake. Drake and his racing partner John W. Gates, 'Bet-a-Million Gates' as he was known in America, had come to England at that time to supervise their investment in Wishard's stable and were then betting huge sums on his horses, as was a man called Charles Dwyer who was connected with a large gambling and racing syndicate in America.

Quite apart from the new methods of riding which gave the Americans such an advantage, these men were able to bet successfully and in great amounts because of the extensive knowledge and experience which their trainers, especially Wishard, had in the loathsome business of doping horses to win. Doping was not then banned in England but it was virtually unknown since no one in racing knew enough about it to practise it to any extent. In America, however, it was widespread especially on minor tracks and had been, in so far as it was possible in those days, reduced to something of a science. This was a situation which these accomplished gamblers well knew how to exploit. Worse still, a whole horde of get-rich-quick riff-raff soon to be known as 'The American Invasion' came over after them to make a killing on English tracks. George Lambton, Lord Durham's younger brother, then just ending one fine career as an amateur rider and starting another wonderful one as a trainer, has told how he remarked to an American at that time that he supposed there were a good many rogues and thieves racing in America. 'There is not one,' was the reply. 'They have all come over here.'

Sievier resented and detested these men and their methods. He hated to see the ruin of good horses by doping and he despised the men who did it for their gain. Most of all he hated what the Americans were doing to his friend and benefactor R. H. Fry.

The plungers from across the Atlantic, casting round for someone to carry their money, soon fastened on Fry as the man to pillage. With his easy-going nature, quiet sympathy for those in trouble, and readiness to extend what amounted to unlimited credit, he was just the man they were looking for. They stepped in and virtually took over his book.

Fry was getting old; he had not seen that the aristocratic or semi-aristocratic plunger such as Hastings, Ailesbury, Baird or Benzon, who either eventually paid up himself or had family resources to fall back upon when his own failed, was giving way to a much more dangerous type of gambler who was prepared to go to the limit, collect if he won and abscond if he did not. The debts these men incurred with Fry rapidly ran into six figures.

Sievier determined to stop them if he could. In this for once he found himself on the side of the Establishment and the authorities. They may well, however, have found him an uncomfortable ally. Slowly, as always at that time, authority was coming to realize that something must be done to call a halt to what was amounting to a public scandal. Lord Durham, who had taken upon himself Lord George Bentinck's self-styled role of cleanser of the Augean stables of the Turf, made a typically hard-hitting and outspoken speech on the matter in October of that year. Newmarket, he said, had become 'a sort of cosmopolitan dumping ground,' and he went on to point a finger directly at the Americans as the cause of the troubles in English racing. They considered racing, he roundly declared, merely as an instrument of high gambling and nothing else. Then he named names and here it was Sloan who caught the full blast of the onslaught. 'This year he was reprimanded for unscrupulous riding in the Derby; he was disqualified for bumping and boring at the Liverpool July Meeting; and he was complained of for unfair riding at Doncaster and suspended for the remainder of the meeting.'

It was Sloan whom the Establishment were really after, and it was Sloan in the end who was to bring the whole house of cards tumbling down. For, protected by Beresford who delighted in his outrages and roared with laughter at his social and other sins, Sloan's behaviour off the course as well as on it was getting out of hand. At the previous Ascot he had hit a waiter in the face with a champagne bottle, splitting his lip and costing Lord William a pretty sum in hush money; his night life was the talk of London; his betting and smart answers were a cause of constant criticism and astonishment on the racecourse. He even went so far as to tell a member of the Jockey Club that he would decide if he would ride his horse 'after he had looked in his book'! To cap it all, from the Establishment point of view, he was now riding with some regularity in the Royal colours and it was being widely reported that Lord William was arranging for the royal retainer to be his next season.

Sievier liked and admired Sloan, indeed they had tastes and characteristics in common and met often at Romano's and elsewhere on the town. It was the Reiffs, Wishard and the dopers he wanted to see banished from the Turf. He was especially contemptuous of the fact that Gates and Drake had been given the freedom of the Jockey Club stand at Newmarket and other privileged places. And, of course, he said so—in public, loudly, dramatically and pungently.

Daylight robbery was what he called the activities of Wishard and the Reiffs, and he was right; they were just that. This, he said, was the only excuse he could find for 'the owls' of stewards seeing nothing. The *mot* was repeated and did not increase his popularity in high places.

The culminating point in his campaign came over the running of a horse called Americus owned by the Irish-American 'Boss' Croker who had deemed it wise to quit the States after Theodore Roosevelt's investigations into the activities of Tammany Hall. Lester Reiff was to ride Americus. It was opposed by only one other runner and appeared a certainty on its previous form. Public money poured in for it and the starting price was 6—5 on. Sievier, however, knew that Wishard had been doping the horse for months and that it had run doped to win in its previous races. He was also in possession of the information that the horse had been doped so often that the stimulant was no longer taking effect and that Wishard and his connections knew this. Thus the horse could not and would not win.

Sievier watched the betting closely; he also watched Drake and Gates. He saw the public money going on and saw, too, that neither Drake nor Gates struck a single wager on Americus. As the horses left the course he crossed to where the two Americans were standing by the rails of the Jockey Club stand. There he offered them longer odds than the book-makers were asking to £5000 against Americus. They both shook their heads and declined to take the bet. Then Sievier turned toward the Jockey Club stand and shouted at the top of his voice, 'Americus does not win for £5000! An even £5000 against Americus!' Gates and Drake rapidly left him and disappeared amongst the crowd.

Americus was beaten by four lengths.

Sievier, as usual, had done himself no good with the authorities. They did not care to be hastened or shown up by an outsider such as he. It was immediately said by the knowing and the would-be wise that he was in association with the Americans, that the scene was a put up job and that he had backed the winner both for himself and them.

But events were coming to a head and the Cambridgeshire of that year saw the beginning of the end of the American Invasion.

In September Sloan won the Prix du Conseil Municipal on a French horse called Codoman belonging to a M. Maurice Ephrussi. Sloan then persuaded M. Ephrussi to send the horse over for the Cambridgeshire and to give him the ride. Once this had been arranged he proceeded quite openly and with his usual audacity to back Codoman for pounds, shillings and pence. At the end of it all he stood to win no less than £66,000. His heedless self-assurance had reached such proportions that he was foolish enough to give Captain Machell a share of his money at 33—1. Machell told George Lambton of this bet, Lambton told his brother, Lord Durham, and then the fat was really in the fire.

Codoman was beaten four lengths by a good horse called Berrill. Sloan had lost his money. He then made what was bad a great deal worse by letting fly a string of abuse at Berrill's rider as they returned to scale.

All these things were duly noted. Soon after the meeting the stewards of the Jockey Club, Lord Crewe, Lord Falmouth and Lord Fitzwilliam, called Sloan before them to explain his betting and his behaviour. It was obvious that he had no valid explanation to offer for either. Even Lord William, his protector, for once had no reassurance to give him. Matters had gone too far for his influence, great though it was, to save his favourite. 'Things look pretty black, little man, but we must hope for the best,' were all the comforting words he could say.

Sloan returned to America. Shortly after his arrival he was informed that if he were to apply for a licence to ride in England the following year it would not be granted. Sanguine as ever he was sure that the suspension would only last for the one season. But in December Lord William died unexpectedly. There was no one then in the seats of power to intercede for him. Lord Durham, especially, did not waver in his determination to rid the English Turf of him and his activities. He paid a high price for his recklessness and braggadoccio. All hopes of a Royal retainer were now, of course, gone. He never rode in England again.

The Stewards then began to move against the Reiff-Wishard-Drake combination. Sievier always maintained that it was due to him and that it was he who shamed and shoved them into it, and there may be something in his contention.

At all events a Stewards' enquiry was convened to look into the whole matter and he was asked to give evidence before it. He had kept a careful note of the form and running of Wishard's horses and had, as well, made an analysis of the betting on them. He was therefore in a position to give to the enquiry ample corroboration of his public statements that the running of these horses constituted a fraud on the public. To his fury, however, the stewards also took the opportunity of examining him on some of his own operations which had also given rise to talk, notably the incident over Americus. Fortunately all his life he was most meticulous in keeping a betting book. He produced this and thus satisfied them that he had never stood to gain over any of the Americans' operations and had no bet on Americus.

The enquiry resulted in the same treatment being ultimately meted out to Lester Reiff as had been given to Sloan. Johnny Reiff took himself off to France. Gates, Drake and the hangers on who followed the movement of their money returned whence they had come.

So the American invasion was defeated and its shock troops dispersed. It cannot be said, however, that in the end its effects were entirely bad.

The jockeys woke racing England from its somnolence and self-satisfaction by their employment of new methods, their lightning judgment of pace and their way of running their races right out, just as Boer rifles and quick-firers were even then jolting the British Army out of the complacence that sprang from easy victories over primitive tribesmen.

The American trainers, too—and Wishard, despite his doping, was one of the most advanced in many respects—brought with them new ideas and a greater understanding of the necessity to study the character and idiosyncrasies of each individual horse. Their attention to detail was much superior to that employed in most English stables, as were many of their methods of stable management. They were, as well, far more receptive of new ideas and more ready to experiment.

Sievier's efforts did little to help his friend R. H. Fry. When the Americans decamped they made no effort to settle with Fry. The original £100,000 owed to him had multiplied rapidly; some said almost ten times. Certainly he was left with enormous sums on his books which he had no hope of recovering. The strain and worry of it broke his heart and ruined his health. He died a little over two years later still liked, admired and respected by all, still contributing lavishly to charity in his native Dulwich and to the hospital he had endowed in Red Lion Square. Comparatively little of the vast sums he had made was left at his death. The debts due to the business were proved at over a million, most of it owed by the Americans. It was never paid and had to be written off.

After all these stirring but financially unrewarding activities Sievier retired to Toddington, the gracious company of Eleanor Master and their families, his hunting with the Oakley and his shooting parties. Toddington was costing a fortune to keep up, not that he ever worried about expenditure or anything else for that matter. Once a friend asked him about his huge expenses at this time—after all he had forty horses in training with Morton as well as the upkeep of Toddington to look after, and no visible means of support—and if this worried him at all. 'Worry,' he answered. 'I don't worry, old horse. I leave that to the bookmakers.' It is, too, a fact that the bookmakers then and thereafter were content to carry him.

When Christmas came there was, of course, a house party at Toddington. Champagne flowed as never before to toast the future success of Sceptre, Lavengro and the rest of the string, the children received gifts on a scale commensurate with the wonderland in which they were living. There were other benefactions as well. Every family in the village received a joint of beef and a Christmas pudding cooked by Sievier's chef. Nor were the village children forgotten for he loved children as he loved animals and by and large they loved him. The estate carpenter put up a Christmas tree laden with gifts rich and rare, in the village schoolhouse. Bob himself played Santa Claus, joking and laughing with all who came and dispensing presents and hospitality to one and all. It was one of the roles he played particularly well and one in which he was at his simplest and most likeable. No wonder the village loved him.

No wonder, either, that the pace was too good to last. The astonishing thing is that it lasted as long as it did.

13

Enter Joel

❊❊❊❊❊❊

In the spring of 1901 not only Sievier and his friends but the whole of the racing world was agog to see how the record-breaking filly would turn out.

Sievier wanted a trial and in April he had one. Leonid, a useful handicapper, was set to give Sceptre, Duke of Westminster, Kaffir Queen and another three-year-old, a stone over five furlongs. Sceptre and Duke of Westminster slammed the older horses, Sceptre winning by six lengths, easily, from the colt who was two lengths in front of Leonid. If that were not enough to prove that they had two exceptional racehorses in the stable, they then ran a trial for Lavengro and he came out of it as well as if not better than Sceptre. Receiving a stone from a four-year-old called Jam Jar and at level weights with Merilla a useful three-year-old, he won by a distance. Morton, waxing enthusiastic for once, assured Sievier that he had in Lavengro and Sceptre a colt and a filly which were likely to astonish everyone in the months to come, and that Duke of Westminster was not far behind. Since Sievier had backed his own judgment in buying them all he had indeed some cause for self-congratulation. There was little talk of 'a dray horse' now.

But troubles, as usual, were encompassing him. He had spent enormous sums on horses the previous year and his gambling, especially during the back-end, had not gone well for him. Then, too, the cost of running Toddington in a manner which would have taxed the resources of a Rand millionaire was at last beginning to tell. Even in the carefree days of the early Edwardian era some tradesmen, especially in the country, liked to see the colour of their customers' money. They saw very little of Sievier's that spring.

Dunning letters, writs and threats of legal action began to fly about again. He paid very little attention to them. 'Tradesmen can always wait,' was a maxim he had borrowed from his betters, the nobility and gentry of the time, but nevertheless ready cash he had to have to keep his racehorses going and there was precious little available.

But, once he had tried most of his purchases, he had sense enough to see that his string could well stand weeding out, and that those that went were likely to bring in some of the ready money so badly needed to defray current expenses. He resolved to put the whole lot, save Sceptre, up for sale, to place large reserves on them and to let go those that made the prices he required.

This proved to be a clever move. With the glamour now attaching to his name and the sensation of his purchases of the previous year still fresh in everyone's minds, crowds came flocking to the auction. The foolish, the ambitious and the easily impressed paid more than the reserve figures for what Sievier regarded as rubbish or near it. The best horses were there to attract the better bidders and focus attention on the sale. This they did but as he anticipated they failed to make the huge reserves he had placed on them. The sale realized 12,350 guineas, enough to pay some of the more pressing debtors and to keep Toddington, the cricket parties and the racing stable going for a part of the season at least.

At first all went well. Lavengro won brilliantly at Manchester and was cheered home by the crowd. Sceptre's début was fixed for the Woodcote Stakes over six furlongs at the Epsom Derby Meeting. This race does not usually attract two-year-olds of her class and just why Morton and Sievier picked on it has never been explained. The Derby that year was not considered to be of outstanding interest and almost as much attention was given to the first appearance of Sceptre as to the Classic. Her record-breaking price was still news; and Sievier had openly talked of the trials she and Lavengro had done. Lavengro had shown his worth by slamming a useful American horse that had been backed to beat him at Manchester, yet Sievier was known to hold that Sceptre was the better of the two. Crowds thronged the paddock to catch a glimpse of her.

Some came from curiosity, some to see what many believed would prove to be the filly of the century, some to gamble and some, un-questionably, in the hope of seeing Sievier humbled, of his boasts and his belief in the pride of his life and his stable being shown up as false, his judgment to have erred and his money to have been thrown away.

Morton had Sceptre turned out to perfection. She walked the parade ring like a queen. Good judges watching her said that there was about her the best of both sexes. She had in her appearance a masculine strength and resolution combined with the grace and suppleness of the filly. As she moved she showed both power and symmetry. But no race-horse is ever perfect. There was no question but that she was straight in front and her feet, as her owner admitted, were inclined to be fleshy. Both these weaknesses were to show to her disadvantage in her subsequent career and indeed made themselves apparent in and after this very first race.

Ridden by Sam Loates, she seemed to be galloping all over her field as they approached Tattenham Corner. There the slight fault in her conformation asserted its influence. Coming downhill on firm ground she found difficulty in negotiating the bend and, despite all that Loates could do, she swung very wide. Ever afterwards she had difficulty in rounding corners on the stretch and this one especially.

The rest of the runners went on from her and she appeared to have been left with too much to do and too little time to do it. Standing beside Sievier in his box and watching through his glasses Morton exclaimed. 'By Gad! She's beat!'

But Loates knew what he had under him. He balanced her and set her going up the straight. In a few strides she settled the issue. To a storm of cheering she cruised home by four lengths from a useful horse called Csardas, whom we shall hear of again.

Next morning she was lame. The iron hard ground at Epsom had jarred her knees and bruised her feet. Morton, typically, was pessimistic about her future and struck her out of her Ascot engagements.

But Lavengro was still astonishing them in his work at home. Even Morton was becoming enthusiastic about him and at this time was inclined to rate him something better than Sceptre as a racing proposition. He was a colt of tremendous strength and substance; he had over nine inches of bone below the knee and so deep was he through the middle that special racing girths had to be made for him. He was the very opposite of Sceptre for in the place of her grace and fluidity of movement he was ungainly in his slower paces, not showing his quality until he really began to gallop and then giving an impression of brute force and almost elemental power. He won the Forty-Fourth Biennial on the first day at Ascot in a canter by three lengths. As they were un-saddling him after it Morton turned to Sievier: 'This is the best horse,' he said 'we have seen since Ormonde.'

At home Lavengro could give Duke of Westminster a stone and hand him out a beating by several lengths. The public knew this for there was never any concealment about Sievier's trials. When on the Wednesday of that Ascot week Duke of Westminster walked away from two good colts in Game Chick and Robert le Diable the potential that lay in Sceptre and Lavengro was clear for all to read. If they both kept sound what prodigal feats might they not perform in Sievier's colours the following year? It was not a prospect relished by the ruling few.

But all this was for the future. At the moment financial clouds were looming again. Despite the good wins he had had on his own horses, that Ascot had been a disaster. He had followed his early winnings on Lavengro by playing them up in his usual manner but he had not waited for Duke of Westminster's win to do it. The fatal attraction of backing other people's horses had plunged him into trouble once again. On the last day he knew that the following Monday he would have difficulty settling. As he left the box towards the end of the meeting, quite by chance he ran into J. B. Joel. It was to prove a momentous encounter for both men.

Jack Barnato Joel was a man of enormous wealth even by the standards of that rich and gaudy time. Aged only thirty-nine, his private fortune, apart from his vast financial interests in gold, diamonds and other enterprises, was estimated at four million pounds. But he had not been born to wealth or riches. He had been named plain Isaac Joel and his family were old-clothes-dealers in Petticoat Lane. An uncle, Barney Isaacs, went on to the halls with his brother Henry. The act involved the playing of two tipsy toffs by the brothers and Barney's cue was the shout by the stage manager of 'Barney too!' Barney contracted this to the elegant and esoteric 'Barnato' and adopted it as his name instead of the common-place Isaacs.

After a few years on the boards Barney and his brother Harry emigrated to South Africa in search of a fortune. This they quickly found for their arrival coincided with the opening of the Transvaal Goldfields. Barney, his brother and a man called Cohen, who was in partnership with them, soon expanded their interests into diamonds and real property. By methods which make the exploits of the American robber barons look like those of the Knights of the Round Table they rapidly became multi-millionaires, amassing one of the greatest fortunes of modern times. After a few years the rapid expansion of his interests and the size they had assumed convinced Barney that he must have assistance in managing them. He sent for his two nephews, Isaac and Solomon, to come out from London. Both eagerly accepted the opportunity offered and took ship for South Africa where Cohen described them on their arrival as 'two neatly-dressed, quiet-looking lads, subdued in manner and respectful to their elders.' In a short time they, too were millionaires.

Young Isaac quickly discarded his given name and assumed the names of Jack Barnato by which he was henceforth known.

Barney Barnato was one of the many financial pirates produced by the *laisser faire* economy of the day, ruthless, grasping, greedy and tough. As such he had made many enemies and the driving nature of his ambitions taxed both his physical and mental stability. When returning to London from South Africa on one of his many business trips he jumped overboard from the liner that was carrying him and was lost at sea.

His nephews, in inheriting the empire, exhibited many of his qualities and characteristics. Jack had the greater ability of the two, Solly was more eager for the social round. The responsibility for the management of the involved and far flung finances of the Joel enterprises which, by the time they returned to London to take control, included theatres and insurance as well as the South African interests, devolved almost entirely on Jack. It was a responsibility readily accepted and discharged for he was possessed of immense ability and financial acumen coupled with an unremitting capacity for hard work. But he was a bitter man to his enemies and an unbending one even to his friends.

Barney had owned a few racehorses in South Africa and had enjoyed the relaxation of racing and the camaraderie of the Turf. In this as in other matters the nephews followed their Uncle's tastes. Back in London both decided to invest in bloodstock and to take up racing in a big way.

In racing as in everything else Jack Joel wanted the best and he wanted to be on top. In this, in the end, success attended his efforts. Just then, however, his career on the Turf had not really started. The horses which he had in training were a moderate lot. He was not satisfied with them and wanted to improve them. There can be no doubt that his eye had fallen on Sceptre and that he wanted her. What he wanted he usually got though it was also his practice to see that his purchases came worth the money. And he did not get Sceptre. What he did get was a mortal enemy and a load of trouble for himself and Sceptre's owner.

As they chatted together Sievier told Joel that he was going to have a rocky settlement. In his usual uninhibited way he went on to ask Joel for a loan to see him through. Joel told him he would think it over and suggested a meeting after the next race. This took place and there and then terms were agreed. Joel was to lend Sievier the money; in return Sievier was to give Joel a bill at ten per cent interest and an undertaking that he would not dispose of any of his horses except those engaged in selling races without giving Joel first refusal, these terms to remain in force until the money was paid.

The following Sunday—the day before settling day—Sievier was dumbfounded to receive a letter from Joel saying that he had changed his mind and would not lend the money. Sievier was furiously angry, his wrath being increased by the fact that, relying on Joel's promise, he had just refused £25,000 for Lavengro. When they met shortly afterwards he upbraided the millionaire and as a result Joel asked him to call at his office where they could discuss the matter further. Sievier did so and found that Joel, so far from offering to lend him money, was now trying to buy Sceptre from him at a knock-down price. He suggested that Sievier should take £10,000 for the filly which was the same figure that had purchased her as an untried yearling. On her trials and her performance in the Woodcote she was clearly worth far more now. Sievier accused Joel of trying to get Sceptre cheap by exploiting his knowledge that he was short of cash. High and loud words followed. Sievier then slammed out of the office with all his vindictive fury and enmity aroused against a man who had wronged him, determined never to speak to Joel again and to do what he could to hurt and injure him wherever and whenever opportunity offered.

His first step was to bestow the nickname of 'Promising Jack' on Joel and to recount his reasons for doing so to all who would listen. Later a very moderate two-year-old of his coming up for naming he called him 'Promising Jack' and registered the name with Weatherbys. The horse ran at Windsor and was beaten by one of Joel's. Sievier thereupon wired Joel: *You have won although you were second.*

Meanwhile, brilliant horses having a habit of bringing their own troubles with them, this was happening in the cases of Sceptre and Lavengro. Lavengro was in the Hurst Park Foal Plate and was regarded as a certainty. Sievier backed him as such, and he desperately wanted a win.

One of Morton's supreme virtues as a trainer was his attention to detail. On the morning of the meeting he went to the stables to supervise Lavengro being plated. As he watched he was certain he saw the blacksmith prick the horse. The smith hotly denied that he had done so but Morton refused to be convinced. He went away to return an hour later and to find, as he thought he would, that the colt was lame. He had the plate removed, the leg poulticed, but it seemed impossible that Lavengro would run.

Going to the Mitre Hotel where Sievier was waiting lunch for him he told him what had happened. Sievier was determined that Lavengro should run if at all possible since the wager which he had on this race put the whole future of his string at stake. When they went back to the stable the colt seemed much better. Under the watchful eyes of Sievier and Morton the colt was re-plated. Morton actually stood over the smith and told him where to put the nails. Then they trotted him out. The further he moved the sounder he went. With a sigh of relief Morton sent him to the post. He toyed with the opposition and won as he liked. Sievier had landed his bets and gained a respite if nothing more from those who were pressing and pursuing him. Out of his winnings he handed Morton a cheque for £500.

At the Newmarket July Meeting Sceptre, still feeling the ground and not moving as freely as she might have done, won the July Stakes with odds of 10—1 laid on her. A fortnight later Lavengro won the Chesterfield at a price of no less than 20—1 on.

Because of the cramped odds these victories were not as financially rewarding as they might have been, for Sievier was now paying the financial penalty for the open way in which his horses were run. Still, the money they brought in allowed him to return to Toddington, secure for the moment, which was all he ever wanted money to do for him. There the fun was even more fast and furious than before. The round of cricketing house parties went on and at one of them he landed a side bet of a sovereign with Archie McLaren who refused to believe any man could give W. G. Grace enough liquor to make him unsteady on his legs.

Starting at luncheon the choicest wines and liqueurs were placed before the Doctor in great goblets and gargantuan measures. Grace accepted them in the manner in which they were offered and readily consumed them. This continued throughout a long, sweltering day's cricket, boys bearing beakers of champagne laced with brandy being sent out to Grace in the field at appropriate intervals, where they went the same way as the lunch-time drinks. After the game there was dinner to the visiting teams when more champagne, port and old brandy was poured down that mighty throat. It did not seem to have had the least effect at all until, in the billiards room afterwards, when proceeding from the table to the piano he was observed slightly to stagger in his walk. Arrived at the piano upon which one of the 'lovely ladies' was performing he leant against it and gazed at her solemnly if a little glassily whilst she finished her piece.

She was in the secret and, smiling sweetly up at him, asked him to hand her another sheet of music from the rack. His great hand, which Sievier described as being well able to reach over any till to collect what was in the counter, stretched out for the music. But the effort was too much. He over-balanced, stumbled and slid to the floor. McLaren with a show of ceremony solemnly handed Sievier the sovereign across the doctor's prostrate body.

But even at Toddington there were troubles. A dispute had arisen over the shooting rights, Sievier alleging that his landlord had infringed on them. Accordingly he issued a writ claiming an injunction and this action was to drag on for some time. Also there were, of course, a succession of 'lovely ladies' and Mrs. Master must have been tolerant indeed and very much in love with him to put up for so long with these and their visits to the house.

Worse still, tragedy was about to strike down one of the stars of the stable and bring more financial peril with it. Lavengro was in the Champion Breeders' Foal Stakes at Derby. Odds of 7—4 were laid on him and Sievier backed him as if defeat were out of the question— as indeed he believed it to be. Lavengro ran like a shadow of himself and was beaten three lengths into second place by Major Joicey's Sterling Balm. Indeed he only just scraped in as second from a moderate colt called Battle Song. Something was obviously seriously amiss and it did not take long for them to find out what it was. Lavengro had become stalliony too soon and was already a confirmed and consistent mastur-bator.

Everything possible was done to cure him including using electric batteries and new-fangled appliances employed by American trainers when the horses in their care were afflicted with this vice. All were equally unsuccessful. Eventually the time came when there was nothing else for it but to cut him. This was done. Except for a small selling race he never won again. From being a potential classic winner and of priceless value at stud, in the space of a few weeks he had become virtually worthless.

As often happens in racing when trouble comes, worse follows. Sceptre was entered in the Champagne Stakes at Doncaster. The only horses of any account to oppose her were Czardas and Game Chick. She had handed out a hammering to Czardas at Epsom and Game Chick was well held by Duke of Westminster who only ranked a bad third in Sievier's stable. The race appeared a mere formality. Sievier gave his commissioner instructions to back her to recover all his losses in the season to date. It seemed quite certain that she had only to gallop over to recover them for him.

But Sievier had been living it up at Toddington and elsewhere and had not been down to Letcombe Regis to watch her in her work. Morton had warned him that she had got her winter coat but added that she was, despite that, very well.

When Sievier saw her on the racecourse he was shocked by her appearance. She was a shaggy mass of hair which had been clipped trace high and she was walking sluggishly. Although he had not yet realized just how much work she needed to get her fit and the amount of racing she required to keep her there once she had reached fitness, looking at her then in the paddock Sievier was of the opinion that she was short of work. He immediately sent a message to his commissioner to call off his bets.

In the race itself she led to the distance and then faltered. Game Chick and Czardas both headed her and beat her, a length and a half and a head separating the three of them.

That was bad enough but then to crown a wretched afternoon his commissioner came along to say that the message to call off the bets had never reached him. Sievier had lost both the race and his money.

He could always take a beating. In defeat he refused to blame anyone. Though he had his private reservations about the wisdom of having run her at all he kept them to himself and accepted responsibility for her being beaten.

The race is interesting if for no other reason than that it shows how difficult Sceptre was to understand and to train in that even one so experienced and astute as Morton had not yet discovered how best to do it. Both Morton and Sievier have left it on record that she should not have run in that race. Since two forceful characters such as her owner and trainer were for once in agreement it is hard to see just why she did run.

All this is of some importance in racing history since it has been said time and again in print and elsewhere that had Sceptre remained in Morton's care throughout her career she would never have been beaten. In this instance she was in Morton's care, she ran under his orders and, as it turned out, clearly short of work and was well beaten.

It is customary to blame Sievier and his betting for all her defeats and in the following year it may well be that the blame is truly laid. But in this case he believed he had called off his bets before she ran. In discussing Sceptre's two-year-old career it is almost always overlooked that Morton, too, was a tremendous plunger, overshadowed only in this respect by his owner. Later in life his betting, not only on horses trained by himself but by others, became so out of hand that he dissipated the fortune his great talents as a trainer had brought him and died a poor man. May it not well have been that he, too, had a huge sum at stake on that race? If so, then assessing her past form and what he knew she could do, he may well have determined that Sceptre, despite the change in her coat and the lightness of the work he had given her, could and would win it for him. At all events the record stands. She was in Morton's care when she was beaten and well beaten in that Champagne Stakes.

Sievier was now in a desperate quandary for money. He had won £11,171 10s. od. in stakes but this was a pittance compared with what he had lost and to put against his vast expenses. His training bill alone was £100 a week to say nothing of what Toddington was costing him. Of the huge sum he had had at his disposal the year before nothing now was left. But a little of it, at least, had been well spent. He had bought a house at Torquay for his mother. He called it Sceptre Lodge and he maintained her in it for the rest of her life.

Because everything he did was done openly, or brazenly as his enemies liked to put it, all the racing world knew he was badly hit. Envious eyes were once more cast at his horses. It was thought that he must sell them and, despite the tragedy of Lavengro, in Duke of Westminster and Sceptre he still possessed, as he said himself, racehorses the like of which 'no man has owned for many a year and such as few have ever possessed since the days of horse-racing commenced.'

Joel, his acquisitive eye still on Sceptre, made another attempt, this time through an intermediary. He sent a man called Honey, who had been in charge of the box-office in one of his theatres, to see if Sievier would now do business. When Honey said 'Mr. Joel will still give you 10,000 guineas for Sceptre and chance it,' Sievier's response was so sulphurous that he said afterwards it was fortunate for Honey he was deaf or else even he might have been shocked.

There was, however, another approach which might well have put him in a quandary had he known on whose behalf it was made. Towards the end of the season Sir Ernest Cassel came up to Morton at Hurst Park and asked him 'very confidentially' if Sievier would sell Sceptre, Lavengro and Duke of Westminster. Morton said that he did not think money could buy the horses for he well knew Sievier's pride in them and affection for them. 'See if £50,000 would tempt him,' Cassel said in his peremptory way.

Anticipating the reception he was likely to get, Morton very reluctantly agreed to approach Sievier with the offer. Finding him outside the weighing room he put the proposition to him.

'Tell him to go to hell,' Sievier said at the top of his voice. 'I'm not selling my horses to him or to anyone else.'

Morton returned to Cassel. 'I'm afraid,' he said, translating the message into terms more suitable, he felt, for a millionaire's ears, 'that Mr. Sievier won't entertain the matter.'

'Offer him another £10,000 then,' Cassel commanded.

This time the reply was couched in even more pungent and uncomplimentary terms and could be heard in the farthest confines of the racecourse.

But Sievier would scarcely have been so peremptory, so positive and so rude had he known on whose behalf Cassel was acting.

Sir Ernest Cassel was one of the new millionaires whom Edward VII as Prince of Wales had made his close friend and confidant. He knew little of Sievier save that he was a gambler and a man of indifferent repute in the circles amongst which Cassel moved. The mares then at Sandringham were, in the words of Marsh, the royal trainer, something less than ordinary. Royalty's racing advisers were aware of this and they knew, too, that in all probability a lean period for the royal horses lay ahead. Fresh blood was necessary and their eyes, along with many others, had fallen on Sievier's string. The new King, too, had always taken the greatest interest in Sceptre who looked like turning out to be the best progeny of his own Derby winner, Persimmon.

Cassel, thinking it was only a matter of money where one such as Sievier was concerned, had rashly volunteered to negotiate a deal for the best two-year-olds in training on behalf of his royal friend and master. He was more than a little taken aback at the reception accorded to him and his millions.

But Sievier might have found himself in some difficulty had Cassel's principal been disclosed to him. Throughout his life he always regarded the English Royal Family, especially as personified in Edward VII, with a respect which amounted almost to adulation. Reluctant though he always was to part with a good horse he might well in this instance have persuaded himself to prop his failing finances and flatter his vanity with a sale to the reigning monarch.

It was not to be, however, and, when the season ended and there was no chance of money from betting coming in for months, it was obvious that something had to be done.

John Porter, perhaps assisted by a hint from Morton that Bob might just then be persuaded to put something on offer to the right person, now appeared on the scene. Sievier always liked and respected Porter and the two men got on well together. When the trainer came to him and asked to be allowed to inspect the string at Morton's stables he readily agreed. Porter went down at the time appointed and found Sievier waiting for him. The horses were pulled out for the trainer to see and Sievier watched him intently as he examined them. After he had finished his inspection the two men, along with Morton, went to the trainer's house and in his sitting-room they discussed a possible deal.

As a result of Sceptre's recent defeat many racing men were now saying that she was unlikely to train on. They pointed also to her straightness in front and the faults in her action at a walk. It was held in some quarters, too, that she was unlikely to act on hard ground next summer and might well break down and not stand training at all. Neither Sievier nor Morton believed this but Sievier hoped that Porter might have been influenced by the talk and rumours which were going the rounds. Moreover, having watched him closely during his examination of the horses, he was convinced that it was Duke of Westminster that Porter really wanted. When Porter asked him to price the horses, naming Duke of Westminster first in his request, this put the matter beyond all doubt in Sievier's mind. At once he decided upon a desperate ruse which appealed to both the actor and the gambler in his nature. He made up his mind to ask less for Sceptre than for the colt, in the belief that this would make Porter certain that Duke of Westminster was the more valuable of the two. It would also, or so he speculated, convince Porter that there was something in Sceptre's recent history known only to Sievier and Morton which had seriously depreciated her value.

'I am asking 25,000 guineas for Duke of Westminster,' he said. Then he hesitated as if he did not know quite how to price Sceptre, just such a hesitation as a man might make who is considering what value to place upon an apparently priceless article which has in it nevertheless an undisclosed defect. The actor in him was uppermost now and he held the hesitation as long as he dared. Finally he said. 'Well, say 15,000 guineas for the filly.' Here Morton, who had not been told what his unpredictable patron intended, almost gave the game away by allowing an audible gasp to escape him. Then he gazed at Sievier open-mouthed as if he thought he was mad, as indeed he did.

Fortunately Porter had his attention on Sievier and no one else.

'Would you put that in writing and leave the matter open for a day?' he asked.

'Certainly,' Sievier replied and requested Morton to bring writing paper and ink to the table at which they were sitting. When Morton produced these Sievier wrote: *I hereby agree to take 25,000 guineas from John Porter for the purchase of Duke of Westminster with his engagements and I also agree*—here he looked at Morton casually and asked: 'Did I say 15,000 guineas for Sceptre?'

'Yes, indeed you did,' Morton confirmed with a grunt.

'Well, let me see, I think I'll make it 14,000 for her.' Sievier was, as usual, pushing his gamble just as far as it would go. Then he went on writing, his pen rapidly covering the paper—*to accept 14,000 guineas for Sceptre with her engagements. This offer to remain open and binding until 4 o'clock tomorrow afternoon. Signed* R. S. SIEVIER. He wrote his name with a flourish and, watching Porter, he was sure he had convinced him there was something wrong with Sceptre.

The following day Porter returned and told Sievier that he wanted Duke of Westminster. The usual wrangle then took place over the price. They finally agreed on 22,000 guineas. Porter told Sievier that he was acting for Mr. George Faber, one of his wealthy patrons, and the next morning he gave Sievier a cheque for the agreed sum. When he had handed over the order to Morton to deliver the colt and the receipt for his engagements Sievier asked Porter if he was satisfied with the deal. 'Perfectly,' Porter said. 'And I hope you are.'

'Yes, John, I am,' Sievier said. And indeed he had reason to be for he had made a profit of 17,750 guineas on a colt he never rated in the same class as his two other flyers and who had, as well, won him £2,645 in stakes. Most important, however, he had kept Sceptre and secured at least her immediate future. 'I offered you both, John,' he went on, rubbing in his victory as was his way. 'And naturally you inclined to the colt as against the filly, but I can tell you this—the first time they meet Sceptre will beat Duke of Westminster.'

In fairness to Porter it must be said that he always maintained that he had not been taken in by Sievier's rodomontade, but that he was under instructions from Mr. Faber to buy the colt and leave the filly. This may be so but Duke of Westminster was a failure as a three-year-old, the story of the choice made by Porter became well known and his judgment was harshly criticised in some quarters, so he may have been attempting to justify himself. It is a fact, too, that he had told friends and was to repeat it that, owing to her breeding on the dam's side, he did not believe Sceptre to be a true stayer. At all events, whatever the truth of the matter, the deal did not disturb the amicable relations between the two men and Porter was shortly to prove a good friend to Sievier.

There was now some cash to keep things going. His hunters were being prepared for the coming season with the Oakley, lists for shooting parties were being made out, and altogether it looked as though he could retire to winter quarters at Toddington with the prospect of a peaceful few months in front of him. But it was not to be.

J. B. Joel was still smarting from the public insults heaped upon him by Sievier, from the 'Promising Jack' affair and from the scathing messages sent back to him when he tried to re-open negotiations for Sceptre. Joel was not a man lightly to shrug off an injury. He was every bit as vengeful as Sievier. Those who crossed him were accustomed to pay for it in tears, blood and coin. And there is no doubt that he still had his eye on Sceptre.

Up till now Joel's horses had been trained for him by William Jarvis. Jarvis had other owners and Joel was not one of the most important of his patrons. Joel decided to increase his investment in bloodstock and to employ a private trainer. To fill this post his choice fell upon Charles Morton of Letcombe Regis. It can hardly have been a coincidence that from amongst all the trainers in England Joel should choose to approach the man who had the care of Sievier's horses, to set him up in sole charge of the powerful string he proposed to acquire and to back him with the fortune which he had at his disposal. Certainly neither Sievier nor the public, knowing the enmity between the two men, read it as such. It was a body blow to Sievier, given by an expert and with all the power and weight of money in millions behind it.

Morton was hardly likely to refuse this wonderful opportunity both for security and success nor, in fact, did he. The partnership thus formed as a counter-move in what was to be a vicious private vendetta remained in being for twenty-five years. It redounded to the credit of both men and the trust they put in each other and, though no part of this book, made Turf history.

Morton behaved to Sievier as well as was possible under the circumstances, giving him long notice of the proposed change and all the time he could spare to arrange for the transfer of the horses. Sievier, it must be said, though he fell out with him afterwards over another matter, never blamed Morton over this affair for he knew that the trainer's best interests lay in his acceptance of the offer. But he recognized the motive behind Joel's move and was, needless to say, furiously resentful of it. At once he began to brood over it and to plot ways and means of hitting the millionaire where it would most hurt him.

Meanwhile he took his time about deciding what to do with his horses. This may well have been in order to annoy Joel but he had, as it happened, other things on his mind too. The law suit over the shooting rights was threatening to come to a head and he had, quite by accident, discovered a promising steeplechaser which he thought might well win him a National.

A year or so before he had seen Ted Robson, who trained at Wantage, riding a good-looking hack. Wishing at that time to make a present to one of his 'lovely ladies' he bought the horse from Robson, called him Bobsie and sent him to London as a mount for the lady in Rotten Row. He proved too strong for her, however, so Sievier took him to Toddington where he used him as a hack, riding him about the park, and occasionally jumping a small fence or two. One day hounds ran through the park. Sievier was actually having lunch but, hearing hounds, he ran out, saddled Bobsie and set sail after them. To his delight and astonishment the horse proved to him that not only was he a natural jumper but that he could gallop as well. He was bold and strong and took his fences as if he had been hunting all his life. Sievier came home convinced that he had something at least good enough to run in a steeplechase.

He had recently bought a horse called Merry Mood out of a selling hurdle at Gatwick. Merry Mood was still at Toddington. Putting some hurdles up in the park Sievier mounted his second horseman on Merry Mood and rode Bobsie himself in a fast school over them. Bobsie beat Merry Mood out of sight.

The Oakley Hunt Races were shortly to take place. Forthwith Sievier entered Bobsie in the Hunt Cup and undertook all the training himself. Ridden by a local farmer, Bobsie won by a distance beating a couple of useful horses. Still trained by his owner he went on to win four open steeplechases in a row. Then he went up to 12st 7lb in the handicap and was put by.

Whether the enjoyment and success he had in training Bobsie influenced him in the decision he made as to the future of Sceptre and the flat-race horses it is impossible to say. It is probable that it at least had something to do with it, other motives no doubt being to show that Joel's body-blow meant nothing to him and that anything another could do he could do better. There was, too, the ever-present wish to keep himself in the focus of public attention and the very real feeling, love and understanding he had for horses especially the finest of them all, the most wonderful thing in his life, the filly Sceptre. Next season he was determined that she would come out and beat everything that birth, breeding, power and riches could send against her. He made up his mind to take the flat-race string into his own care and train them himself. This meant that as an inexperienced amateur in his first season as a trainer he would have in his charge a filly entered in all four classics who might well start favourite for each of them. It was a prospect which might have daunted many men far better qualified to train thoroughbred racehorses. It was one which he faced with pleasure and lively anticipation.

But Sceptre's three-year-old career deserves and shall have a chapter to itself.

14

The Year of Sceptre

❧❧❧❧❧❧

Toddington Park was admirably situated for cricket and shooting but it was no place in which to train racehorses. There were no gallops, no adequate yards or stabling, no quarters for the lads. It was essential for him to move and to do so quickly for he had not allowed himself much time in which to prepare Sceptre for her first race. She was in the Lincoln and he had already made a tentative decision to run her. Suitable training quarters are never easy to find in a hurry and now it was lucky for Sievier that he had preserved Porter's friendship.

Some years ago Porter had bought Elston House, Shrewton, in Wiltshire, for his son George. Not long after he had moved into it George died and Porter was left with the place on his hands. Hearing of Sievier's predicament Porter offered him the goodwill of Shrewton, its stables and gallops, at a reasonable price. Sievier immediately accepted the offer. He settled his action over the shooting rights with his landlord and effected a surrender of his lease of Toddington on the terms that he be paid £600 for possession, £300 for improvements and £197 for some tenants' fixtures. Considering the amount he had spent on the place these were scarcely favourable terms but time was now pressing and he was in no position to argue. Children, hunters, horses, Mrs. Master and all were swept up and moved to Shrewton.

It was in fact a splendid place in which to train. He had all Salisbury Plain on which to work his horses. Porter, too, had made sure that the appointments lacked nothing and fine gallops had been laid out. With typical desire for innovation Sievier put down a new one at Lavington which came to be known as Sceptre's gallop. The others were altered and extended and a head lad called Spittle was engaged who proved to be a loyal and devoted servant.

So far so good. He then made up his mind that he would definitely run Sceptre in the Lincoln. It was an ill-advised decision much criticized at the time and it has never been satisfactorily explained.

Later he justified it on the grounds that she required and could stand as much work as two other racehorses. This of course was the case but at that time it is clear that even he had not yet realized just how much work it was necessary to give her.

Then he did something else. Despite the fact that he hated the Americans and had played a part in ridding the Turf of the worst of them he was an admirer of many of their methods. He saw that much of what they did in matters of stable-management and horse-mastership was an improvement upon the out-moded ways used in England. Private and financial worries were pressing him. He felt that he could not manage this string of valuable horses, his only remaining asset, without some skilled help. He employed, as his assistant to supervise the stable, an American who had been with Duke when he was Sir John Thursby's private trainer.

Four weeks before the Lincoln was due to be run, for a reason that has never been divulged save that it was an urgent private one, he went to Paris and stayed there for a fortnight. The American was left in charge of the horses—and of Sceptre.

On his return the first thing Sievier did was to go to Sceptre's box. To his astonishment he found her tucked up and sickly, off her feed, snappish and bad-tempered. Obtaining no satisfactory explanation for this state of affairs from the American he sought out Spittle. Quickly then he learnt the reason for her condition.

Taking him at his word that she wanted more work than the ordinary horse the American had not only given it to her, he had nearly killed her with it. In four days this is what she had done—first a mile gallop at racing pace with Lavengro, and Lavengro although now a gelding could still go a bit especially at home; next a mile at the same pace with two fresh horses; then another mile with Lavengro; finally a trial with Lavengro and the two others, giving them a stone. 'Four severe races on four consecutive days,' was Sievier's comment to a friend. 'And that was the swine's notion of training!'

Immediately, in a flurry of the most blistering language he could muster some of which is said to have frightened even the stable lads, he sacked the American. Afterwards when asked why he had not only employed the man but given him such complete authority in the stable he answered, 'Because I was a bloody fool,' and beyond that no one ever learnt the true explanation either of the extraordinary incident or of his absence in Paris. Having dispensed with his trainer's services Sievier sat down and wrote a letter striking Sceptre out of the Lincoln.

But he did not send it. He and Spittle took over the care of Sceptre themselves and she quickly began to respond to their care and sympathetic treatment. It was Sievier who persuaded her to eat again, feeding her from his own hands, and his boast that he knew her and her peculiarities better than anyone else dates from that time. Soon she began to come back to herself and to show them something of her old fire and ability.

But there were only fourteen days in which to put her right. During that short space of time he had first to nurse her back to physical and mental health and then start again to give her the work she required. The magnitude of the task facing him if she were to run and do herself justice can be appreciated. Nevertheless, watching her improvement each day and the way she went in her work, he tore up the letter striking her out and resolved to let her take her chance.

He has been widely condemned ever since for doing this. It certainly seems an act of recklessness at odds with his avowed love for the filly. One is forced to the inescapable conclusion that the reason he ran her was that which lay behind almost all the major moves in his life and over-rode everything else—shortage of money. He is said to have spent some time during that spring at Monte Carlo and to have lost a fortune at the tables. Certainly everything he had received from Porter for Duke of Westminster had now gone and a lot more with it. In order to recover he had backed Sceptre to win him between £30,000 and £40,000 on the ante-post market. This and other inspired betting, for of course he made no secret of his confidence, resulted in her being favourite in most bookmakers' lists. Not to run her would have caused disappointment and loss to many small punters and this was always a consideration with him. It was one of the factors that made for his popularity with the public. But just the same it cannot readily be accepted that this was, as he was sometimes later on to claim, what weighed most with him in his decision to run.

If he ever worried he was worried then. Despite all he could do by way of persuasion, tempting her beforehand with a carrot or an apple, she was not feeding up properly. When he took her over she was only consuming a measure and a half of oats a day amounting to 5 lb 4oz. He succeeded in doubling this. But it wasn't enough and he knew it. There is no doubt that she was still far below her best when the day of the race came round.

He had hedged a little by backing her each way and, in order to lighten the weight on her back, engaged to ride her a leading apprentice

5. The crowd watching Sievier leave the Court at the luncheon interval

6a. Rufus Isaacs and Sir Edward Carson arriving at the Law Courts

6b. Bob Sievier and Rufus Isaacs outside the Law Courts

called Hardy. The allowance which Hardy could claim put her pretty well in at the weights for she was then set to carry 6st. 7lb.

The Lincoln in those days was of course still run on the Carholme. It was a useful field that year and included a good colt of Harry McCalmont's called St. Maclou who had won the previous Manchester November Handicap beating Volodyovski the 1901 Derby winner pointless in the process. Sceptre was receiving nineteen pounds from him. She was favourite at 11—4, much of the money to make her so being her owner's. He still thought she could pull it off. And, in the event, she very nearly did.

It was his attempt to try to ease the weight on her that cost him the race. In a desperate finish with St. Maclou, Hardy, who had also allowed her to run too freely in the early stages of the race, was not able to produce the strength required to get the best out of her. She was beaten a head.

In the stand his friends were telling Sievier that his jockey had thrown the race away. He would have none of it. As has been said, he could always take a beating. In fact he was a far better man in defeat than in victory, for the call to battle brought out the best in him. He went straightaway to the weighing-room. There he found Hardy downcast and depressed, knowing what the race had cost his owner. 'Well ridden, Hardy!' he said, patting the boy on the back. 'Bad luck!'

Defiantly he announced that he had not lost anything in the race and that his place bets had saved him. But what he did not say was that he had not won anything either and that, in his present position, was serious indeed. He also told the press that she was a certain starter in both the Guineas. Then he went back to Shrewton to superintend her preparation.

He was much criticized but that was something he was used to and of which he took no heed. He might well have ruined his lovely filly for life. Whether, in the event, the race did her any harm is another matter, for so superb was her constitution that she does in fact appear to have survived unscathed the appalling treatment she received from the American, her hurried preparation and her hard race.

The public remained loyal both to him and the filly but in many knowledgeable quarters they were both now derided as serious contenders for the season's classics. Amongst the knowing and the wise and with considerable satisfaction in Establishment circles it was said that he was a bungling amateur with too little knowledge or experience successfully to supervise a classic candidate and that, if they had not done so already, his unconventional methods would soon put an end to her career. In addition, rumours of all sorts flew about concerning Sceptre, her conformation, her condition and her temperament.

Sievier was determined to disprove all this, both for himself and for Sceptre. Gone, for the moment at any rate, were all thoughts of high living, of card and cricket parties, of lovely ladies and gay Bohemian days and nights. Now his time was spent quietly at Shrewton following the dedicated routine of a trainer's life. He was up early each morning and rode out with the first lot. He supervised morning and evening stables and took Sceptre into his personal care.

At first he gave her the rest she both needed and deserved. She was given light work in the morning and if the weather was good enough was brought out in the afternoon to walk about in one of the paddocks and eat grass. As her health and appetite returned so did her strength. Gradually he began to put her back into full work. She was, as he said, 'A high-blower, clean-winded when thoroughly wound up, yet she would roar as she walked if she did no work for a week.'

For his jockey in the coming classics he had discarded Hardy not, as he took care to explain, due to any fault of his own, but because of his light weight, and had engaged Herbert Randall in his place.

Randall, like Hardy, was relatively inexperienced. He was the son of Sir Henry Randall, a Northamptonshire boot manufacturer, and until that season had ridden as an amateur. It is one of the mysteries of Sceptre's career and was never explained by Sievier why he did not engage a leading jockey to ride her. He had, of course, his own ideas about the riders of his day, their honesty and ability. He knew most of them personally and of those with whom he was not acquainted he had the means through his book-making friends of finding accurate information concerning their finances and their trustworthiness. It may well be that he preferred to employ one upon whom he knew he could rely rather than another whose skill was greater but whose probity less. For Sceptre was now everything to him, not only as a beloved piece of horseflesh but also as an investment to restore his shattered finances.

On the Sunday before the Two Thousand Guineas, Randall came down to Shrewton and rode her in a gallop. In this she delighted them both. At Newmarket it was immediately seen that she was far stronger and better in every way than she had been at Lincoln. Sievier was full of confidence but so bad now was his financial position that he appears to have been unable to back her the way he wanted and indeed needed to.

One of Sceptre's peculiarities was that, ordinarily placid and contented in temperament, as the work given her increased so she became excitable and fretful, especially on the racecourse. Oddly enough, too, she appeared to know who was responsible for this and the presence of her trainer near her caused these symptoms to increase. At home in the yard as the time for a race approached and the immense amount of work she needed was being given her she would turn on Sievier and almost chase him out of the box.

Now, when he brought her into the paddock at Newmarket she broke into a profuse sweat. He took her outside and saddled her there. One of his lady friends coming by, he paused in his exertions, for Sceptre in this state was not easy to saddle, and told her she was looking at the winner of the first classic. His openly expressed confidence and the tremendous improvement in her looks and condition impressed everyone. She started joint favourite with Duke of Westminster now, of course, trained by Porter.

Duke of Westminster had not wintered well. Neither in looks nor in substance had he improved in the interval. Remembering how Sceptre had slammed him at home in their two-year-old days Sievier anticipated no danger from him. In fact he feared nothing despite the fact that a good colt called Ard Patrick who had won twice as a two-year-old and only just failed in the Dewhurst behind Game Chick was also in the field.

Newmarket was Sceptre's spiritual home. There were no turns to bother her; she could lay herself down to go and gallop her opponents off their legs. In the Two Thousand Guineas of 1902 that was just what she did. Her fretfulness gone and forgotten once she strode out on that galloping ground she won as she liked in the record time of 1 min. 39 secs. Ard Patrick was third, beaten two lengths and three lengths.

On Friday she came out and gave the same treatment to her own sex in the One Thousand and established a record time in that race, too. This performance was even more meritorious than it appeared. Sievier had been given permission to saddle her at the Scrubbing Houses not far from the start. When he had finished and she was walking away he saw, to his horror, that she had twisted the plate on her near fore so badly that it was protruding a couple of inches. His blacksmith, whom he had told to be present, had not arrived. The only others there were Randall, and Spittle who had helped with the saddling. There was nothing for it, the plate would have to come off.

Lifting her fore leg Sievier took hold of the plate and by main strength wrenched it partly free. But do what he could it would not come the whole way. Time was running on, there were only the three of them there and Sceptre, though submitting with surprising meekness to the treatment, might at any moment elect to give one of her displays of temperament. At last, with a final heave, the plate came away, just in time to get her down to the start.

This fact was not generally known at the time. The manner of her performance, however, without a plate on her near fore, increased her owner's confidence in her for the Derby.

The exact nature of his betting commitments about this time is far from clear. Undoubtedly he won something over the Guineas and this he appears to have used to enable him to strike further bets on Sceptre in the Derby, backing her to win him another £33,000. But he was still very short of ready cash and about this time he received a writ from Gilbert, the Newmarket saddler, claiming payment for saddlery supplied to him when he went to Shrewton. It was a comparatively small amount but even so he seems to have had trouble in settling it though at the same time he had subscribed substantial sums from the stake money to the Newmarket Coronation fund and to charities in Shrewton.

Sceptre was now a raging favourite everywhere for the Derby. Press and public almost unanimously agreed with her owner's opinion that she could not be beaten. Very quietly however, and with the minimum of publicity, Sam Darling, one of the shrewdest trainers in the business, was getting Mr. Gubbin's colt Ard Patrick ready for the day. The fact that Ard Patrick had been beaten in The Guineas did not worry Darling in the least. The big colt wanted time and his trainer was determined that he should have it.

Again, at first, Sievier allowed Sceptre a rest before he began her Derby preparation. Then he set about giving her all the food and all the work she would readily take. Even now he and his helpers were only beginning to realize how much she could stand of both. Indeed it was not a question of what she could stand but of what she required to make her racing fit especially if the race were over a distance of ground. Inevitably much of this preparation was accompanied by a blaze of publicity. A biograph company which was operating a primitive form of newsreel obtained permission to photograph the filly and her owner. The operator omitted to warn Sievier that the camera when started to work by revolving a crank handle made a series of sharp noises 'rather like a machine-gun' as William Allison, who witnessed the incident, put it.

These noises, naturally enough, upset Sceptre. They also upset her owner who addressed a series of pungent and uncomplimentary remarks concerning his parentage to the cameraman and was photographed in so doing. 'Mr. Sievier,' Allison wrote, 'expressed his displeasure in fairly adequate terms which, had they been retained by a phonograph, would have imported a still more vivid image to the picture . . .'

Allison, as a friend and a favoured member of the press, was constantly at Shrewton during that time. He admitted in print that, along with most racing people, he had had considerable doubts that Sievier could succeed as a trainer of first-class thoroughbreds, but he went on to say, which many another would not, that those doubts had now been proved wrong. He saw Randall ride her in a gallop over nine furlongs with Doochary who was receiving 9lb, and was tremendously impressed. 'Sceptre has the lithe, stealing action of the thorough stayer,' he wrote. 'Every movement is suggestive of absolute ease, and as she slipped along past me with her ears pricked and no indication that she was really exerting herself I wondered what manner of filly can this be for did not we see Doochary beat Pekin last year?'

Randall, too, confirmed what Allison watching her had perceived. 'The strange thing is,' he told the journalist, 'that she never feels as if she was going fast. She does it all so easily.' But, in talking to Randall, Allison sensed that the boy was nervous about the responsibility which had been thrust upon him. Although he believed that she had had a stone in hand in both the Guineas he was worried about getting Sceptre round Tattenham Corner in the Derby. He told Allison he wished it were being run at Newmarket. 'I shall do the very best I possibly can,' he said. 'And one can't do more than that.' It was not perhaps the best of moods in which to contemplate riding what was likely to prove the hottest Derby favourite for years.

On his last visit to Shrewton, Allison was let into a carefully guarded secret. A few days earlier Sceptre had been stopped in her work and had been three days in the stable. One of her feet, always a weak point, had been giving trouble. She had pulled up lame from a gallop, either from treading on a stone or from some other unknown reason. She had bruised a foot and the trouble went along her leg and into her knee. She was given treatment and, when the heat went, was shod over felt. After a little while the trouble passed and she became quite sound again but not even Sievier realized at the time just how vital the stoppage was. He gave Allison permission to publish a full report on her injury and, a week before the race, when she was back in work, he did so. No one took any notice and she remained a raging favourite at 2—1. Allison himself at the time did not realize the full significance of the short lay-off and, having watched her again in her work and receiving a handful of green food from Sievier in her box, reported her in the very zenith of condition.

The night before the race Sievier took a party to a box in the Gaiety Theatre. The show was *The Toreador* which had been running for a year and which had extra songs added from time to time. One of these was *The Miller's Daughter* with its chorus:

> *She was a miller's daughter*
> *Who sat beside the mill*
> *Fast was the current of Water*
> *But she was faster still!*

That night the management varied the song and Gertie Millar, looking roguishly up at the box, sang:

> *Sceptre is Persimmon's daughter*
> *She's trained on the Wiltshire Downs*
> *Wednesday's the day she ought to*
> *Fill Bob Sievier's pockets with pounds!*

He was delighted of course though few there knew just how badly he needed those pounds if he were to keep Sceptre.

It was the Coronation Derby. There was no Royal runner and what then more appropriate if the most famous daughter of the Monarch's winner should gain the prize? But it was not regal weather for it rained steadily all night and showed no sign of ceasing when morning came. This was, however, held to strengthen Sceptre's chances by taking the sting out of the ground.

His Majesty himself was there looking happy and at his ease as he always was amongst his sporting friends and the plain people of England who loved him. Despite the rain an enormous crowd had turned out to cheer him at his Coronation Derby and to bet on the famous filly. Those were the days of simple enthusiasms and undivided loyalties, of hero-worship of the great in any sphere, when Englishmen believed in their country, their horses—and themselves.

It was, in its upper reaches, indeed a gilded throng. No less than seven Indian princes were present, the Prince and Princess of Wales had come, as had the Duke and Duchess of Connaught, Prince Charles and Prince Christian of Denmark and the usual racing Dukes and Lords led by the

Dukes of Portland and Devonshire each of whom had a runner.

Mr. Gubbins, the owner of Ard Patrick, crippled by an attack of gout, was hobbling about on two sticks. Lily Langtry, the former *maîtresse en titre* of Edward VII and still his firm friend, who raced under the name of 'Mr. Jersey', had asked him to watch the race from her box. On paying a visit to her there before racing began the King was full of confidence in Sceptre. Mr. Gubbins warned him that Sam Darling, having watched the early morning workout, had said to him, 'I do not fear Sceptre's chances today'. So impressed was the Monarch by this that, meeting his friend Harding Cox in the club a few minutes later, he told him not to plunge too heavily on Sceptre but to have a saver on Ard Patrick, advice which Cox gratefully accepted.

The public, however, would have nothing but the filly and her owner exuded total confidence. He had won £900 on the two earlier races and instructed his commissioner to put the lot on Sceptre, thus increasing even more his already heavy commitments. Now he stood to win over £40,000 on her. Others were not slow to follow his lead. Her price quickly shortened to even money.

On the form book everything looked right. Pekin, the horse Doochary had slammed the year before, was second favourite at 6—1 and Allison had already told his many readers what Sceptre could do to Doochary at home. Ard Patrick, well behind in the Guineas, occupied third place in the betting at 100—13. The others included Czardas and Duke of Westminster who appeared to have gone back still more in his condition since the Guineas. 'He didn't look worth 22,000 guineas today' was one racing reporter's pointed comment.

Sievier had obtained permission to take Sceptre out of the parade. He saddled her in the Durdans, Lord Rosebery's Epsom estate beside the course. Then, led by Barberstown, a stable companion whom he was now sending everywhere with her, he brought her into the paddock. Her entrance, as managed by Sievier, was that of a star performer on a stage as, of course, at that moment, she was. 'Let Cheers' (another runner) 'come through the gate please,' Sievier said, addressing the crowd. 'And then let *her* come.' As she approached he requested those pressing nearest to stand back. 'You will see a lot of her very soon,' he said. 'And you can see her next week at Madame Tussaud's for sixpence.' Then, still accompanied by Barberstown, she went out on to the course. When she broke into her preliminary canter she was seen to move with the deceptive stealing ease which confirmed the confidence of her supporters.

Sievier went up to his box to watch her bring home his money for him and fulfil the greatest ambition of his life. He was quite sure that the next few minutes would see him win the supreme classic of the Turf with a filly bought, owned and trained by himself. Had he been twenty years younger and a stone or so lighter he would probably have ridden her.

The Epsom preliminaries provide a severe test of the temperament of both horse and rider. There can be no doubt but that anxiety as to the outcome of this race had been steadily building up in Randall's mind. Now he was to be denied the company of others in the parade and the walk across the hill. Instead he had been told by Sievier to take what someone sarcastically referred to as 'an Irish short cut' and to bring Sceptre slowly round the course in the reverse direction. He obeyed these instructions all too well and took her the whole way at a walk. As a result the rest of the field had arrived at the start and were kept waiting for fully fifteen minutes in the rain and the cold.

Arthur Coventry was the starter that year and had the responsibility of getting them away by means of the new-fangled starting gate which had only comparatively recently been introduced and which was still the subject of severe criticism in some quarters. He was not best pleased at the delay. He had been a leading amateur rider in his day; he was accustomed to control and to command and he had ready for use a flow of blistering language not far behind Sievier's own. Some of this rang out across the Downs to greet Randall on his approach. It cannot have had a soothing affect on the jockey's nerves.

When she did join the others she was well enough behaved so Sievier's object in settling her down by bringing her the long way round appeared to have been achieved. The rest of the field, having waited so long, were, however, inclined to cause trouble and there was difficulty in getting them into line. And, whatever about the filly, her jockey unquestionably was far from settled down. The nervous tension of the preceding weeks, the long and lonely walk around, the tongue lashing he had received and now the further delay with horses wheeling and riders cursing all about him, were combining to upset his nerves and his temperament.

At last, after nearly another five minutes of backing and swinging, of swearing and shouting, Arthur Coventry effected a brilliant start getting them off in a near perfect line.

Immediately Czardas, who had been drawn on the inside, dashed into the lead, followed by Fowling Piece. Sceptre was slowly away and this, together with all that had gone before, appears to have completed the disintegration of Randall's temperament. Without allowing her to settle at all he drove her up to the leaders and kept her there. He had been worrying all the time about how she would come around Tattenham Corner and appears to have decided that she must be in the leading group when they came to it in case she had to give away ground. In the event she had no trouble rounding it, and when the field turned for home appeared to those on the stands to have her race won. The crowd began to cheer. But much can happen between Tattenham Corner and the post. 'Skeets' Martin on Ard Patrick had been riding a cool and calculated race. Now he brought the big colt up in one steady, sweeping run. All at once Sceptre was seen to falter. To the dumbfounded astonishment of the watchers her stride suddenly began to shorten. Ard Patrick swept past her and went on to win as he liked from Rising Glass and Friar Tuck. It looked at one moment as if Sceptre would run into a place but William Allison recorded that she 'almost stood still' from the bell.

The victory was received in silence. The crowd could not believe the evidence of their eyes that their idol had not only been beaten but humiliated.

Almost immediately after the result was announced Randall and Sievier were sent for by the stewards. They both received severe reprimands for the dilatory progress of Sceptre to the start and for the delay caused by it. This was the only occasion in his entire racing career that Sievier was before the stewards about one of his horses and in this instance, of course, the running and riding were not in issue. But the fact that owner and rider had been sent for coupled with her astounding defeat set the course afire with rumour. Tongues began to chatter and the wildest stories flew around. It was said straightaway and repeated over and over again that Sceptre had been stopped and that her owner had laid against her, thus making money on her defeat. His many enemies took care to fan the flame and this slander persisted in some quarters for many years and for all one knows may indeed persist to this day. To the end of his life Sievier fiercely resented this and it is probably the one accusation levelled at him which had the power to penetrate the armour of his self-confidence and really hurt him. His integrity on the Turf and the straight running of his horses meant everything to him. Whatever he did elsewhere it was always his pride and boast that no finger could ever be fairly pointed at him concerning his racing career. There can be no question of doubt that when Sceptre failed, the cause did not lie in her owner's motives or instructions. No one who knew racing accepted the stories or believed the rumours though there were many who, through ignorance or malice, repeated and embroidered them. When in a subsequent slander action this accusation was said to have been made it was the one portion of the slanderous statement which was denied and then withdrawn, and the sixth Marquess of Ailesbury, who had no reason to love Sievier, writing of him long afterwards said: *He has been accused of having her pulled for the Derby, but this I do not believe. He was too good a sportsman in that way and was also too fond of a great mare to try to spoil her record.*

But, for the moment at any rate, the crowd, up to now his most enthusiastic supporters, believed it. They were demonstrating in the uninhibited way Edwardian crowds could demonstrate and were baying for his blood. The situation looked ugly enough.

Sievier always afterwards said that what quietened the demonstration and turned the crowd once more in his favour was the action of King Edward VII.

The King was a sportsman himself and an owner of racehorses. He had a kindly and understanding streak in his nature which was never nearer the surface than when he was on a racecourse or with his sporting friends. He liked unconventional characters and he knew from bitter experience the trials and disappointments of an owner's life. He came down to the Club enclosure, sent for Sievier and shook him by the hand. From that day onward Sievier's veneration for his King stopped only just this side of idolatry.

Some sort of racecourse acquaintanceship appears, too, to have developed between the two men. When racing, the King often would stop and chat to him, asking his opinion of horses and their running. This acquaintanceship, such as it was, was treasured by Sievier and for once he was discreet about it. His enemies, however, and those around the King who disliked him could scarcely be expected to look upon it with favour. Someone, perhaps Dudley, Sievier never quite found out who, attempted to turn the King against him by telling him Sievier had made insulting remarks about Lily Langtry. He had not; it was pure fabrication. It was not Sievier's way to make insulting remarks about women in any walk of life. He kept the deadly weapons of his voice and tongue for use against men and then against those whom he disliked and who were well able to hit back. The attempt failed and, commenting on it to a friend, Bob said, 'If I'd been such a bloody fool to have done that I'd have deserved whatever I got for it.'

Discussions about the reason for Sceptre's defeat, acrimonious, slanderous or sympathetic, went on all that day and long afterwards. Morton told Allison that it was all very simple, she just didn't stay. Porter was of the same opinion and said that it only reinforced the earlier judgment he had formed of her. Both soon lived to eat their words. Allison remembering, too late, the bruised foot and the stoppage in her work, advised against condemning her too soon. Randall said she was never going like herself at any stage of the race.

Sievier blamed Randall's riding though he never said so in public until years later. It was certainly a disastrous afternoon, for he was now in real financial trouble. But he still held to his belief in Sceptre. Immediately he announced that she would run in the Oaks on Friday, probably in a hood, and in the Grand Prix in Paris after that. He also confirmed that Randall would ride her in both these races. Certainly he could never be accused of not being loyal to his servants. Then he sent out a challenge to the world that Sceptre 'shall run any horse at weight for age and sex for £10,000 over from $1\frac{1}{4}$ to $1\frac{3}{4}$ miles.' He might have lost everything else but he had not lost his nerve. The challenge was not accepted.

Then he waited for Friday. Seeing Sceptre work that morning he very wisely decided to run her without a hood. She started favourite at 5—2, took part in the parade and although drawn this time on the extreme outside and fractious at the start was allowed by Randall to settle down. But Randall was a mass of nerves before and during the race and Sievier afterwards always said that he owed his win to William Halsey. Rounding Tattenham Corner Randall, strung up as ever, was about to go for home. Seeing this, Halsey, riding Sir Edward Cassel's Doctrine, shouted across 'Hold her in. What do you want to go on for?' Randall held her up and when he did let her go she simply galloped the rest of them off their legs. Amidst a storm of cheering she won as she liked by three lengths. Admittedly, she took rather longer to do it than had Ard Patrick two days before and thus the question of their respective merits was as open as ever. When Sievier announced that she would take on the colt in the St. Leger interest became intense.

Only after this race did he finally appreciate the amount of work she required to get her into racing trim. Although every expert said he was mad he decided on a tough and ambitious programme for her. He was now quite certain that her defeat in the Derby had been caused by the stoppage in her work coupled with Randall's injudicious riding tactics. He decided to run her at Paris, Ascot and Goodwood. In the meantime cash was so short that he had to ask Messrs Pratt to advance what was due to him for the prize money in the Oaks so that he could make some sort of a settlement on Monday.

Then he took her to Paris for the Grand Prix. He made some money on the earlier races and had 26,000 francs on her to win. Once again Randall's riding tactics, whether caused by nerves or not, were deplorable, and she was beaten. The French jockeys of those days were a pretty ferocious bunch. A generation before they had made Archer, who feared no man, go the long way round to preserve his skin. Now Randall emulated him. Sievier said that he thought Sceptre must have covered at least two hundred yards more than the winner.

Still Sievier refused to put Randall down. It was misplaced loyalty. He took Sceptre straight from Paris to Ascot and ran her in the Coronation Stakes. Randall again rode a terrible race, lying so far out of his ground that he left her with an impossible distance to make up at the finish. Carrying 9st. 10lb and giving over a stone to the rest of the field she was flying once she started to go but she could only secure fifth place. Afterwards Sievier found out that she had bucked Randall into a blackberry bush at the start and run loose. But Randall himself did not tell him this, he heard it from another quarter. Furious at having what he considered vital information withheld from him he sacked Randall on the spot.

Sceptre was in the St. James's Palace Stakes the following day. He engaged Hardy to ride her and she won in a common canter beating, among others, Rising Glass who had been second in the Derby.

After that she had a rest but she was soon back in strong work and, amidst the usual criticism that he was murdering her, he brought her to Goodwood and ran her in the Sussex Stakes. So far from her being over-worked, in fact she needed the race and was beaten two lengths by a good colt called Royal Lancer belonging to Sir Blundell Maple. She blew so much after the race that many said she had gone in the wind. Now Sievier was more than ever convinced that she needed the work of two ordinary horses. Fortunately for him it was a damp, moist summer, the ground was soft and he was able to give it to her.

There was the usual chorus of criticism when the next day he had her out and with Hardy up gave her a fast gallop over six furlongs, and, after a short rest, another over a mile and a half at three-quarter speed. The following morning before running in the Nassau Stakes he had Hardy send her along for a mile 'as fast as she would go'. These were, to say the least, unconventional methods, but they proved themselves when she won the Nassau Stakes with consummate ease by four lengths giving the second no less than 17lb.

But what he won over those victories was no real help to his finances. That night playing in a billiards flying handicap in the County Club at Brighton the marker called out: 'Mr. So-and-So receives six. Mr. Sievier owes two.'

'Owes two, you fool!' Sievier said. 'I owe thousands!'

There were then about six weeks before the St. Leger. He brought Sceptre back to Shrewton and kept her in strong work.

About this time Horatio Bottomley, financier, lay lawyer and demagogue, came into his life. 'England's Orator' as he became known in the First World War, had started racing on a large scale in 1898 but some years before that he had formed an association with J. H. Batho, a stable lad in William Jarvis's yard. For some time Batho leaked stable information to Bottomley and with Bottomley's money behind them they ran a profitable betting syndicate. Then, after a successful financial operation when money was flush, Bottomley set Batho up as his private trainer at Alfriston near his country residence The Dicker. Unlike Sievier to whom it was his whole life, racing was only a hobby with Bottomley, an excuse for gambling, drinking his favourite beverage, champagne, and entertaining his 'pretty ladies'. He never mastered its technicalities nor tried to, though he had a considerable opinion of himself as a manipulator of the betting market which cost him a lot of money from time to time. Sievier disliked and despised him and called him 'the fly-mug'.

Bottomley and Batho had a useful horse called Wargrave which they fancied for the Cesarewitch. Wargrave had been unplaced in the Derby the previous year when owned by Sir James Duke who had been on the fringes of the Sievier-Deerhurst affair in Australia as a youth of seventeen. He was the second baronet, his father, who had made a fortune as a coal merchant, having been Lord Mayor of London. At this time and for some years past Duke had been trying to make a name for himself on the Turf first as an amateur rider and then as an owner, and failing on both counts. But very soon he was to be, either wittingly or unwittingly, the cause of the greatest set-back Sievier was to receive in his tumultuous career.

Wargrave won the Ebor Handicap at York and Bottomley conceived that the best way of testing his Cesarewitch chances was a private trial with Sceptre. For reasons known only to himself Sievier agreed to this. Bottomley insisted on the strictest secrecy. Wargrave was brought down and stabled at a nearby farm and the horses were out before day-break.

When they reached the gallop Sievier had intended to use he found that the ground was too firm and a move was made to another which was of two-and-a-quarter miles and had in it one fairly sharp turn. Bottomley and Batho wanted them to go a mile and six furlongs. Sievier agreed but he pointed out that although Sceptre had done regular work there she had never gone round the turn. Being accustomed to stop on reaching it and being a filly who always knew her own mind she would almost certainly do so again. This, in fact, was exactly what happened. Sceptre, in the lead at the turn, recognized her stopping place and eased up. Wargrave went on and won the trial easily.

Sievier warned Bottomley that the trial was incorrect and even offered another trial at a later date. But Bottomley and Batho, suspecting a trick, refused to accept this and commenced to lay against Sceptre for considerable sums of money. Sievier's contempt for them, freely expressed, knew no bounds.

As the day of the St. Leger approached Sceptre was seen to be thriving on her work. She was now eating 21 lb of oats a day, a strange contrast to what she could only be persuaded to take before the Lincoln. Sievier brought her to Doncaster the Saturday before the race. On Sunday she went the full St. Leger distance. The next day he repeated her Goodwood regime—six furlongs and then a mile. On Tuesday Hardy came down to ride her in her winding-up gallop. Yellow polo-necked sweaters had just appeared and become popular wear for jockeys. When Sievier arrived on the course he found Hardy decked out in one of these, up on Sceptre waiting for him. He did not approve. 'Come down off your perch, you bloody little canary!' he roared. Hardy, chastened, joined him on the ground and was told he was to go the full St. Leger distance, that three different horses would jump in with Sceptre at five furlong intervals and that if he did not beat them all he would not get the ride in the race. The reason for these Draconian instructions was that Sievier knew the criticisms being levelled at him everywhere for working her off her legs. Convinced though he was that he was right, he feared that Hardy might have heeded the critics, believe he knew better than her owner and ease her in her work. However, all went well. On the morning of the race he sent her along for just over a mile and then went off to breakfast confident he had done all he had to do, that she was ready and racing fit and that she would win.

Her task was made easier by reason of the fact that the long awaited clash with Ard Patrick was not going to take place. The colt had leg trouble and was out for the season.

Once again Sievier was fortunate in the weather. Rain had started about ten o'clock the night before and continued up to the off. Thus the ground was in the filly's favour, the going, in fact, being officially returned as yielding. Some, still unconvinced that she was a true stayer, thought this would tell against her. As a result of this and also of the fact that Bottomley was telling all and sundry how Wargrave had slammed her in the trial and because stories concerning the Derby were still current, casting suspicion on all that Sievier did, she jumped about in the betting. The Irish horse, St. Brendan, was at one time a shorter price; the Duke of Portland's Friar Tuck, on whom Randall had the mount, was also well backed as were Rising Glass, the Derby second whom she had already beaten, and Cupbearer which was the name that had been given to the colt by Orme—Kissing Cup that had made second price to Sceptre at the Westminster sale. Eventually she steadied in the market as favourite at 100—30.

The rain kept the crowd from being a record one and the convenience of the newly installed electric tram service which conveyed racegoers to the course for the modest sum of sixpence was much appreciated.

Sceptre was again drawn towards the outside and once more she caused trouble at the start. Sievier had given instructions for her to be led about until the line began to form but this did not prevent her playing up once her head was freed. Cupbearer, too, was fractious and, lashing out, all but caught Rising Glass. During all these unsettling preliminaries Hardy remained commendably cool. Eventually he coaxed Sceptre up to the gate and Mr. Coventry let them go in a perfect line just five minutes late.

Caro, who had been put in as a pacemaker for Friar Tuck, immediately shot into a two-length lead and was ten to twelve lengths ahead by the time they reached the mile post. St. Brendan, closely attended by Friar Tuck, came next a few lengths in front of Rising Glass. Peering through the mist, those on the stand could see that Sceptre was well back in the ruck. At the Rifle Butts Hardy had moved her quietly into fourth place behind Rising Glass, Friar Tuck and St. Brendan. He was riding a perfect race, exactly to instructions, and he knew even then that he had it won.

Below the distance he sent her on. She won in a canter, ears pricked, by three lengths amidst tumultuous cheering. The time was three minutes twelve and two fifths seconds and she hardly seemed to have had a race. Sievier wearing 'a long-sleeved hat' against the weather, went to lead her in. Cheer upon cheer rolled out across the Town Moor as she came into the winners' enclosure.

He had every right then to be pleased and proud. He had regained his position with the crowd as a popular favourite as had his beloved filly. He was 'Good old Bob' again and they proved it by the reception they gave him. But, better still, he had shown the nobs, his enemies, and his many bitter detractors that he could own, manage and train high-class racehorses as well, in fact better, than any of them, for had he not just established a record likely to stand for years if not for ever of winning four classics with a filly owned and trained by himself? It was something to boast about all right and he did so. When one of the Vanderbilts asked him what he would take for Sceptre his reply was: 'Well, we'll start with New York on account.' He also ordered fifty cases of champagne to be sent to Shrewton for the celebrations.

Then he made a mistake brought about by misjudgment and over-confidence. The St. Leger had looked an easy victory; Sceptre had seemed not the least distressed from her exertions. Knowing what she could stand in the way of work he decided to run her in the Park Hill Stakes only forty-eight hours later. It seemed a mere formality. Odds of four and five to one were laid on her winning and he backed her for the certainty she looked. But she was set to carry 9st. 8lb and to give a good filly called Elba 12lb.

Like many high-couraged and highly strung horses her races took more out of Sceptre than was immediately apparent. Elba beat her by a length. It is at least in Sievier's favour that he at once admitted his mistake and said that he should not have run her. It was not in him to make excuses for failure, his own or anyone else's. Thereupon he retired her for the season. The villagers drank the champagne and ended up, according to one witness, 'unconscious to a man'.

When flat-racing ended he was at the head of the list of winning owners with £23,686 against his name. He was the first owner-trainer to head the list and the last, too, for that record still stands as does the record of Sceptre in winning four of the five classics. It was something he never forgot nor did he allow many of his acquaintances to forget it, either. But just at that moment it brought him little satisfaction, for, once again, he was broke.

The prize money, large though it was, had been far outstripped by his expenses. His betting losses on the Derby alone had been immense; coupled with those on the Lincoln, the Grand Prix and the Park Hill

7a. J. B. Joel at the 1911 Derby. Joel on right of picture; Solly Joel on the left congratulating him   7b. F. E. Smith entering the Law Courts in or about the time of the first Wootton case

8. Monarch: Joe Childs up

Stakes, they were staggering.* The sums lost had not by any means been covered by what he had won on cramped odds in her victories. The other horses in the stable had most of them been failures. Splendid though the season had been it had brought financial disaster with it. There had, too, been the desperate disappointment of the defeat in the Derby, the one race it meant everything to him to win.

It was a strange anti-climax that at the end of a season which should have given him the fulfilment of all but one of the ambitions any racing man could aspire to reach he was as near to being depressed in spirit and finished financially as he had ever been in his life.

* A list of the prices paid by Sievier for yearlings, and stakes won together with prices received is given in the appendix. These show a profit of £56,235 which sum alone indicates the huge figure his losses and expenses must have amounted to.

15
Last days with Sceptre

❧❧❧❧❧❧

Defeat and despair were, however, not words with which Sievier had any close acquaintance. Although hard pushed for ready cash with writs flying through the air like leaves in an autumn wind he refused to give up. He still had old Bobsie down at Shrewton. He had an idea, too, that Barberstown, Sceptre's companion, might well make a steeplechaser.

Despite the fact that, whatever about the flat, save for the few runs he had given Bobsie earlier in the year he had no experience at all of training steeplechasers he decided to maintain himself during the winter by running his horses over fences and betting on them when they ran. What is more he conceived the idea that it would fittingly enhance the legends now attaching to his name if he were to win the Grand National with Bobsie after winning four classics with Sceptre, and decided to train him for that race. As a matter of fact, as will be seen, Bobsie had considerable qualifications for doing so had luck been on his side.

But before he could get these steeplechasers going the financial pressures became too great for even him to resist. With the greatest reluctance he promised his creditors that he would send Sceptre to the December sales at Newmarket and settle with them out of the proceeds. This gave him a short respite and in that time he managed to pick up one or two small steeplechases. Though the betting market on steeple-chases in those days was limited in the extreme and the prize money negligible, nevertheless what he cleared over these enabled him to cover current expenses and to quieten one or two of the more demanding creditors.

He kept his promise to send Sceptre to the sales but he did little to encourage prospective buyers. She always looked horrible in her long shaggy winter coat and he seems to have made no effort to improve her appearance. Furthermore, once again the wildest rumours had been flying about ever since she had been beaten in the Park Hill Stakes and had been taken out of the rest of her engagements which included the Cambridgeshire. He was widely held to have ruined her constitution by the work he had given her, some said she had broken down, others that her wind had gone. In fact, nothing was too bad to say of her and him in certain fashionable quarters. These rumours went undenied partly because he despised those who invented them and passed them on but also, it seems certain, because he did not want to see Sceptre sold and the more the stories gained credence the less likelihood there was of a sale.

At the sale he placed upon her the substantial reserve of 24,000 guineas. He must have been fairly confident it would not be reached and he was right. There was in fact practically no interest shewn in her at all, demonstrating how well rumour had done its work. He took her home happy still to have her.

Things then began to look up a little. Bobsie won the Hampton Steeplechase at Hurst Park and then at Kempton, receiving 15lb from Drumcree and, starting equal favourite with him, beat him into third place by ten lengths. Since Drumcree had started favourite in the National the year before and would probably have won it but for being knocked over, Sievier realized tha the had indeed a live Grand National candidate on his hands. From that it was but a step for his sanguine nature to conjure up the vision of winning the spring double with horses owned and trained by himself. He put Sceptre into the Lincoln once more and began to train her for it. Financial pressure was back again and although the steeplechasers were enabling him to carry on for the moment he soon came to realize that he had to win one or the other of these races if he were to keep Sceptre and remain in racing during the coming year. It was money, as always, or rather the lack of it, that compelled him to run Sceptre in that Lincoln. He knew the distance was too short for her and the time of year too early. It would have been kinder and wiser to have cut his losses and sold her then but this the gambler in him would not let him do. After all there was always the chance that one or the other of them would come up against the odds.

He took Sceptre to Lincoln himself, leaving behind him detailed instructions for Bobsie's final gallop which was to take place the day before he was to be sent to Aintree.

Despite her owner's freely expressed misgivings the public made Sceptre favourite for that Lincoln. She had 9st. 1lb to carry and the best she could do was to finish fifth. That was bad enough but then, just as he had seen her in, he was handed a telegram from Shrewton. This told him that Bobsie had bolted in his final gallop, unshipped the lad, gone loose and fallen. The horse was badly hurt and had to be taken out of the National. Sievier went to Liverpool and had the mortification of seeing Drumcree win the great race with 11st. 3lb on his back. It was a bad week.

Now there was no question but that Sceptre had to go. His friends urged him not to delay his decision. Already the rumours and stories of the year before were multiplying, the current one being that she made a noise. If she was to maintain her value she should be sold quickly.

Sievier's friend Arthur Chetwynd was at that time managing the horses belonging to Mr. William Bass, a wealthy young man from the brewing family then serving with the 10th Hussars in India. Arthur Chetwynd and Sievier stayed together at Liverpool during Grand National week. Chetwynd told Sievier he was sure that Bass would buy Sceptre if Sievier would price her. After considerable hesitation and more pressure from his friends Sievier put a price tag of 25,000 guineas on the mare. In those days it was customary for the middleman in a private sale to collect the guineas as commission. Chetwynd waived his right to this sum and cabled Bass that he could buy Sceptre for £25,000. The answer came by return accepting the offer subject to Sceptre passing the vet. Sadly Sievier returned to Shrewton to make arrangements for her transfer.

Chetwynd then, on instructions from Bass, interviewed Alec Taylor who had succeeded his father 'Grim Old Alec' in charge of the famous stables at Manton. He asked Taylor if he would take and train Sceptre for Bass in her four-year-old career. Taylor agreed, though he may well have had mixed feelings in accepting the responsibility knowing, as he must have done, the stories that were circulating about her. He told E. H. Leach, the Newmarket vet, to go down and examine her and wired Sievier advising him of the date and time of the visit.

Save for her wind Sievier had not the least fear of her failing to pass the veterinary examination. He knew that Leach would be particularly careful on this score in view of what was being said about her and no one knew better than he did how thick-winded she was. On the morning of the examination, just before Leach was due to arrive, he galloped her full stretch over two miles with another of his string. That did the trick. Leach had no trouble in passing her sound. A day or so later Taylor himself came along to collect her.

Sievier was never a man to admit his faults or his failures or indeed to blame his luck but there was a great sadness in his heart and an emptiness in his life as he watched her being taken away from him, as he thought, forever. But, as it happened, he was not quite done with her yet.

Alec Taylor's father had been notorious for the severity with which he treated his horses and the toughness of the preparations which he gave them. On succeeding to the control of the stable 'Young Alec', as he came to be known, had gone to the other extreme. The horses in his charge were very lightly raced as two-year-olds, their preparation being worked-out and graded with exceptional care. The most stringent precautions were taken against anything approaching over-racing or over-work. His horses looked well and ran well especially in long-distance races, earning for him later on the sobriquet in the Press of 'the wizard of Manton', but some of the older school of trainers were wont to complain that he kept them in cottonwool. He was a quiet, retiring man, cautious by nature and careful with money, and a greater contrast to her recent owner and trainer it is impossible to imagine. A true professional at his trade and coming as he did from a family steeped in racing lore for generations, Taylor was not unnaturally sceptical about the methods employed by Sievier, the amateur and outsider, in training the mare.

Sceptre always looked her worst in the spring and autumn of the year. Taylor decided that she had been subjected to far too much work and that she needed nursing. He put her in light work and gave her two gallons of milk a day. Her first race under his care was the Jockey Club Stakes at Ascot. She won this all right but she had very little to beat and she blew very hard after it. Her next appearance was to be the Eclipse Stakes at Sandown.

The Eclipse that year aroused enormous interest for Sceptre was to be opposed not only by her old rival Ard Patrick, but also by Rock Sand who had just won the Derby. Taylor had continued his careful preparation of her, as was his practice with the horses in his care, gradually bringing her back to her full health and racing fitness. He engaged Hardy to ride her.

It was a glorious summer day and the Sandown enclosures were crowded. Duke of Westminster and Oriole were also in the field but everyone knew that the cracks would have the race to themselves.

Once into the straight Rock Sand was beaten and the two four-year-olds, the colt and the mare, came on together. Half-way for home Sceptre was seen to hold a slight advantage. But Otto Madden on Ard Patrick was a genius at judging pace especially over a distance of ground.

He nursed the big colt, timed his effort to perfection and then drove him for the post. They passed the line locked together in a storm of cheering. When the numbers went up Ard Patrick had won by a neck.

In the unsaddling enclosure she was again seen to be blowing very hard and Sievier, watching her and sadly reflecting on her gallant defeat, was sure she was short of the work she needed and that he could have given it her had she still been his. There were others, too, and George Lambton, no lover of Sievier, was amongst them, who commented on her condition and felt that if Taylor had known as much about her then as he did later she would not have been beaten.

Her next race was the Jockey Club Stakes at Newmarket and Arthur Chetwynd, who was frequently at Manton, was not entirely happy about the light preparation she was getting. In the race she would be opposed by Rock Sand and, at 9lb worse than weight for age, she would need to be at her best to beat him. Ard Patrick had broken down again and been sold to Germany as a stallion. Chetwynd consulted the owner and then went to see Sievier. As a result of these consultations and conversations it was agreed that Sievier should be on hand to advise during the final few days before the race. What Alec Taylor thought about this is not recorded but he apparently consented to it with a good enough grace. What is more he allowed himself to be persuaded into sending Sceptre along in some really testing work. She was galloped a mile and a half at top speed accompanied by a sprinter at first and then picked up by Grey Tick, a subsequent winner of the Cesarewitch. She blew hard after this. When Lord Falmouth, coming by, stared at her dubiously, Sievier said to him: 'Do not worry, my lord, you are looking at the winner of the Jockey Club Stakes.' Next morning she had the same treatment and this time she was much clearer in her wind.

Rock Sand had just won the Leger and become one of the few winners of the Triple Crown, but Sievier did not believe he was good enough to beat Sceptre. He never stopped backing the mare to recover some of his losses over the Eclipse and Charles Clark, the bookmaker and his close friend, who believed in Rock Sand, never stopped giving him the odds he wanted. It was Newmarket where she was always supreme and, to help her once again, the rain came down before the 'off'. Cappa White, William Rufus and Cheers were also in the race but they were not held to matter nor did they. Amidst tumultuous cheering Sceptre won as she liked by four lengths having well and truly slammed one of the few Triple Crown winners of the century, a colt held by many until then to be a world-beater. 'Mr. Sievier,' Sir Theodore Cook, the

Turf historian wrote, 'was completely overcome. Lady Noreen Bass and Mr. Arthur Chetwynd were within the barriers while the mare, with her head up and the eyes of a queen, waited outside the weighing-room door.' She was indeed a queen come into her own for she was never beaten at Newmarket, the galloping course she loved so well.

The money he won over her victory helped but Sievier was far from prosperous that year. He was now trying his luck as a public trainer and had amongst his patrons Lord Fermoy, an eccentric Irish nobleman, and a Mr. H. Sleath Skelton who owned a horse called Happy Slave.

Sievier put Happy Slave into the Duke of York Stakes at Kempton and trained him for it. He backed him, too, at long prices. Then it became known that Sceptre would also contest this race. Were it not for her he felt he had the race at his mercy. On the morning of the race he met Arthur Chetwynd who told him that Sceptre was lame and that he doubted very much if they could run her. Sievier asked if he could see her. When she was pulled out he recognized that she was not truly lame at all but was exhibiting one of her many peculiarities. This was that on occasions she would walk behind in a way that Sievier described as 'half-lame and half string-halty.' He told Chetwynd that when she cantered she would be sound in a couple of strides and that he should run her. As he said himself, had he not been there in all probability they would have taken her out. Even then they had not time to plate her and she ran in soft ground in her exercising shoes.

Taylor had engaged Madden to ride her. Sievier thought this a mistake for he always believed she went better for Hardy than for anyone else. He instructed Butchers, the apprentice who was riding Happy Slave, to make the most of his 40lb pull at the weights and to come for home as hard as he could.

Madden, for once, rode an atrocious race. He didn't know the mare, he dreaded being beaten on her and he was very much on edge about the whole thing. Taylor warned him again and again not to get shut in, that this was the only thing that could bring about her defeat. These admonitions increased Madden's nerviness, and, during the race, he did indeed get shut in, not just once but no less than three times. When at last he burst through he had to get at Sceptre in real earnest and show her the whip. Driven desperately by him, displaying every ounce of courage and every inch of speed she had, she just got up on the line to beat Happy Slave by a short head.

Sievier scarcely knew whether to cheer or cry. By his advice he had cost himself the race and lost his money. Perhaps the mare's victory was reward enough. And there was something else too. He never forgot Chetwynd crossing to him in the unsaddling enclosure, holding out his hand and saying for all to hear. 'Well, Sievier, by God, you're a sportsman!'

It was the end of his long association with her and, in his heart, whatever about his pocket, he must have rejoiced for he left her at her best, gallant in victory and poised for success.

16

Sievier v. Duke

$\rightarrow\rightarrow\rightarrow\rightarrow\rightarrow$

Now the abyss was yawning in front of him though he did not know it.

For the second October Meeting of 1903 Sievier and Arthur Chetwynd went together to Newmarket where they stayed at the Rutland Arms. There they met a party of friends and, after racing on the first day, sat down in Chetwynd's rooms to play baccarat. One of the party was a Major David Sellar, an officer in the 4th Dragoon Guards then stationed at Shorncliffe. All those playing save Sievier were members of the Raleigh Club, a sporting club which enjoyed a fairly cosmopolitan membership and occupied extensive premises in Lower Regent Street.

Stakes ran high and the game continued during the next two evenings. There was, however, at no time any suggestion that the game was not properly conducted nor was a finger of suspicion then or thereafter pointed at anyone who took part in it.

On the third evening Sievier was the banker, and when the party broke up Major Sellar owed him £7000. Sellar did not then settle and on the following morning Sievier told another member of the party that he had no wish to take so much off Sellar. He suggested a settlement of £3000. This was not an unusual or suspicious procedure for in those days of high play and heavy betting on credit it was quite customary for considerably smaller cash sums to be accepted when settlements came to be made.

Sellar, on being told of Sievier's gesture, expressed his gratitude and arranged to meet him in the Carlton Hotel on their return to London and to settle with him there.

After racing, Sellar and Sievier made their independent ways back to London. That evening Sellar was in the front room of the Raleigh Club known as 'the gazing room' when Sievier came in. He was looking for Tommy Lushington, a well-known racing man and gentleman rider who had bought Ambush II for King Edward, and who was a mutual friend. He spoke casually to Sellar, then Lushington approached, bought Sievier a drink and they started to discuss the matter which had brought Sievier there. Sellar went home, dressed for dinner and returned to dine in the Club. As he entered he was met by Sir James Duke, then a member of the Club committee, who said that he had something private to say to him. They went into a room off the hall where they were alone. There Duke said: 'Major Sellar, members tell me that Bob Sievier is from time to time in the club and members, Tommy Lushington for one, object to his presence here.'

'That's strange,' Sellar replied. 'I've just seen Sievier and Lushington having a drink together in the gazing room.'

Duke then said: 'You must know what character this man has. You know he was a murderer, a card-sharper and a thief. A man was found murdered under his window in Australia, and it was reputed that Sievier had murdered him. I myself saw him thrown from a boat into the water for cheating at cards. I unmasked him before the stewards of the Jockey Club, and had him turned out of the Jockey Club Stand at Newmarket. He was also turned out of Boodles Club. I am surprised that you should know a man like that. Sievier made money by Sceptre not winning the Derby.'

These were certainly, to say the least of them, serious allegations to make, and, over dinner that night, Sellar pondered them. The following morning he saw Lushington in the club and asked him if it were true that he objected to Sievier's presence there. Lushington replied that he did nothing of the sort, and Sellar told him of his conversation with Duke. Both of them then sought out Duke and confronted him. Duke promptly repeated all he had said about Sievier the night before and maintained that, as a member of the committee, he was right in warning Sellar not to bring him into the club. Sellar said that Duke then went on to say: 'You can tell all this to Bob Sievier with my compliments.'

After that Sellar went round to the Carlton. There he met Sievier and handed him an open cheque for £3000. Sellar was a highly strung and excitable man. He appeared upset during the interview and Sievier asked him if anything was wrong. After some hesitation Sellar said: 'If I believed what I have just been told I would be perfectly justified in refusing to settle.'

Never one to leave the possibility of an insult over-looked Sievier then demanded that Sellar should repeat to him just what he had been told and who told it to him. The result of this was that Sellar gave him, word for word, what Duke had said. Thereupon Sievier required that Sellar take him to the Raleigh Club so that he could confront Duke.

Since Sievier was now in a towering rage and his rages were frightening to look upon, Sellar very wisely refused to do this, saying that in view of what had happened he could not possibly bring Sievier into the club.

Straightaway Sievier went to Sir George Lewis, the great society solicitor, and instructed him to write to Duke claiming damages for slander. In this instance his rage was surely justified. Many true and damaging things could have been said against him but this statement was a tissue of lies. Duke seemed to have chosen the very stories and statements which could not on any account be justified. And what hurt most of all was the repetition of the slander that he had had Sceptre stopped.

When Duke received Lewis's letter he consulted his solicitors who sent a case to advise to Frederick Gill. In the interval since he had last appeared in Sievier's life Gill had prospered. He had been senior Treasury Counsel; he was standing counsel to the Jockey Club and enjoyed a steady and lucrative general practice. Gill had not forgotten Sievier, the enmity was still there and the grudge still rankled. Having read the papers he advised Duke to adopt a certain course which was both clever and cowardly, which could scarcely fail and which was calculated to do Sievier the maximum harm.

Gill knew that the statements made by Duke were untrue and could not be substantiated. On the other hand Duke was a member of the committee of the Raleigh Club. The statements therefore would almost certainly be held to have been uttered on a privileged occasion when Duke was acting in what he conceived to be his duty as a member of such committee. Thus, although they were untrue, unless Sievier could show that Duke was activated by malice in uttering the statements he could not recover damages for them. This Sievier was hardly likely to be able to do since the acquaintanceship between the two men was of the slightest. When Duke was attempting—and failing—to make a name for himself as a gentleman rider he had once challenged Harding Cox to a match and lost it ignominiously. Sievier, watching the two men come in, had remarked at the top of his voice that the betting should have been 100—8 on Cox; and they had on another occasion exchanged pleasantries at Lewes where Duke, who was a steward there, thought Sievier should have told him to back one of his horses. But these incidents were hardly a firm basis on which to ground an accusation of malice.

Gill advised Duke against attempting to maintain any plea of justification so that the statements would be allowed to go as the lies they were, and suggested relying entirely on the plea of privilege. He then went further. He pointed out that if this course were taken a statement in mitigation of damages could and should be filed. This statement would set out in full all the doubtful or allegedly dishonourable acts in Sievier's past. He could then be cross-examined upon it to show that he was a person of such low and disreputable character that he was not entitled to damages, even if the plea of privilege were to fail. Gill, having advised Sievier in the Hawk case, knew something of Sievier's career. This knowledge he was only too ready to exploit and he was able to suggest to Duke what he was sure would prove profitable lines of investigation.

This advice was eagerly seized upon by Duke. It relieved him of the task of attempting in court to justify his lying statements and appeared to offer a guarantee of a successful outcome of the case. The fact that to hide behind a legal technicality to protect himself from the consequences of his untruths was dishonourable to say the least did not appear to occur to the second baronet.

Immediately Duke set about employing detectives to investigate every likely incident in Sievier's history in Australia, on the Continent and in England. Since Sievier lived his life in the full glare of the public eye, careless of the consequences, the task was not as difficult as it might have been, but it was expensive. Whether Duke paid the expenses will never be known. Sievier always maintained that once the action had been launched, Duke was a mere catspaw and that other richer and more powerful enemies guided and financed him.

When the defence of privilege was raised and that of justification abandoned the dangers were readily apparent to Sievier's advisers. They told him flatly that he would not succeed in proving malice and that he could not win his case.

He would have none of it. It was sufficient for him that he had been slandered and that the slander had not been withdrawn. It was a serious slander and it was all untrue and now the bloody lawyers, whom he despised anyway, were telling him he could not succeed owing to a legal technicality. He could only see the wound he had suffered and that he had been falsely accused of having his beloved Sceptre pulled. Never to the end of his days did he understand what the plea of privilege meant nor did he make any attempt to. He instructed his lawyers to proceed.

Things looked even more serious when the plea of mitigation came in. Every single incident in his life which could possibly tell against him had been dredged up and set down with malice aforethought, and by going on, if he went on, he was offering himself up to be examined on them all. The prospects of success, never good, became much worse when it was known that the case was to be heard before Mr. Justice Grantham.

Grantham's accession to the Bench had been due to blatant political preferment and his personal friendship with Hardinge Giffard, the Lord Chancellor. No less than six of his fellows with far better credentials were passed over. Once there he displayed a singular lack of judicial temperament, a profound ignorance of law and the rules of evidence and a considered disregard of anything other than his own prejudices in deciding a case or addressing a jury. In addition he spoke out too often, too foolishly and too publicly so that his *obiter dicta* became famous for their fatuity. Husbands were advised to box their wives' ears, the public never to take a cheque from a bookmaker, publicans were told that when drunken people committed crimes a universal fine should be levied upon all owners of licensed premises, and he scarcely endeared himself to his brothers at the bar by announcing in open court that barristers were paid to raise false issues before a jury.

Grantham was a friend of Sir James Duke and lived near him in Sussex. There was, too, a strong bond of friendship between the Judge and Charles Gill who acted for him in personal matters. It may indeed not have been entirely an accident that the case came into his list at all for Gill had been known before to approach higher authority with a view to taking a case from one judge's list and putting it into another's.

At all events Grantham's prejudices were hardly likely to sway him in Sievier's favour. He was an Establishment man; he had been made by them—one of them has recently referred to him in his memoirs as 'a great character on the Bench'—he copied their ways and wished to stand well with them. Every morning when weather permitted he could be seen riding to the Law Courts on a grey hack. He was a puritan of the strictest sort and a snob.

When Sievier heard that Grantham was going to try the action he asked Eldon Bankes, who with Norman Craig had been briefed to appear on his behalf, if he would make an application to have the case taken out of Grantham's list on the ground of his known friendship with Duke. Bankes refused, believing that the application was unlikely to be successful and if made, would only further antagonize the judge.

So, on the 6th May 1904, before a special jury and a hostile judge, Eldon Bankes K.C. rose to open the case of Sievier v. Duke.

By abandoning the plea of justification, pleading privilege and filing the statement in mitigation, Duke's advisers had secured the enormous advantage of turning the case right round on its axis. Though nominally the plaintiff, Sievier had in fact been made to take the position of defendant. Duke had to prove nothing because he admitted the statements to be untrue, but Sievier had to disprove or at least disarm the many and varied allegations in the statement in mitigation which had been lovingly and carefully drafted by Gill into an impressive dossier of villainy. To give Sievier even more cause for alarm, if he was inclined to alarm which he was not, Gill, during his investigations into the past, had been studying the reports of the bankruptcy hearings. As a result of this he let it be known that, whatever the outcome of the action, he intended to advise that a prosecution for perjury committed during them be instituted against Sievier immediately after it.

In his opening Bankes attempted to secure for his client the sympathy of the jury. The style of advocacy adopted by Bankes was some thirty or forty years in advance of his time. The hectoring and bullying tactics of his fellows were not for him. His weapons were charm and persuasion and so successfully did he use them that he ended his career as a Lord Justice of Appeal. Although, especially in the context of the time, this suave approach in a bitter and sensational defamation action was to a large degree unprecedented, it was probably the only one which held out any prospects of success in view of the known attitude of the Judge and the tactics of the defence. Bankes told the jury that it was not now possible to fight what was the real issue in the action, namely were the words spoken true, for Duke had abandoned any attempt to prove this. Instead he was attempting to defend his pocket in another way, that of hiding behind the law of privilege and filing the statement in mitigation. He was using, Bankes said, 'the dagger of the assassin and not the sword of the warrior.' It was not an inapt quotation.

Bankes first called Sellar to prove the slander. Nothing really turned on his evidence for the uttering and publication of the words were largely admitted save as regards what had been said about Sceptre. This was the only point upon which he was cross-examined to any purpose.

Lawson Walton, a future Attorney-General with a fine common-law practice who had in his chambers a promising junior called Rufus Isaacs, had been brought in to lead Gill and to conduct the important cross-examinations. Gill's career, though about that time it appeared to be poised for the highest success, was, in fact, faltering, and during the next few years he was to fall behind in the race for the very top.

There was somewhere in him a curious lack of self-confidence and self-sufficiency. As he grew older he preferred to be led by another more forceful man and to operate behind the scenes, advising, assisting, scheming for the best lines of approach but seldom taking the foremost part in the conduct of a case. When he was left on his own he would see the dangers ahead all too clearly and he became such a confirmed settler of actions many of which ought to have been fought that his popularity with clients suffered and his practice fell away. Here he was to leave all the cut-and-thrust to Lawson Walton.

'Did Sir James say in a later conversation with you,' Walton asked Sellar, 'that however big a blackguard or scoundrel he might have thought Sievier, he never said any such words about Sceptre because his opinion was that Sievier would have given anything to have owned a Derby winner?'

'He said the substance of the last part of that.'

So at least it seemed that Duke was flatly admitting there was no truth in any allegation about pulling Sceptre. It was a small gain for there was everything still to be faced but to Sievier it was the greatest satisfaction. These words to him had contained the real sting of the slander for it is true to say that, despite the seriousness of the other allegations, this one, though the least damaging in law, had hurt the most.

After Sellar there was only one other witness for the plaintiff and this was Sievier himself. The actual slanders were now to all intents and purpose out of the action. The whole kernel of the case when Sievier entered the box was the statement in mitigation and here he stood in great peril. Virtually no incident in his life, however small, that could lend itself to his discredit had been left unrecorded. There were minor assaults, one in defence of Lady Mabel during their brief married life, a loan of £300 from his clerk in Australia, the Deerhurst affair, his divorce, his cancelled presentation at court and then the three main items upon which the defence would base their full attack—the *Hawk* libel, the Renton-Kavanagh incident and the Horn affair in Monte Carlo.

Many of these matters were of little account and the attempts to make use of them went more to the discredit of Duke than of Sievier, for they could have been shrugged off at the time of their occurrence and easily dismissed now. Others, set in the circumstances surrounding them, were perhaps susceptible of explanation but, examined in the cold light of a court of law before a judge and jury impregnated with the strict conventions of Edwardian middle-class morality, they were unlikely to receive either sympathy or understanding. It may well be that some deserved neither of these things but a litigant, however unworthy, is entitled to a fair hearing which is what Sievier did not get.

He was handicapped, as always in his law cases, by the faults of his temperament and character. Despite the fact that he had had the statement in mitigation in his possession for weeks before the hearing he had not bothered to check it through nor to get up the necessary exact information to use in its rebuttal. Instead he trusted to his memory on the day and his own native wit and ready tongue to see him through. These are doubtful weapons to be relied upon by a witness especially when defending his character and life history. He was not of course assisted by Grantham allowing the defence to introduce extraneous matter which had been omitted from the statement in mitigation and to cross-examine him upon it.

As may be imagined he was far from overawed by the panoply of the law, the majesty of its ceremony or the threat implicit in the wigs and gowns of the lawyers appearing against him. These to him were the trappings of a stage upon which he was about to be called to play his part. The actor in him welcomed them, and his nerve, of course, was as unshakeable as ever. In answer to Bankes he gave his explanations of the various matters alleged against him clearly and, so far as they went, plausibly. It could, however, be commented that they did not go quite far enough. He had not gone on with the action against *The Hawk*, he said, because he had taken the advice of his counsel to discontinue; he had not pursued Renton to the end because Renton had apologized and paid him £100; the suggestions about him swindling Horn were all nonsense, and he had stayed on in Monte Carlo while Horn had to leave. But he made no mention of the cheque to 'Tricky' Williams nor had he told Bankes about it.

When Lawson Walton rose to cross-examine him the battle was really joined.

The initial questions were concerned with his book-making operations under the name of Sutton, and the loan from his clerk which enabled Grantham to set the tone for his many subsequent interventions by staring at Sievier aghast and saying, 'What! You owed a common clerk all that money!'

The Deerhurst affair came next but the defence were not on very good ground here though they attempted, with Grantham's active assistance, to stress the result of the first hearing and to gloss over the reversal on appeal and the fact that Deerhurst had run away. It is an interesting illustration of the sycophancy of the times that throughout the case, when Deerhurst's name was likely to be introduced, he was always referred to as 'a certain noble lord' or 'Lord X' despite the fact that he was then making his living as a butcher in Rhodesia.

When it came to the undefended divorce case it was seen that no mud was to be too dirty to be stirred up and flung in Sievier's face. The defence had brought from Australia certified copies of the wife's affidavits filed in this matter. All the salacious allegations that a vengeful women could make which were contained in this, including the averment that he had had two illegitimate children when married to her, were read aloud for the edification of the jury, Grantham from the Bench accompanying this reading with exclamations of shock and horror. It was useless for Sievier to protest that he had been in England at the time and had agreed not to contest the case. He was curtly informed by the Judge that this was an admission of guilt and of the truth of the statements in the affidavits. In the climate of sexual morality then pertaining the impact of this upon a jury of respectable burghers can well be imagined.

While Walton's cross-examination was proceeding Gill was behaving in a most extraordinary fashion. Sitting near the jury box he was making audible comments on the evidence and encouraging his leader with exclamations such as, 'Now, you have him!' and 'Ah, that's it! That's got him!' Since Grantham added to his other disabilities the fact that he was partially deaf, as Gill well knew, this conduct went completely unchecked.

Walton then came to the cancellation of the presentation and *The Hawk* case in which Gill had, of course, advised Sievier.

In the answer to a question Sievier said that as far as he knew the cancellation was not commented on in the press. This was a minor blunder since *The Hawk* had commented on it though four years after it had taken place. But it was a major blunder caused entirely by his not having checked his facts to say that he had not contemplated a criminal prosecution against *The Hawk*. Immediately, however, he qualified this by saying that he thought Mr. Gill might know more about it.

'I have the benefit of Mr. Gill's recollections in the matter,' was Lawson Walton's reply. The propriety of Gill's disclosing what had been told to him in confidence by one client for the benefit of another and using it against the first may well be queried as it was indeed by Sievier in print later on.

Walton went on to read the affidavit Sievier had sworn for the purpose of obtaining a writ of criminal libel against *The Hawk*.

'Do you still say the fact of the presentation was not commented on in the press?' he asked.

'Not in the press. In one paper edited by a man Mr. Gill told me was the dirtiest writer on the press.'

'Mr. Gill,' remarked Bankes drily, 'Drew the affidavit in question.'

Gill was instantly on his feet. 'My friend has no right to say that,' he declared. 'Counsel cannot refuse to act for a man until he knows what his real history is.' Perhaps, but once Gill had obtained that 'real history' for the purpose of acting for Sievier he should not have used it when acting against him.

'In order to vindicate your character it would be necessary to go to court would it not?' Lawson Walton asked.

'Well, I thought so, but Mr. Gill did not.'

Gill had been continuing his audible remarks to the jury during these exchanges. Bankes rose and said to the judge. 'I must object, my Lord, to Mr. Gill making running comments on the evidence in the hearing of the jury. It is a most unusual course to take.'

'Nor is it usual,' Gill said, on his feet once more, 'For a witness to introduce into his evidence the advice he got from his counsel as to going into the witness-box or not.' Which was scarcely a convincing riposte.

'I heard nothing,' Grantham said. 'Besides, Mr. Gill knows very well how to behave.'

'You took the advice given you?' Walton said to Sievier.

'I took it with great reluctance and Mr. Wontner, my solicitor, wanted to go to another counsel.'

Grantham immediately interrupted again. 'As I understand it,' he said to Sievier, 'You wanted to go into the box and Mr. Gill advised you not to.' Then he looked significantly at the jury. 'Well, Mr. Gill usually gives very good advice,' he said.

So it went on. When the Renton case came up Grantham broke in once more. 'Let me see,' he said. 'The date of the incident was almost simultaneous with your bankruptcy?'

'Yes.'

'And how would you have paid if you had lost?'

'I would not have lost.' He meant of course that he would have got out if he was going badly. Apart from the fact that it was probably untrue for it was most unlike him to have done anything of the sort it was a singularly foolish answer for it left itself open to many interpretations most of them adverse, and it gave the Judge another opportunity he was unlikely to miss. 'I see—a sort of heads you win tails I lose game,' Grantham said.

But the Renton case was damaging enough without any of Grantham's assistance to the defence; 'You stopped an action against a man who said you were a card-sharper?'

'Yes.'

'*The Hawk* affair was in April and May of the same year?'

'Yes.'

'So that in April, May and June you had been posted in the newspapers as a card-sharper and in the records of the court in the Renton case and in neither case had you gone on with the action?'

'I have given you my reasons before and I will again if you like for not proceeding with the prosecution or the action.' And of course he had. Whether they were convincing ones and whether the jury, especially when guided by Grantham, would believe them was another matter.

Then the Horn case came to be dealt with. 'Now let us go to Monte Carlo,' Walton said. 'It will be a refreshing change. Do you remember this man Horn?'

'Yes.'

'Was he called Drinking Horn?'

'Either that or Hunting Horn. His brother was one name and he the other.'

'Did the name Drinking Horn describe his habits?'

'I do not know.'

'Was he not in a state of hopeless alcoholism most of the time he was there?'

'No, but I have seen him screwed once or twice in my life.'

'Was he not found next morning in his room in a state of helpless coma?'

'No. After playing we sat in the hall. I left Horn there and went to bed.'

'What had you won from him?'

'I had won £700 at billiards.'

'Was not his cheque book found in his room with six cheques torn out?'

'I do not know.'

'Was a cheque drawn in Williams' favour for £700?'

'I do not know. Yes, I remember now. It was.'

'Have you ever heard Williams called "Tricky" Williams?'

'No.'

163

'Why were the cheques drawn in Lady Mabel's favour?'

'I cannot remember.'

'They were drawn in Lady Mabel's favour,' Grantham said, 'because she had a banking account and he had none.' This was the only reasonable interjection made by Grantham throughout the trial. It is the obvious explanation and would have done Sievier no harm had he admitted it. Why he did not do so is known only to him. He may however have had in mind Gill's threat of a perjury prosecution and thought that any admission made by him relevant to his bankruptcy could be used against him.

'These are incidents not likely to slip the mind of a man who was careful of his honour?'

'We are dealing with matters of ten years back and more. You have given me notice of some incidents and you bring forward a number of which I have not had notice.'

This was true enough but he had had notice of the Horn case and could well have refreshed his memory about it had he bothered to or—as was suggested by the defence—had he been able to offer any plausible explanation for his conduct that night, especially for that damning cheque to Williams.

The cross-examination was continued for another day and a half. Nothing was spared him, however trivial. But it was noted by many that there was one aspect of his life, and that to him the most important one, which was studiously avoided by the defence. His career on the Turf was left untouched. No mud was hurled here for there was none to stir and throw. His racing life was blameless and his enemies knew it. However hard they must have tried they could not uncover the smallest thing to impute against him. In view of the detailed examination and exploration of all his actions, had there been anything discreditable it cannot be doubted but that it would have been uncovered and exploited. Neither in England nor Australia could his racing career be questioned. His name and his pride here were intact. It must have been a grave disappointment to Gill and Duke and whoever stood behind them in the shadows. Also, although he had made no preparations to withstand the attack by way of checking his facts, he stood up to a severe and prolonged cross-examination from an experienced counsel with plenty of material at his disposal better than might have been expected. His memory betrayed him and his anxiety to score a point carried him away once or twice but by and large his courage and his nerve saw him through.

Nevertheless the facts elicited had been terribly damaging and the judge's loathing of him, coupled with his freely expressed horror at the disclosures, was plain for all to see. It was generally expected that the jury would stop the case as soon as Sievier's cross-examination ended. But when Grantham asked them pointedly if they wished to hear any more, after a short consultation, they required Sir James Duke to go into the witness-box. As often in Grantham's cases his obvious bias went in some way to defeat its own ends.

In his evidence-in-chief Duke gave his version of the conversation with Sellar. 'Is he the sort of man you would introduce to your wife if you had one? You must know his reputation' was, he said, the way he opened the conversation. 'Major Sellar,' he went on, 'Did not appear to attach sufficient importance to what I said and said that I had no right to speak like that unless I gave him my reasons. I then told him . . .' He repeated the words complained of save only those relating to Sceptre which he denied having spoken: 'I said however big a blackguard Sievier was I had always held the opinion he would have given his ears to have won the Derby and so have his name enrolled amongst honourable men.'

In cross-examining Duke, Bankes had an unenviable task. There was really nothing at all which he could ask him that would assist his client's case. The slander was admitted as was its untruth, but the defence of privilege stood out like a rock and quite unassailable. Still, he had to ask him something. As an experienced counsel will, even when he has little or no material, he probed away, and in his opening questions he made at least a few small gains.

'You have said you did not know Mr. Sievier to speak to?'

'Yes.'

'You had heard of Mr. Sievier as the owner of Sceptre?'

'Yes.'

'He was a very successful owner was he not?'

'I'm sure I don't know.'

'He was top of the list of winning owners in 1902?'

'I have heard so.'

'Was Sceptre favourite for the Derby?'

'At one time I think she was a long price.'

'She did not win?'

'I know that.'

'You do not suggest there was anything unfair or improper about her running?'

'I have never said there was.'

'And it was your honest belief there was nothing wrong with it ?'

'That is so.'

'You had heard rumours to the contrary ?'

'Yes.'

'Which you did not believe ?'

'That is so.'

If Sir James Duke, a prominent racing man in his own eyes at least, really expected anyone to believe that he did not know that Sievier was a prominent owner or that he was telling the truth when he said that he thought Sceptre had at one time been at a long price he was naïve indeed. Had these questions done nothing else, at least they established that Duke was not a candid witness. They did, however, do something else, not much, but a little. They hammered home the fact that here in open court where he could do so with safety, Duke did not dare to query Sceptre's running in that Derby.

There was one more witness to be called for the defence and he was one who should never have been permitted to give evidence. Inspector Edward Drew had been in charge of the Vine Street police station for sixteen years. He said in evidence that there was a special class of men in the West End who were particularly under his observation. He had known the plaintiff—he said—by sight and reputation since 1893.

'Speaking from your knowledge, what is his reputation ?' he was asked.

'Bad, sir,' was the reply.

This evidence had nothing whatever to do with the issues in the case, nor had it any direct bearing on the particulars filed in mitigation. It is a measure of the bias displayed by Grantham that he allowed it to be given. The damage done to Sievier's case in the minds of the jury by this evidence from an experienced police officer must have been immeasurable. They might, however, have been less impressed had they known the true character that lay behind Drew's imposing presence and impressive rank. He had sporting predilections which led him to the racecourse and his activities there and elsewhere had earned him the sobriquet of 'Tricky' Drew. This was a *nom de guerre* which he shared with Williams of the Monte Carlo escapade and which, along with Williams, he had done everything to earn. And the reputation of the Raleigh Club was scarcely enhanced when, after the case, Duke and the members of the committee entertained Drew to a dinner in the club. We shall meet Drew again in this story.

When Drew left the box an attempt was made by the defence to call

Froome, the valet Sievier had dismissed, to give evidence about what had happened in Monte Carlo. Bankes objected on the grounds that this had nothing to do with the pleas of privilege. When Gill persisted Grantham looked at him and said it was 'hardly necessary' to press the evidence and then further reassured him by saying: 'I think, Mr. Gill, that since this evidence is objected to it is better to run no risks by admitting it!'

After this the jury took the hint and stopped the case, the final speeches were made and Grantham summed up. It could scarcely be called an impartial address. It was a bare-faced polemic against Sievier much of which had no basis in either law or fact. What he did was to turn his own opinions into evidence and to pronounce them. 'Now, who is this man?' were his opening words. 'You have heard of a false name, his career in Australia, how he had become the father of two illegitimate children in two years and how he had been divorced for cruelty and adultery. You must know, gentlemen, that he has been constantly in the company of gamblers, card-players, card-sharpers, and the greatest scoundrels on earth. . . .'

It is unnecessary to dwell at any length on the remainder of the summing up save to say that Grantham put the worst possible interpretation on the Horn affair, referring throughout to 'this young man Horn' when it had been proved that he was fifty-six years of age, and going on to say: 'There was the incident where the plaintiff played billiards up to two or three in the morning with a young man and sat talking until six or seven o'clock doing nothing. If they were doing nothing, how was it he was found drunk or drugged hours afterwards?'

Here Eldon Bankes was moved to protest. 'There is no evidence of that, my lord,' he said.

'I hold it to be a fair statement from the evidence,' Grantham said. Since there had been no testimony save Sievier's and he had denied the allegation of drugs, one wonders just what Grantham would have considered to be an unfair statement. But his crowning fatuity came when he dealt with the cancelled presentation to court. 'Her Majesty,' he said. 'Would rather give up her throne than be addressed by such a man!'

Grantham then told the jury that the occasion on which the words were spoken was a privileged one. They took fifteen minutes to deliberate and, in view of what had gone before, it is surprising that they were out for even as long as that. They returned, as they were bound to, with a verdict for the defendant. Grantham then asked them that, supposing they had found a 'Technical verdict' for the Plaintiff, at what amount they would have assessed the damages.

'One farthing,' was the answer.

Always a gambler, Sievier had put his character into hazard and had lost it.

17

Warned Off

He was finished now, or so his enemies thought. He was known to be penniless and the costs of the case should complete his ruin. Besides, the sensational disclosures and the conclusive result of the action ought, by any rules and precedents, to leave him no other course but to drop entirely out of the sporting and social life as it was lived by him and his like in those days and quietly to disappear.

But paradoxically enough, public opinion swung round rapidly in his favour. Throughout his career Sievier's personableness and character saw to it that he was never without friends, some of them in high places. It was about this time, for instance, that he made the acquaintance of the eccentric Earl of Shrewsbury who introduced him to the young Bend Or Westminster. Both of them stood by him and remained his friends for life. They were not alone. The ordinary Englishman, at that time and in every walk of life, had a great sense of fair play. It was not the fact of Sievier's losing the case but the manner of its winning that rankled in men's minds.

Grantham's ridiculous bias had been too blatantly displayed as had the subservience shown by him and the whole court to Sir James Duke and the proprieties. To the real grandees Duke was a jumped-up nobody. Nor was his standing or popularity increased when, shortly after the case, a notice appeared in a weekly called *Land and Water* saying that his friends were opening a fund to assist Duke in defraying the heavy legal expenses he had incurred and that subscriptions would be received at the Raleigh Club. The fund was heavily under-subscribed.

In addition it had not escaped notice in the racing world that, as has been mentioned, try as they might, the defence had failed not only to make any accusation stick as regards racing but to uncover grounds for an accusation at all. And racing was his career; it was his public life, that part of his life which provided his living in which from day to day he rode out the worst and revelled in the best when it came. Here he was blameless. It was felt by many, especially on the Turf, that his private life was his own affair. The cowardliness of Duke's conduct, too, became more apparent as the case was discussed. Many thought and said that since Sievier had had the courage to face him out he should have been man enough to stand over his words. There was also another aspect of the matter which disturbed people and that was the employment of a high-ranking police officer to give evidence of character in a civil action. Mr. Atherley Jones, M.P. put this disquiet into words when he gave notice that he intended to ask a question in the House regarding it and later on he did: 'Will the Rt. Hon. Gentleman,' he enquired of the Home Secretary, 'frame regulations which will in future prevent officers of the police doing what has been done by that officer? Such conduct is reprehensible and I hope the Rt. Hon. Gentleman will be able to give the House some assurance that steps have been taken to prevent its recurrence.'

Sensing the swing in public opinion, Sievier's enemies resolved to strike again and this time where they thought they could really finish him off. If the racecourses of England could be barred to him it was felt that he must be ruined once and for all, for, as has been said, racing was his life, and then he would have no means of living it.

That year the senior steward of the Jockey Club was the Earl of Durham, the champion of purity on the Turf, straight running of horses and strict interpretation of the rules of racing. It does not appear, however, that the initial moves in the matter came from him for he told Lord Rosebery long afterwards that he was never happy about what followed. It seems that pressure from other members of the Club was exerted against Sievier and that finally Durham consented to a case being sent to Gill to advise on whether Sievier could or should be warned off the Turf.

As an experienced lawyer Gill must have known that on the face of it to warn Sievier off was an impossibility, for he had committed no racing offence. Worse still, from the point of view of the Jockey Club, he had never been before the stewards on any matter connected with racing or the running of his horses. They could hardly warn him off because he had been rebuked by the local stewards for delaying the start at Epsom. Again, it is a cardinal principle of English law that no man can be expelled from a club or barred from entrance to or user of certain private facilities to which he has a prima facie right without being allowed to state his case or to be heard in his own defence. Any hearing over which the Stewards of the Jockey Club could preside must be concerned with racing and nothing else. At such a hearing no racing crime could be proved against Sievier.

Then Gill either discovered for himself or was told of a precedent for another course of action that obviated the necessity for a hearing at all. It was a very doubtful precedent indeed. Whether he was blinded by malice or not cannot of course be known but there seems no doubt that he advised Durham to follow it for Durham, having consulted him and being reluctant to act in the matter, anyway, would hardly have proceeded unless under the instructions and guidance of counsel.

Forty-seven years earlier, a man called Atkins, who was then of some prominence on the Turf, had been found guilty of cheating another out of £6,000 by playing with loaded dice. The then Lord Derby had proposed a resolution at a meeting of the Jockey Club which ran as follows: 'The Jockey Club, having taken into their consideration the facts proved in evidence in the late case of Sidebottom *v* Atkins, direct that Mr. Atkins be warned off the Heath at Newmarket and that no horses of which he may be in whole or part ownership be allowed to run on any ground over which the Jockey Club exercise jurisdiction.'

This resolution was passed unanimously and adopted by the Stewards and Atkins was warned off the Turf without a hearing.

After considering Gill's opinion the Stewards decided to follow this forty-year-old precedent. Durham throughout voiced his hesitation; he was not a weak man; overwhelming pressure from somewhere must have been brought to bear upon him.

The Racing Calendar of May 19th 1904 bore the following brief notice: *The Stewards of the Jockey Club have warned Mr. Robert S. Sievier off Newmarket Heath.*

To say that the racing world was astonished is an understatement. It was dumbfounded. Sievier himself only received notification the day before publication and then merely by way of a curt copy of the official notice typed on Weatherby's writing paper. It had been addressed to Shrewton and forwarded to him in London.

Immediately he read it he went around to 6 Old Burlington Street and demanded to see Mr. E. M. Weatherby, then head of the firm and secretary to the Jockey Club. Throwing the piece of paper on to Weatherby's desk he enquired if it was correct.

'Yes, it is,' was the reply delivered in the most chilling tones. The incident of the firm having been held up to ridicule at Newmarket when Sievier had refused their cheque had not been forgotten.

Sievier asked what offence on the Turf he had committed and why he had not been given a hearing. As he had every right to do he demanded an explanation. None was offered him either then or afterwards. He was merely informed that the stewards had arrived at their decision and that it was final. Seeing it useless to pursue the matter further he left the office, slamming the door behind him with a crash that shook the place almost to its foundations, as he was to use every effort to shake the firm itself in the years to come.

He could, had he wished, have taken an action against the stewards for reinstatement in which there is little doubt that he would have been successful. No man can be condemned unheard and no judge—save possibly Grantham—would enforce such a ruling. But, to Sievier, racing was sacrosanct. It and its rules almost took the place of religion with him. He had always preached that a racing man, once he trod the Turf and ran horses, accepted the jurisdiction of the stewards and must abide by their decision right or wrong. Now he was in a position to prove the sincerity of that preaching and he did so. He took no action. Ever afterwards he maintained that he was right, and he was the first to criticize Sloan who sued the Société D'Encouragement in France when he was put down by them.

So, it seemed, the enemies had won. He had been successfully stripped of the one thing that really mattered to him. His way of life had gone. Also his financial ruin appeared to have been completed since he must now sell the few horses that remained to him as his only asset. They would fetch far less than their value, small though it was. The horses of a man who is 'off' carry with them complications in the way of entries and forfeits, apart from the air of disrepute cast upon them by the sentence on their owner, which do much to lessen their value.

But once more the public sensed the existence of what Sievier afterwards melodramatically referred to as 'a hidden hand'. Everywhere sympathy swung enormously in his favour and the stewards' ruling was seen to be what in fact it was—a naked exercise in the misuse of power.

John Corlett was one of those who sensed the swing and put it, to some extent at least, into words. Corlett, son of a serjeant-major in the Carabineers, through industry, knowledge and integrity in sporting journalism had written himself into the confidence of the great. His paper *The Sporting Times*, known as *The Pink 'un* from the colour of its newsprint, was read everywhere there was racing. At its masthead Corlett had placed the motto: *High Toryism, High Churchism, High*

Farming and Old Port forever, and to these sentiments he was true. He was a welcome guest in great houses, his advice was sought over social and sporting problems by men as diverse as Abingdon Baird, Leopold de Rothschild, Baron Brampton and the then Earl of Rosebery. His voice was a power in the world of sport, but it was a power which had to be tactfully wielded were it to maintain its influence, for Corlett knew that he lived at the whim of the Establishment and openly to affront those who made it up meant the end of his paper and his position. It took courage then to make even the muted protest that he did: *With the exception of Atkins,* he wrote, *we cannot call to mind an instance of a man being warned off the Turf for an offence not committed in connection with it. . . . With regard to Mr. Sievier, however much we may condemn him, it is impossible not to feel some admiration for his ability and pluck. Here we have a man, possessed of small means to start with, paying prices which had never before been heard of for untried yearlings and, as showing the excellence of his judgment, winning the greatest races on the Turf with them. He is a professional gambler and yet in connection with his racing transactions there is no one ready to cast a stone at him. . . . It is only two years since he won the Two Thousand Guineas, One Thousand Guineas, Oaks and St. Leger—and now the Turf will know him no more.*

Sophisticates, too, in the world in which Sievier mixed, knew that Horn, Taylor, Renton and the like whose accusations had been thrown in Sievier's face were bad men and that his word was at least as good as theirs. At that period of social history there was a division of creed quite unknown now and which had nothing to do with class. The aristocracy itself was cloven by it, there being on the one hand the strictly moral successors to the evangelical tradition begun by Queen Victoria and, on the other, the fast set, at whose head, setting its tone and dictating its pace, was the King himself. The worldly men cared very little about the disclosures concerning Sievier's private life. Many of them had mixed in the same company themselves and most had much in their own lives they would not care to have stripped bare under cross-examination. Besides, Sievier had charm and cheek, and an abundance of what an earlier generation had known as bottom, which we call guts and Corlett wrote down as pluck. These were the qualities that went to make a man in their eyes and which they admired. It was left to a well-known figure in sporting life, easily identifiable from his initials, to sum the whole thing up and to express the widespread feeling of the world in which he moved by a letter to Corlett's paper which is worth quoting in full:

'To the Editor of the *Sporting Times*.

'Sir,—You take such an impartial view not only of old port, but life in general, that I hope you will let me "voice" the opinions, not only of myself and the "man in the street", but of many others who think themselves gentlemen as well as sporting men.

'Mr. Sievier, if an adventurer, and confessedly a gambler, was never proved in his recent ill-advised action to have pulled a horse, loaded dice, or kept a card up his sleeve, and yet he is treated as if he were convicted of both chicanery on the Turf and cheating at the card table.

'He could not, it is true, get a verdict; but an average English jury would at once decide that any man who admitted winning £3000 at cards at a sitting was a scoundrel of the deepest dye. They are not used to gambling, and such tales fill them with horror.

'I can see nothing in Mr. Sievier winning money from the "Jubilee Plunger"—who would not have done the same thing? Mr. "Drinking" Horn was not too drunk to make 98 out of 100 at billiards, and apparently was too accustomed to the bottle to be readied with whisky for this occasion only.

'If when the Duke played and Mr. Renton played some of "the Boys" were present, the Duke and Mr. Renton were equally discredited with Mr. Sievier by the company they kept.

'The judge allowed it to be shown that the Plaintiff had been in the Divorce Court and had lost his wife's money in speculation. Is he warned off the Turf for this? His Lordship also allowed a detective to be called and asked what Mr. Sievier's reputation was. The answer was "Bad". I could have called half a dozen detectives who would have said his reputation was "Good", and have given reasons for it.

'We heard of Mr. Sievier's winnings and it was assumed that he always won, and large sums. He said himself that he lost £6000 in one sum at Liverpool. If his losses were known and contrasted with his winnings it would be patent that he had no infallible method of play. Before a man is warned off the Turf he should at least be heard in self-defence. As far as I am aware he has been given no opportunity to defend himself. The Jockey Club, no one can doubt, should take instant cognisance of a criminal conviction as well as of racing fraud but if they are going to "warn off" unsuccessful litigants in libel cases we do not know where the line will be drawn in the future, and the absurd rule disqualifying

Sceptre has also hit her present owner most unfairly,—I am, Yours—F.C.P.'
'Harpenden'.

The reference to the nomination of Sceptre concerned the fact that since Sievier had been her nominator for the Princess of Wales Stakes at Newmarket, once he became a disqualified person by the rule then pertaining, though he no longer owned her, the nomination was void and she could not run. In an effort to overcome this Bass had written Sievier this letter:

'Dear Mr. Sievier,—I hear you are willing to forego your claim to the £400 you get as nominator of Sceptre in the Princess of Wales's Stakes at Newmarket, should she be able to run, and win it. If this is so, will you write to Messrs. Weatherby, or wire them to that effect, and also write or wire me too?

'There is a meeting of the Jockey Club in London at 12 o'clock on Monday, so that if you are willing to give up your interest in the race your letter or wire should reach them Monday morning.— I am, yours truly,—(signed) William Bass.
'145 Piccadilly, W.
'June 3 1904'

Still smarting from the whole affair Sievier might well have refused to assist in any way. Instead he decided to do what he could and wrote to Weatherby's as follows:

'To E. M. Weatherby, Esq.,
'Sir,—With regard to the entry of Sceptre in the Princess of Wales's Stakes at Newmarket, and the rumour that she is not eligible to run as I might benefit by her success as nominator, I have duly considered the situation; and, though dissenting from the present interpretation by the Stewards of the spirit of the rule, and precedent shows that the spirit—might I say the "meritorious meaning"? —of a rule has often been acted upon as against the wording of it, I am writing to forego any benefit I might as Sceptre's nominator anticipate according to the conditions of the race; for I feel it would be unfair that Sceptre should not run, and unsportsmanlike towards Mr. William Bass that any action of the Stewards or of mine, right or wrong, should debar him of the chances of those anticipations he must have counted upon when he bought the mare from me.

'I should like to add, as an expression of hope, that the Stewards of the Jockey Club will cause the nominator's money to be given to charity, a moiety each to the King's Hospital Fund and the Bentinck Benevolent Fund, if Sceptre is successful.—I am, your obedient servant,—(signed) R. S. Sievier.
'Elston House, Shrewton, Wiltshire,
'June 4, 1904.'

To which he received this reply:

'R. S. Sievier, Esq.
'Dear Sir,—In reply to your letters of the 3rd and 4th inst.:
'PRINCESS OF WALES'S STAKES
'The Stewards do not consider that the fact of your foregoing any interest you may have as nominator of Sceptre is sufficient to remove the disqualification which your nomination has attached to her.
'As regards Lavengro, so long as he is the property of a disqualified person he is not qualified to run for this race.—I am, yours faithfully,—(signed) E. M. Weatherby.
'6 Old Burlington Street, London, W.
'June 6, 1904.'

The stewards were, of course, entirely within their rights in refusing to stretch the rule. But when Bass, in answer to enquiries as to why Sceptre could not run, released the explanation together with Sievier's offer their popularity was not increased in the eyes of the public nor was sympathy with Sievier lessened.

None of this was at all to the taste of the forces who had combined to bring him down. The damn fellow had been ruined financially, warned off and disgraced socially yet he still refused to disappear. At Shrewton he seemed to be keeping up Elston House much as before, entertaining those friends who had stood by him, and still welcomed by the locals who refused to dun him. When in Town he was about Romano's and all his old haunts, breezy as ever, apparently unaffected by it all, hailed by acquaintances as 'good old Bob', his stories laughed at and his drinks accepted. There was even a rumour going around that he was thinking of starting a racing paper. The story was absurd, of course, because no one now would dream of putting up the financial backing and, since his experience of journalism was negligible, even if it were floated it could not succeed. But if by any remote chance he did manage to start up,

Sievier with a pen in his hand and the pages of a racing paper at his disposal might well be a force to be reckoned with.

It wouldn't do at all. There was only one thing for it. Sievier must be put where he could no longer do harm or cause offence and embarrassment to the proprieties. There was only one place for him—in prison and for as long a term as possible. His enemies set about getting him there.

18

Perjury

꩜꩜꩜꩜꩜

Although Gill had resigned the office of Senior Treasury counsel in 1899 when he took silk he still retained an interest in Treasury prosecutions and influence with the Home Office. Now he pressed that a warrant for Sievier's arrest on a charge of perjury committed during the bankruptcy proceedings be issued without delay.

Meanwhile Sievier was spending much of his time at Elston House, relaxing in the sun with Mrs. Master and the children, arranging for the sale of his horses, trying to raise the money to pay the costs of the action and contemplating his future. It was correct that the idea of starting a racing paper was already taking shape in his mind. He had written occasionally for Corlett's *Pink 'Un* and he had to his credit the ill-fated playlet *Stone-Broke* and the mysterious novel *A Generation*, but beyond that he had no knowledge of journalism nor experience of writing at all. He knew nothing about the technical problems of putting up a paper, handling contributors, advertisers or printers, nor had he ever before in his life shown that he could devote himself to the consistent hard work such a project would demand. And he was now forty-four years of age, penniless and in debt.

It is typical of him that none of these difficulties daunted him. Throughout his life and never more so than at this time Sievier was a living illustration of Hemingway's maxim that a man can be defeated but not destroyed. He began to put out feelers to find a backer.

One of those whom he approached told him brusquely that had he made three fortunes of over a quarter of a million before he was forty-four (as Sievier had) he would not be looking for money now for he would have kept most of it. 'You wouldn't,' Sievier told him contemptuously, as he left the office, 'for you would never have made it.'

News of these approaches came to the ears of his enemies. It was borne on them that Sievier might well succeed in his project. He seemed to succeed in most things he set his mind to. Gill harried the Home

Office for the warrant. The result was that on Saturday June 18th a warrant was issued for the arrest of Robert Standish Sievier charging him with wilful and corrupt perjury during a private examination in bankruptcy on December 6th 1898. This warrant was handed to Chief Inspector Arrow of Scotland Yard to execute and the next day, Sunday, he travelled down to Shrewton to do so.

Sievier had not been left in ignorance of what was going on for he and his friends had their own methods of obtaining information and Gill, besides, had been neither wise nor reticent concerning his intentions. On the Sunday morning a friend wired Sievier to be on his guard, that an attempt would in all probability be made to arrest him that afternoon.

Sanguine as ever, Sievier scouted the warning. A tennis party had been arranged for that afternoon and he saw no reason to postpone it. He was on the court, playing a set, when he saw a fly with two men in it, strangers to him, turn into the drive. Unperturbed he went on with the game until his daughter, Gogo, came running from the house. The two gentlemen from the fly, she said, had obtained entry to the house and were demanding to see him. It was only then that he woke up to the reality of the position in which he stood. Robert Topping, a leading bookmaker of the day, was in the party and Sievier sent him off to find out what was afoot. Topping returned in a few minutes to say that the two men were Chief Inspector Arrow and a junior and that they held a warrant for his arrest.

Sievier had no intention of being taken out of his own home in handcuffs and being bundled into a train from Shrewton station with two police officers in attendance. He sent Topping back to tell Arrow that he would meet him at Scotland Yard at one o'clock the following day. Then, still in his flannels, while Topping and the police were parleying, he made his way to the stables, saddled a hack and rode across the Downs to where his friend, Fred Hunt, had a training stable.

Finding the bird flown, Arrow and his junior returned to London but not before they had left instructions with the local constable to seek out Sievier and arrest him on sight. Men were posted at the various stations on the way to London with similar orders. The authorities were certainly treating an alleged six-year-old perjury as a serious crime.

Mrs. Master sent over a change of clothes to him at Hunt's house. Late that night he was driven to Swindon where he caught an early-morning train to London, the police watcher having apparently been withdrawn by then. Once back in town he went to Topping's house and had a bath. Then he consulted with his solicitor, Mr. Blanchard Wontner, and instructed him to prepare his defence and brief counsel on his behalf. After that he strolled round to Romano's, had a drink and an early lunch with friends. He had had no sleep at all the night before but sleep was something he never appeared to need. Perfectly dressed as usual he looked as fresh as if he had been resting for a week. He was also quite unconcerned and no one who shared that lunch with him was given the slightest inkling that he was about to face a charge engineered by powerful enemies which, if it succeeded, could well lead to his spending the next few years of his life in gaol.

Lunch over, he walked along to Scotland Yard. There he met Wontner, Topping and Clark Frost, another leading member of the Ring who had agreed to stand bail for him. He informed Arrow that he was surrendering himself to answer any charge that might be brought against him and then asked what the charge was and who was prosecuting. Having had it read over to him he was told that the matter was in the hands of The Public Prosecutor. 'Paid by Sir James Duke, I suppose,' he remarked when he heard this.

Before leaving for Bow Street, Arrow told Sievier that he thought bail would be only nominal but a few minutes later he returned and warned him to prepare himself for a fight on the issue of bail. The Home Office, he said, had just run up to say that bail, if granted at all, must be in a very large sum.

When formal evidence of arrest had been given, Archibald Bodkin, who was prosecuting, opposed bail. He gave no grounds for his opposition, merely stating that these were his instructions. Wontner contested this saying that no attempt to arrest Sievier had been made for the previous five and a half years and that it would be utterly inequitable and unfair to refuse bail now on so stale a charge. With obvious reluctance Marsham, the magistrate, then granted bail but he fixed it at sums he clearly thought would be prohibitive, a very usual ruse in such cases by magistrates when they wish to defeat the ends of justice without appearing to do so. Sievier himself was asked for personal bail in the sum of £6000 and two independent securities were required to bind themselves in sums of £3000 each. Wontner was commencing to argue against the punitive nature of the sums so fixed when Robert Topping jumped up from the back of the court and called out. 'Never mind about that, Bob, I'll go the lot!'

'Sit down, sit down,' Charles Coburn, who was also in court, said to him in a voice that could be heard everywhere. 'This isn't baccarat! You can't do that. You can only go half!'

Go half is what Topping and Clark Frost did with the result that Sievier walked out of court and into Bow Street, at least temporarily a free man. The fact that another alleged perjurer on a far more recent charge who immediately followed him into the dock was freed on his own bail of £50 and one surety of £50 was not lost on the public.

Wontner sent the case to defend Sievier to Horace Avory K.C. Avory, one of the finest criminal lawyers of that or any other day, was later to be the fairest if the sternest English judge of the present century. He had a mind that was as finely honed as the best cutting steel which went straight to the heart of a case and stayed there. He was unswayed by emotion or prejudice, impatient of irrelevance, inaccuracy or inexactness in pleading. His comments at the bar were as biting as they were later to be sarcastic from the Bench. A better man to fight a case of this sort could not have been found. Having read the papers he pronounced the charge ridiculous, one which should not have been brought, and which should not succeed.

Perjury is a notoriously difficult crime to prove. Apart from the many technicalities surrounding it 'assignments in perjury' setting out the exact nature of the instances alleged must be made and should be given to the defence. As Avory was quick to point out there were none such here.

When the hearing was resumed the following Monday Bodkin still led for the Treasury though it was noticed that Gill had come along and was in counsel's benches beside him. Bodkin was an able man and, as a prosecutor, allied fairness to persistence and firmness but he had been given a singularly difficult case to conduct. Apart from the lack of any 'assignment in perjury' the whole charge was so vague and the distance of time since the alleged offence had been committed so great that the prosecution was largely discredited from the start.

Bodkin's opening address made this doubly clear. It consisted of a generalized investigation into Sievier's past from which it was apparent that he was unable to define the reality of the offence charged. In the end it all seemed to boil down to the fact that Sievier had said in one of his examinations in bankruptcy that he had never subscribed to the fund to start the Bedfordshire County Cricket Club but that his mother had made the subscription. Evidence, Bodkin said, could be produced to show that he had in fact subscribed £100 from his own account. Since Avory was immediately on his feet pointing out that if the payment of £100 was all that was relied on to prove the prosecution's case he could produce incontrovertible evidence that this sum had been paid after Sievier had obtained his discharge, a more farcical accusation upon which to base an indictment for the serious crime of perjury can scarcely be imagined. 'I am still waiting,' Avory went on, 'for Mr. Bodkin to state what the assignments in perjury are.'

'I would refer my friend to paragraph two of the written information,' Bodkin answered. But here he was being disingenuous and he must have known it, for a paragraph in the information did not constitute an assignment.

'That is not sufficient,' Avory barked. 'We cannot embark on a roving enquiry. I shall object to every bit of evidence until we know exactly what the assignments are. I never heard of a case of perjury being launched without an assignment.'

'I think I have,' Marsham, the magistrate, said and allowed the case to proceed.

For four weeks, the Magistrate sitting on the Monday of each week, Sievier was kept in suspense and the farce went on.

At first the prosecution attempted to show that Sievier during his occupancy of Park House had been the real owner of the lease. This, as Avory, grim-faced and cutting as only he could be, steadily reminded the magistrate, was not evidence for the charge concerned a statement alleged to have been made in 1898 and had nothing to do with the possession or non-possession of Park House. Marsham admitted the evidence and the prosecution called the solicitor who had prepared the lease on behalf of the owner of Park House.

Avory demolished him with one question. 'Had the defendant any rights under this lease? he asked.

'So far as Mr. Sievier was concerned he had no rights whatsoever under the lease I prepared,' was the reply.

The next attempt on the part of the prosecution was to try to show that Sievier had operated his mother's bank account for his own benefit. He undoubtedly had but this had nothing at all to do with the charge as brought, as Avory was quick to point out. 'I do not object to my friends prying into all these details,' he said, 'but they are, as I submit, irrelevant.' In which, of course, he was absolutely right.

But Marsham over-ruled him. 'Very well,' Avory said. 'I cannot argue further because I do not know what the assignments in perjury are.'

'That is my friend's misfortune,' Bodkin said and called the witness to prove the bank accounts. He was able to show that £34,929 11s. 6d.

had passed through Mrs. Sievier's account between July and December 1898 and that some of the cheques had come from Clark Frost and other bookmakers.

'Had the defendant an account in your bank?' Avory asked the witness.

'No.'

'Therefore his statement in his examination that he had no account there is correct?'

'Yes.'

'How old is his mother?'

'Nearly seventy years of age, I believe, and I understand that Mr. Sievier looks after her affairs.'

That ended that line of approach. The prosecution were being confounded by their own witnesses. Bodkin was now driven back upon the final absurdity of the cheque to the cricket club. He called the secretary to prove the receipt of the cheque. This put the case no further at all for it was clear, as Avory had said, that Sievier had obtained his discharge when he issued the cheque. Bodkin—one wonders who was behind him for it was unlike him to push a bad case to such ridiculous lengths—was now driven to the desperate expedient of trying to show that Sievier's lavish way of life at Toddington was inconsistent with that of an undischarged bankrupt. To do this he called John Alfred Marchmont, formerly secretary to the Dunstable Cricket Club, who had played on visiting teams and enjoyed Sievier's hospitality.

Avory's cross-examination of Marchmont is a perfect example of how to pulverize an already reluctant witness:

AVORY: 'What have you got to complain of?'

WITNESS: 'Nothing. Quite the reverse.'

AVORY: 'So far as you know has the defendant ever said he has not played cricket?

WITNESS: 'No.'

AVORY: 'What did you have—Champagne and truffles?'

WITNESS: 'No. An ordinary lunch.'

AVORY: 'Cold meat and shandy gaff?'

WITNESS: 'Yes, and a little Scotch.'

AVORY: 'Do you know why you have come here?'

WITNESS: 'No.'

AVORY: 'Neither do I.'

And he sat down.

Bodkin was rash enough to attempt to re-examine.

'Did you ever in the course of your visits to Toddington Park see the defendant's mother?' he asked.

'No.'

'It is not suggested that she played cricket,' commented Avory, flint-faced, from his seat.

That concluded the evidence such as it was, for the prosecution and Avory rose to address the magistrate. His speech, as usual, was short, succinct and to the point and in it he scarified the prosecution's case. This was, he said the most trumpery charge of perjury ever to be heard in any court. Such a case as this after the lapse of time and in such circumstances was unprecedented. He then mercilessly stripped bare the pretences that had been put up of applying the law, analysed the evidence given by the witnesses and annihilated it and them together. 'This case,' he ended by saying, 'is a perfect illustration of the way in which the criminal law in this country is degenerating into a practice of making a flimsy case against a man and calling upon him to prove his innocence.'

There were some in high places who must have squirmed when they read or heard those biting words delivered with the incisive vehemence of which Avory was a master.

Then the magistrate rubbed it home. The charge, he said, had been made after so long a lapse of time and the wilful and corrupt perjury necessary to sustain it not having been substantiated, that he had come to the conclusion no jury would convict. The defendant would be discharged.

Sievier left the court amidst loud cheering from the public gallery. His step was as springy as ever after his ordeal, his dress as immaculate, his smile as jaunty, and he went out into the sunshine a free man once more. But he was facing an unknown future. He had done that before on countless occasions and it did not daunt him. During the weeks of enforced idleness waiting for the case to end he had had plenty of time to think. He had had opportunity to see and sound out his friends, too. Charles Clark and Bob Topping were prepared to provide the financial backing for the venture he had in mind. He would indeed start a weekly racing paper and he would call it *The Winning Post.*

19

The Winning Post

The first number of *The Winning Post* was published on August 20th 1904. It was written, with some very little outside help, by Sievier himself. The price was one penny and it was an immediate success. The initial printing sold out almost before it reached the hands of the news boys. Once it was with them they announced it to the public by shouting 'Ere y'ar. Bob's *Winning Post* for a penny! A bob for a penny! Twelve to one your money! What more do you want!' No doubt they had been carefully coached beforehand and it hardly needs much guessing to name the fertile brain that thought that one up.

What Sievier did in *The Winning Post* was to take the formula developed by Corlett for the *Pink 'Un* of combining racing notes, news, comments and selections with gossip of stage and society, saucy jokes and paragraphs full of sexual innuendo, and push it much further than ever Corlett dared to do. He was hampered by none of Corlett's inhibitions. He cared nothing for standing well with the nobs save for those few who were his friends. He was free to castigate whom he wished and as he liked. His whip was at large and its lash could fall at his will and his will alone.

Corlett, as it happened, was not best pleased by the appearance in the field of this newer, brasher rival. More especially was he ruffled since in taking the title *The Winning Post* Sievier had calmly appropriated without permission the name of an earlier paper started by Corlett which he had allowed to die without taking the precaution of registering the copyright. The airy acknowledgment on the first page of the first number did little to soothe his offended susceptibilities: *We extend our hand to the 'Pink 'Un'* Sievier wrote,—*the staff and Master in particular— and if, in choosing the 'Winning Post' as our title, we have resuscitated one that once belonged to our Pink Pals, the coincidence suggests the old axiom that 'Great minds think alike.'*

Every successful paper takes on something of the character of its editor or proprietor, and *The Winning Post* was no exception to this. It was, like Sievier, breezy, witty, informed, knowing and knowledgeable—and entirely outrageous.

The front page consisted of a banner title in big, black letters:

THE WINNING POST
EDITED BY
ROBERT S. SIEVIER

Beneath this was a drawing of a sceptre lying on its side and below this again, under the dateline and the price, were the saucy stories or 'Tabasco tales' as Sievier was to dub them when, with success, they grew hotter and hotter. Inside were short stories and sketches, all written by Sievier; London, Paris and Irish notes, 'motobilia' and the like.

But the real kernel of the paper was contained in the centre pages which were also, with very few interruptions caused by illness or other unavoidable reasons, throughout the life of the paper written by the editor himself. Under the inside masthead Sievier had placed, once more emulating Corlett, a line which would set out the policy and nature of the paper. But his was no reassuring jingle about High Torism and old port. It was a quotation containing a brief statement of fact, and in that statement a threat was implicit which no one who knew him could miss. *I possess no Sceptre but I do possess a pen— Voltaire* were the minatory words in which he set out how he would use the weapon he had forged for his hand and in which he served clear notice on his enemies that they had better look to their moats.

On this centre page, too, were his leaders, and his racing notes in which he set out his comments and selections. Though barred from the racecourse he had at his disposal a multitude of sources of information and in his writing here he amazed everyone by the depth of his knowledge and the accuracy of his perception. It was immediately seen that he knew the rules, he knew racing with the inner acquaintance of the professional, and that what he said on that subject and on horses— their breeding, running and riding—made sense. Indeed it made a great deal too much sense for the comfort of some readers.

Moreover, when writing about racing he pruned his style. Gone were the flowery paragraphs and high falutin' monologues he often used elsewhere. The racing articles were set down in hard, sinewy, purposeful prose. They were written by an expert and were read as such with admiration or, in some cases, trepidation, for, fearless as usual, what he thought he said and what he or others saw he reported.

What was, however, the most sensational and controversial page of the paper and which contributed in a large measure to its success was the page entitled *Celebrities in Glass Houses*. This was an open letter purported to be written by 'Tweedledum and Tweedledee' to a prominent person of the day usually, but not always, connected with racing. To call it frank is an understatement for in it Sievier set out his views on the character, career, attainments, probity and private life of the subject in a manner—when he wished—uninhibited by considerations of taste and unfettered by fear of libel.

The scandalous nature of these articles has in fact been much exaggerated by the publicity given to the few that did land him in court. It was only in a small proportion of them that he poured out the full flow of vitriol contained in his ready pen and vengeful mind. There can however be no doubt that he used them as a threat and enjoyed doing so and that those who had wounded him in the past or were to offend him in the future were to feel the full force of a scurrilous, clever and unbridled talent for invective. The worst of these letters were seldom other than witty which made them even more damaging, and the abuse, though tough, was usually true for he had a retentive and probing mind and his knowledge of the foibles and follies of the Establishment figures he pilloried was encyclopaedic. That is what kept him in business for so long and enabled him to survive the onslaughts of his enemies and the traps they set for him. That, too, is what made him so feared.

Sievier had ability and brains; he was no tuppenny-ha'penny mudslinger such as had briefly thrived during the closing years of the nineteenth century. He was a man of tremendous talents which he rode on far too loose a rein. But he pursued his vendettas too long and in doing so carried his lust for vengeance almost beyond the bounds of normality and into the insensate. The trouble was that, as in everything else here, too, he was larger than life. But considering what he had just been through, it is impossible to withhold some sympathy for him in the course he took.

No man, even one as physically and mentally tough as Sievier, could have gone through the ordeals of the past three months without in some way being affected by them. In that short period he had lost a disastrous and sensational libel action in which he had been held up to public odium by the Judge, he had been unjustly warned off the Turf, thus suffering the greatest injury and humiliation that can be brought upon a racing man and had, as a result, lost his livelihood as well. Close upon the heels of that, entirely through the machinations of his enemies, he had been put in the dock on a trumped up criminal charge during which for four weeks he did not know whether he was to go free or stand convicted as a felon.

Up to this point there had always been something boyish in his escapades. A bit of the boy was there still but not very much. Even his fondness for getting his own back had heretofore an engaging quality of recklessness and bravado about it. Now in his conduct of *The Winning Post* something almost of pure wickedness came into him and flowed out of his pen. His vindictiveness in certain cases went far beyond the bounds, even given his justifiable grievance, that could be condoned by normal men. Those three months had twisted him. Now that the world of the great and the would-be respectable, and the forces of the Establishment, had done their worst to him and failed, it was his turn to hit back. That world owed him something and it was going to repay it in hurt and fear. *Oderint dum metuant* he might well have said and placed that tag from Cicero at his masthead instead of the quotation from Voltaire.

But, as always, he retained his flair for the unexpected. The advance publicity for *The Winning Post* had announced that the first of the Celebrities would be The Earl of Durham, the man who had signed Sievier's warning-off notice. Those who turned to it confidently expecting a flow of abuse were disappointed. Instead of a personal polemic Sievier printed a reasoned, well-thought-out and soberly argued article dealing with certain aspects of racing such as the lack of amenities compared with Australia and other countries, the looseness of the system then used for declarations, and the anomalies attaching to the position, rights, and duties of the stakeholder.

So impressed was old John Corlett with this that he wrote: 'Mr. Sievier's article, we are glad to see, contains nothing of a personal nature but, on the other hand, in a temperate manner points out many shortcomings in the working of the Turf and is so well worthy of consideration that we print it.' And he did so, calmly appropriating the whole lot without Sievier's permission, informing his staff that it was only his due since Sievier had stolen his title. Honours were then even and Sievier sealed whatever breach there was by printing a eulogistic 'Celebrity' of Corlett in a forthcoming number.

All this was disappointing for the seekers after sensation as was the open letter to Mr. Justice Grantham which the public were certain would produce fireworks. Here he contented himself with using one column of the paper only. This was left entirely blank save for the heading: CELEBRITIES IN GLASS HOUSES: MR. JUSTICE GRANTHAM, and in the very centre of the empty column, the words 'OH UPRIGHT JUDGE.' SHAKESPEARE. As a journalist Sievier, at times, knew the value of restraint.

Mr. E. M. Weatherby, too, must have been somewhat surprised and taken aback to find in the open letter to his firm that there was not one word which could be possibly construed as libellous. Instead there was a serious, balanced, well researched and absolutely deadly examination of their antiquated methods of running English racing, far more damaging than any polemic could be.

Sievier, then, had not yet unleashed his thunderbolts. He himself had no doubt upon whom, when they were ready, they were going to fall. Duke had been dismissed with a few contemptuous paragraphs as being not worth powder and shot. Dudley was no longer in the arena against him for he had removed himself to the Lord-Lieutenancy of Ireland. He had not been forgotten but he could wait. Gill, too, though high on the list, and his advocacy, whenever he lost a case, never escaped adverse comment, could come later. There was one man whom he blamed for it all, whom he believed to have been the watcher in the shadows, the provider of funds to pay for the detectives and the Australian research in the libel action, the moving figure behind his warning off, the hand that had guided Gill to search through the records of his bankruptcy to find evidence to ground the perjury proceedings. Rightly or wrongly, but it must be remembered that he had sources of information in all walks of life, he blamed for his troubles his old enemy Jack Barnato Joel. Slowly, lovingly, with care, attention and skill he was investigating every detail of Joel's past. He would not move until he was ready and when he was he would strike straight for the jugular.

In the meantime, still following the pattern Corlett had set, he was gathering a staff about him. As Corlett called himself 'Master' he took the title 'The Chief' and, attracted by his success, men of talent in journalism asked for employment on the paper. Determined, however, to keep absolute control in his own hands, he selected only a few. Archie McLaren, the old friend from Punch & Co. and Toddington days, came in to do the cricket, F. J. Sellicks, the all-round sportsman, was enrolled as secretary and stayed, loyal, true and trusted to the very end, Fred Wisdom, 'Tea-Leaf' of the *Pink 'Un,* crossed over to the newer paper and helped out with his professional knowledge and also did the dramatic criticism. A brilliant cartoonist, Starr Wood, who signed his work 'the Snark' was taken on to do the illustrations and hold the celebrities up to ridicule, with another younger man, 'The Jabber-wock' to help him.

With success, too, came advertising revenue. Thomas Henry Dey, the former clerk in Punch & Co. and now a leading bookmaker in his own right, took a whole page to advertise in huge letters his honesty and standing. Pierrepont 'Enquiry Agent to the Nobility and Gentry of England' also displayed his services:

WHEN BLACKMAILED GO TO PIERREPONT
WHEN WATCHED GO TO PIERREPONT
WHEN TROUBLED GO TO PIERREPONT
ALL SORTS of confidential work and enquiries undertaken
for RACING MEN TRAINERS and all SPORTSMEN and
WOMEN

Teofani, the then fashionable cigarettes, had a page. Bookmakers, saddlers, racecourses, purveyors of high-class grocery and consumer goods and publishers of books with a sporty flavour, all sought space in his columns, some of the more favoured being rewarded with ill-disguised puffs in the letterpress.

There were others with a different type of book to sell:

RIPPING VALUE said W. P. Gold & Co. of Bishopsgate. '*The Bride of The First Night*' *156 pages, well-illustrated. 20 photos of pretty Paris girls. 1s. An equivocal love letter. Awful Disclosures of Maria Monk in a Nunnery Revealed, cloth and gilt 40 illustrations. 12 real photos of a Parisienne taking her bath. 15 positions of matrimony. Splendid value 3 stamps.*'

L. Jackson, Publishers, of 126 Tottenham Court Road offered RARE AND CURIOUS BOOKS including *Revelations of Girlhood. Fanny Hill, profusely illustrated,* could be bought for ten shillings, and it was also suggested that you should '*try one of our 10s. assorted parcels of spicy books unobtainable elsewhere for less than 25s.*'

As the paper prospered and circulation increased the jokes became more and more blue and the short stories more risqué as did other parts of the paper which was full of *double entendres*. The gossip from Paris was headed OUR FRENCH LETTER. Adam and Eve jokes were much in vogue at this time and Sievier used this theme over and over again. One of the better of these rhymes was:

Eve stood in the Garden
(Mother of us all)

> *Examining her trousseau*
> *Fig leaves—that was all !*
> *There stood poor old Adam*
> *Up against the wall,*
> *'What oh,' said he, There's work for me,*
> *When the leaves begin to fall !'*

The jokes kept up the same strain:

The Major: Who's that long-haired individual at the next table?
Miss Simkins: He's Herr Hammerstein the great pianist.
The Major: And who's the dear little fair with him?
Miss Simkins: I don't know her name but I believe she turns over for him.

As the success of these tabasco tales increased, unsolicited contributions of the stock exchange and smoking-room variety came pouring into 15 Essex Street where *The Winning Post* had its offices. This gave Sievier the idea of starting an 'answers to correspondents' column which in turn provided an opportunity for sexual innuendo which he exploited to the full.

The column bore at its head the stern warning that unsolicited contributions were never paid for unless previous arrangement was made. In fact even the members of *The Winning Post* were never quite sure where their next week's wages were coming from since from the very beginning the editor and proprietor had his hand deeply in the till to pay for his gaming debts. It was really the fact that the whole operation was a hilarious one that kept them going at all. Frequently they would gather round the Chief's desk inventing and bandying about more and more outrageous answers to fictitious correspondents before adjourning to Romano's to spread the news of Sievier's latest audacity. Buried amidst apparently innocuous items were such as these:

J.H.C. Your 'three with spouts and one without' is very venerable.
OLD SPORT. That 'pealing of the organ story' is as old as marriage itself.
NIBLICK: Golf stories are all balls.

It was really no wonder that in a very short time the *Winning Post* went to a circulation figure of 50,000, nor was it a matter for surprise that Edwardian papas, eagerly scanning it each week, did so in the privacy of their smoking rooms and hid it hastily beneath cushions when female members of their family were about. What sold the paper was the mixture of good sense about racing and scandal about people. Lord Derby, giving evidence in the Wootton case a few years later, said, 'I think on the whole your comments on racing are very fair.' Coming from one who had no reason to love Sievier and who had been called for the opposition this was a testimonial indeed. And it was true. From the very first he demonstrated that he knew racing and could and did write sense about it. The trouble, of course, was that his comments on the people he disliked were very far from fair. The cleverness in them—diabolical cleverness his enemies said—lay in the fact that they almost always had at least a foundation in truth. This was certainly so in the case of Joel against whom he was just about to be in a position to unmask his batteries.

The *Winning Post* of October 15th 1904 informed its readers that the next *Celebrity in Glass Houses* to be dealt with would be none other than Mr. J. B. Joel of Grosvenor Square. Joel was not greatly loved and the issue was looked forward to in the sporting world and elsewhere with considerable anticipation.

By this time Joel was not only a man of immense means but also of position and substance. His mansion at 34 Grosvenor Square was packed with treasures acquired by his wealth from all over the world; his racing enterprises had prospered too; he had already the winning of one classic to his name for Morton had trained Our Lassie to win him The Oaks in 1903. He was a member of the Jockey Club Stand at Newmarket and had gained admittance to the Royal Enclosure at Ascot. In the city, of course, the manipulation of his millions brought him ever-increasing wealth and power.

The open letter which Sievier penned to him was a frank polemic and scurrilous to a degree. He set out in detail Joel's lowly origins in Whitechapel; he revealed that he had been christened 'Isaac' and had taken the names of 'Jack Barnato' without the formality of a deed poll, and was thus—so Sievier said—presuming to practise his affairs and to race on the Turf under an assumed name. The question of an assumed name always rankled with Sievier ever since he had been pilloried for using the name of Sutton to trade under in Australia. If he were to suffer for it he did not see why others should not do so as well.

Much worse than all this, so far as Joel was concerned, was the fact that Sievier had discovered in the files of the British Museum and the *Police Gazette* a diamond-buying offence which had been charged against Joel as a young man in South Africa. Joel had been remanded on bail and when the charge came on for hearing it was found that he had absconded leaving his uncle Barney to pay up a heavy sum for the estreated bail. He had never since returned to South Africa.

Joel was, as might be imagined, extremely sensitive about this incident in his past. Sievier set it all down in full for the delectation of his public.

In this article about Joel venom dripped from Sievier's pen and he went far beyond the bounds of ordinary decency and well into the realms of gutter journalism. It has to be remembered, however, that he himself had just faced out a criminal charge trumped up as he thought at least in part by Joel and had also just been warned off the Turf by a flagrantly unjust ruling. In his position of humiliation he saw the man he believed to be responsible for most of it, a man whom he thought he could show to have a far worse record than his own, lording it in the Royal Enclosure at Ascot, mingling with the good and great and prospering mightily from one million to another.

Joel took no action for defamation or otherwise on account of this article. It was therefore assumed by all who read it that the statements contained in it must be true and Sievier, emboldened, increased his attacks. Scarcely an issue passed without some scurrilous reference to one or both of the Joels though Jack was the chief target. He was branded as 'Joel, the notorious dealer in illicit diamonds,' and there were other, minor references. In the answers to correspondents column 'Constant Reader' was told *Consult columns of 'Daily Telegraph' for information as to where to sell old clothes, or write to the Joels. We give them away*. And such jingles as the following constantly appeared:

> There was a crooked man
> Who went a crooked mile
> And he found a crooked sixpence
> Against a crooked stile
> Whereupon he sadly soliloquized, 'Being crooked,
> why am I not a
> South African millionaire?'

It was, of course, considered astonishing that Joel did not move at law and he stood no higher in men's eyes for not doing so; but at the same time it was widely felt that Sievier was going much too far. To start with, it had perhaps been no harm to give Joel's pretensions a knock but this campaign of vilification passed beyond the common reader's conception of fair play and it was the common reader who made up most of Sievier's circulation. He was beginning to forfeit much of the sympathy and admiration he had won for his courage and enterprise in fighting back from all his misfortunes when Joel took a course so extraordinary and ill-advised that one can only speculate on the mentality of the man who conceived it.

The front page of the *Winning Post* of December 17th 1904 bore one headline, the word JOEL in huge capital letters. Beneath this headline Sievier set out in detail a plot hatched by Joel to have him attacked, mauled and disabled even to the extent of throwing vitriol over him. The agent employed by Joel to carry out this plot was one, Dan Murray, a broken-down pugilist. Unfortunately for Joel, Sievier's underworld connections were more extensive than his. An informer told him of the plot. He saw Murray and won him to his side. It was agreed between them that Murray should send off the confirmatory telegram arranged with Joel *Have done the job properly. Dan,* and claim from Joel his reward of £200 paid in £5 and £10 notes. Sievier obtained the notes from Murray, photographed them and published facsimiles of them and their numbers in the article. He ended with the words: 'Joel has tempted others with his filthy lucre to do that which he was too cowardly to attempt in person, and thus proved himself worse than the ruffian he employed.'

All this, of course, if untrue, was scandalously defamatory of Joel. But no action at law from Joel followed. The public was not slow to draw the deduction that what Sievier had written was true and that Joel had hired a desperado to cripple him. Pressing home his advantage Sievier then issued a challenge to Joel in the columns of the *Winning Post* to take an action for defamation against him. Joel was known to have consulted Gill on the matter, but, presumably as a result of the advice given him, he did nothing.

Sievier had accused Joel of a number of criminal offences none of which had been repudiated. He took it that he had secured for himself a licence to libel Joel with impunity and of this he was to make full use. The vendetta was now out in the open and it was to be pursued with the utmost ferocity on both sides until it culminated in a resounding *cause célèbre* at the Old Bailey just over three years later.

20

Reinstatement

In order to devote his time to the paper Sievier left Shrewton where Elston House and its stabling stood empty waiting for a tenant. In its place he rented a charming town house at 8a Hobart Place and bought a country cottage at Taplow from D'Arcy Baker, the first Fiat agent in the United Kingdom.

Soon he moved his country quarters from Taplow to Hillmorton Manor, a small Elizabethan House some miles from Rugby. Here he and the children hunted with the Pytchley and the Warwickshire. In fact he kept hunters all over the place including a few at Brackley which he hunted with the Bicester and the Grafton. There he made the acquaintance of F. E. Smith, the future Earl of Birkenhead, before that worthy quitted the hunting field forever with the immortal words, 'In future that vermin may pursue its way unmolested by me'.

Sievier wrote of Birkenhead that 'he sat a horse as well as he was to sit the Woolsack later on'. According to Birkenhead himself he once, in an impromptu steeplechase, defeated Sievier and another famous sporting character of those days, Charley Thompson, known to all and sundry as 'Bonnety Bob' from the fact that his mother kept a hat shop in the Walworth Road under the title of 'Madame Louise'. The three men found themselves thrown out in a hunt with the Bicester. In order to improve the dull moment 'Bonnety Bob' suggested that they should ride to the nearest church steeple which could clearly be seen a mile or so away for stakes of £10 a head. F.E. agreed but insisted that he should hold the stakes since he doubted his opponents' willingness to settle if they lost, and that the first obstacle should be a five-barred gate immediately confronting them. When F.E. told the story he said that the others were riding blood horses and he considered it unlikely that they would take on the gate first time in cold blood. He proved to be right. His staid old hunter sailed over the gate while both of the others refused. Having got first run Smith made the best of his way home and had a clear lead of two fields by the time 'Bonnety Bob' smashed the top rail of the gate and set out after him. He won by a distance and afterwards could and did boast of how he cut the two top-sawyers down and handsomely defeated them across a country. He pocketed the stakes, too.

Sievier and F.E. used on occasions to share a carriage to London together and Sievier remembered that the great barrister had on one of these journeys proposed that he should buy him a horse to win the Heavyweight Race at the House of Commons point-to-point. The price F.E. suggested paying was not, however, Sievier said, commensurate with the fees he marked on his briefs, and the idea was dropped.

The *Winning Post* did in fact brief F.E. in one of the libel actions in which the paper was involved. It was a singularly silly action, the identification of the gentleman rider who was the plaintiff with the man named in the article being remote in the extreme, but F.E. had one of his off days and damages were awarded against the paper for £500. After that the friendship, if it could be called such, between the two men became noticeably cooler and the references to F. E. Smith in the *Winning Post* considerably less complimentary.

By and large Sievier, not unexpectedly, hated lawyers and the legal profession and made no bones about saying so. Gill, of course, was fair game throughout his career, and Sievier saw to it that he was never spared. 'The atmosphere of the court' he wrote on one occasion, 'was putrid with prejudice repeatedly injected by counsel Gill, and instead of the case being kept to its legal aspect and points, it was transformed into mud-slinging which did not bear on the charge at all.' This was the sort of thing that Gill had to put up with on almost all of his appearances in court, especially if he lost his case, and, overdone though it was, it did his practice no good. Sievier's enemies had been wise when they tried to put him in prison to prevent him starting the *Winning Post*, for they were now finding out just how ferociously he could hit back. Already he was making himself a man to be feared, and he continued to do so for the *Winning Post* continued to prosper.

Throughout the life of the paper he went on with his campaigns as to what was wrong with racing. These campaigns were controversial but were almost invariably founded on commonsense, for it was very seldom that his prejudices or enthusiasms led him into writing rubbish. He wanted the ridiculous rule abolished that nominations became void on the death of the nominator; he pointed to the inefficiency or worse of much of the stewarding especially at local meetings and pressed for the appointment of stipendiary stewards as in Australia. He lived to see both these reforms come about but he had to wait for over thirty years to do so. He thought that the powers of Weatherby's should be curtailed and said so in language both pointed and strong; he hated the instructions concerning the standstill start from the gate and what he said about its impracticability read like the voice of reason to those who rode and trained horses. He inveighed ceaselessly against the excessive use of the whip, which then went unchecked, and pointed out its dangers in the hands of inexperienced jockeys.

Soon the *Winning Post* was being taken in regimental messes and men's clubs all over the Empire. His name was now a household word and he made sure of its remaining one by commencing to write his 'Autobiography' in serial form for the paper early in the New Year. It need scarcely be said that his own version of his adventures lost nothing in the telling and a highly-coloured gloss was put upon the more discreditable of the episodes in his past which he could not avoid recounting. In effect the Autobiography was an *apologia sua vita* designed to offset the disclosures in the Duke case and the effect of the warning-off. It dealt in great detail with the injustices he had suffered during the hearing of the case and sought to set the record right. He still did not or would not understand that legally he had no hope of winning anyway. It also indulged in some typical sideswipes at Gill, Grantham, and the members of the jury, one of whom was described as 'an alien lodging-house keeper living in the vicinity of the notorious Percy Street.'

Later the Autobiography was published in book form where it attracted a surprising amount of critical attention and sold well enough. It is far from a good book, being scrappy, episodic, tendentious and wildly inaccurate when it suited its author's intentions, but the fact that it was written and published at all goes to demonstrate the astonishing range of ability of the man. He appeared to be able to turn his hand to anything and bring it off. Certainly, too, the *nom de plume* of *Robert le Diable*, which he assumed when writing most of his articles for the *Winning Post*, appeared to many who felt the bite of his pen as singularly apt. In those days his invention never seemed to flag. Soon *The Winning Post Annual* appeared in time for the Christmas trade and went on doing so for year after year.

The annual was a compendium of short stories, sketches, jokes, jollities and tabasco tales, almost all of them written by Sievier himself. It was racily illustrated by Ralph Rowland and Starr Wood, one of whose full-page pictures entitled 'The First Mixed Bathing' showed

Adam and Eve, nude and hand in hand wading into a lake while the head of the serpent rose from the waters regarding them with a lewd and knowing eye. Most of the stories, too, had the covertly sexual slant so beloved by the raffish edge of Edwardian Society.

In November 1905 things were going so well that the *Winning Post* was formed into a limited company. Charles Clark took most of the issued shares though Sievier himself had some and these, together with others acquired later, were the only securities he ever owned throughout the whole of his long life. F. J. Sellicks was the secretary, Sievier, Archie McLaren and a man called Willett the directors. Soon the £1 shares, such of them as could be obtained, were changing hands at 45s. When, a year later, Bottomley started *John Bull*, the paper that brought fame, fortune and disaster to him, he took a whole page in the *Winning Post* to advertise the initial number. He also borrowed Sievier's idea of putting celebrities into glass houses. He called his page an Open Letter but the direction and effect were much the same as Siever's, which did not further endear him to the editor of the *Winning Post*.

Sievier now had success on his hands. He had an income ample for any ordinary man and, recognized and hailed wherever he went, as 'good old Bob', fame such as few men knew. Moreover it was conveyed to him that many of those in authority were far from happy about his continued disqualification from the Turf. Durham in particular was having second thoughts which were both hard and long. He told Rosebery when discussing the case long afterwards that the more he pondered it the more he saw the dangers of the precedent which had been set. If Sievier were to be banished forever for an offence unconnected with racing how many others should go too?

Once Durham made up his mind he was accustomed to act on his decision. When he became a steward again he was in a position to throw all his tremendous influence into righting the wrong which had been done and to which indeed he had lent his name. His was the obverse of Dudley's misuse of power and privilege for it seems clear that Durham had no personal liking for Sievier. He acted out of principle and made principle prevail. *The Racing Calendar* of July 4th 1907 bore the following entry:

> The Stewards of the Jockey Club have withdrawn the notice published on May 19 1904 warning Mr. R. S. Sievier off Newmarket Heath.

At his first appearance on a racecourse after the withdrawal of the warning-off he was welcomed back personally by Lord Downe the then senior steward of the Jockey Club. Immediately he set about getting together a stable of horses once more. His first runner was a two-year-old called Cream of The Sky in a seller at Derby. When the famous colours 'black, gold facings and sleeves, red cap' appeared once more on the racecourse the crowd cheered them all the way to the start. They cheered again as Cream of the Sky came back and the cheering turned to a mighty roar when she was seen to be winning. The uproar of cheering and applause went on as Sievier came down to the sale ring to buy her in. He stood taking off his hat and smiling and waving back at them as they clapped and huzzaed about him. It was indeed a triumphant return.

The world was now at his feet could he but have controlled his wild gambling. He had, of course, many claims on his purse. There was his mother in Torquay for one thing, and the £2000 payable to Lady Mabel for another. He was never anything other than a generous man; many of his kind acts were done by stealth, some to those who appeared to have no claim upon his bounty. About this time he undertook to pay for the education of a young cousin whose father had died suddenly and left the family ill-equipped to face the world. The boy was sent round to Hobart Place to be introduced to his benefactor and he never forgot the atmosphere of quietness and good taste in that charming little house, so unlike the brash public image Sievier presented to the world outside. The obligation thus undertaken was punctiliously discharged despite the fact that before his death the boy's father and Sievier had not been speaking for years.

His vindictiveness seemed to be reserved for his public life and here it appeared all but insensate. He was still, for instance, pursuing Joel with a deadly enmity. During his researches in the British Museum into Joel's past he found a picture of him in *The Police Gazette*. He pencilled a moustache on to this as a guide to Starr Wood the caricaturist and wrote on the back of it 'Sultry Stories—Peppery Paragraphs—Tabasco Tales' for the purpose of making up the paper. When the block for the reproduction of the picture had been made, Sellicks or someone in the office suggested that there might be trouble over copyright. Legal advice was taken which had confirmed that this could well be the case. Sievier shelved the idea and put the whole lot, including the blockmaker's receipt, into the office safe and left it there. It was fortunate for him, later on, that he had done so. But this was then only a minor incident in the campaign for the harassment and embarrassment of Joel in every possible way. He had additional copies of the initial open letter to the millionaire printed. These were advertised in almost every issue of the *Winning Post* and widely circulated. Whenever any particularly offensive reference to Joel was about to appear he employed men with sandwich boards to walk up and down Grosvenor Square outside Joel's house. Under the name of the paper these boards bore only one word JOEL printed on them in huge letters. Neither Joel nor the public therefore knew just what was going to appear except that it was bound to be both meaty and derogatory.

Sievier still believed that Joel had used both his money and his influence to help keep him in the wilderness and off the Turf for those three years. Certainly, considering Durham's expressed wish to see him back, there can be no doubt that strong forces were in the field against him though whether Joel had any means of influencing or controlling these, since he was not a member of the Jockey Club, will never be known. It was sufficient for Sievier to hold the belief that he did to focus all his vindictiveness against him.

Joel, naturally enough, struck back in every way he could though whether he was actually behind the campaign waged against the *Winning Post* by the upholders of public morality and virtue in the person of one Robert Philip Cother Corfe is at least doubtful. Be that as it may, Messrs. W. H. Smith declined to sell the paper on its bookstalls, which denied him one of his chief outlets, though it in no way interrupted the steady increase in circulation. Shortly after this the guardians of public morality scored another victory in having him fined £10 10s. in the Magistrate's court and ordered to pay five guineas costs *for sending through the post a packet enclosing certain indecent articles, to wit —five numbers of a newspaper called the Winning Post*. The actual offending paragraph was contained in the issue of February 29 1908 and was as follows:

> In writing to his best girl describing a sham fight, an enthusiastic militiaman of the Haldane type said, 'On reaching the village on the plain we were surrounded by superior numbers and forced to copulate. I hope during my training you are as true to me, love, as I am to you.

It was not, as Sievier said afterwards, one of the *Winning Post*'s wittier efforts and, as he also said, he fully deserved to be fined for letting it go in at all.

But whether or not Joel had a hand in all this, the vendetta continued.

Joel stated publicly that Sievier was trying to blackmail him. Sievier countered by publishing in the *Winning Post* details of the visits paid to him by emissaries from Joel bearing bribes to tempt him to cease his attacks. One of them, he said, was Arthur Newton, the police court solicitor who defended Crippen and then got into trouble himself. He had refused all these offers with contempt, he said and sent their bearers back with rude messages to their master. Again Joel took no action on foot of these statements nor did he issue any denial. He was, however, biding his time and waiting his opportunity. In the Spring of 1908 it appeared to have come and he moved in, as he thought, for the kill.

21

Arrest

꧁꧂

On Saturday June 27th 1908 Chief Inspector Drew of Scotland Yard, in circumstances ensuring that the maximum publicity would be given to the action, arrested Robert Standish Sievier in the paddock at Sandown Park on a warrant charging him with attempting to obtain £5000 from Mr. J. B. Joel by proposing to abstain from publishing a certain libel concerning him.

The circumstances leading up to this sensational and dramatic event are so extraordinary and have been so often misrepresented that they will have to be set down in some detail.

On April 29th at the Epsom Spring Meeting Sievier met a man called Albert Bendon whom he knew slightly and with whom he had had some transactions. Bendon was a stockbroker, he owned a few racehorses and appears to have done racing commissions for others as well as pursuing his profession. Amongst his clients was Solly Joel whom he knew well and with whom he was on terms of friendship. His acquaintance with Jack Joel was of the slightest. Although Jack had been the main target for Sievier's attacks in the *Winning Post* he had from time to time shot arrows at Solly too. Some time before this Bendon had asked Charles Mills to use his influence with Sievier to bring about a truce between him and Solly. This Mills had done and both he and Bendon were to swear at the coming trial that no element of extortion entered into this transaction and no money passed between Solly and Sievier.

Sievier and Bendon fell into conversation in the course of which Sievier told Bendon he was going very badly betting and might have difficulty in settling. He then asked Bendon to go to Solly Joel to enquire if Solly would advance Sievier £2000 on the security of certain shares in the *Winning Post*. Bendon went to Solly and was met, as he expected, with a flat refusal.

Bendon then said that Sievier asked him to approach Jack with the same request. Sievier denied this and said that the suggestion came

202

from Bendon. At all events here in Joel's own words is what happened between himself and Bendon: 'At the beginning of May Mr. Albert Bendon called at my office. He said that Sievier had sent him to ask me to lend him £2000 on 5000 *Winning Post* shares. I said "It is extraordinary that he should send to me. Why have you come?" Bendon replied: "He is a villainous scoundrel and I am afraid of him. That is why I came." I said: "You must give me time to think it over." After he had gone I consulted my solicitor. Mr. Bendon came to see me next night at my house. I told him I was willing to do business if Sievier would give me a letter promising to abstain from attacking me and my family again.'

It will be seen that even at this very early stage the proposal to abstain from the attacks came from Joel. Immediately he heard of the suggested deal Bendon felt that Joel was up to something that was not above board. He resolved to get out of the affair altogether, but he did not want to offend the Joels or to lose their business which came by way of Barnato Brothers though it was Solly who actually instructed him. Very foolishly, as he afterwards admitted, he suggested that Charles Mills, who had fixed the thing up for Solly, should take his place.

Joel agreed to this suggestion. Bendon then went to Mills, and told what was going on but warned him to be careful in his dealings with Joel. Next Bendon informed Sievier that he was dropping out and Mills was taking his place. Sievier thereupon said that he would have no dealings with Joel at all and that if any money was coming 'my loan will be from Mills'. But in fact no loan was then made nor was anything further done in the matter at that time. Sievier must have raised the money elsewhere to pay his debts for he never approached Joel, Mills or Bendon again. He did not forget, however, and the libellous attacks on Joel continued, indeed they increased in intensity and viciousness.

Naturally enough Joel hit back. On June 19th Sievier had a runner called Waterloo in a seller at Windsor. Waterloo won and Sievier went down to buy him expecting, as was the usual custom, that there would be no opposition. To his fury and astonishment he found Charles Morton, Joel's private trainer, also in the ring and bidding vigorously against him. He was unable, of course, to match Joel's resources and he lost his horse.

The six weeks since the original conversation with Bendon had not been good ones for Sievier's gambling. He was again broke or very near it. He wanted to keep the horse and his rage was terrifying. When

Sievier was in one of these tempers all the racecourse heard him. At the top of his voice he announced to the world at large what he was going to do to Joel and what he was going to say about him in the next issue of the *Winning Post*.

Hearing of this Joel became apprehensive. But he also knew that Sievier was short of money and he quickly realized that here could be another chance of buying his silence. He sent for Mills. At the interview between the two men he told Mills that the articles were making life hell for himself and his family. He knew, he said, that Mills had great influence with Sievier and he begged him to see Sievier and to try to fix it so that the attacks would stop. 'Get the business done as reasonably as you can,' he said to him.

Mills went to Sievier and returned to tell Joel: 'Sievier is mad at you for what happened at Windsor last Saturday because he thinks that Morton bid against him at your instigation; and I hear he is going to publish some very nasty things against you in next week's issue and also a copy of the warrant against you.'

Joel sent him back to try to find out what Sievier would take for his silence. A series of complicated negotiations then took place in which Joel deceived Mills and Mills double-crossed everybody. Joel did not tell Mills that he was laying a trap for Sievier which he hoped would result in a successful prosecution for blackmail. Mills for his part pretended to Sievier that he was getting a loan for him and that he, Mills, could make the actual loan. He actually advanced Sievier £1000 of his own money as an earnest of his good faith. He told Joel none of this but said that Sievier wanted £5000 or he would publish his picture between two murderers. During these negotiations Mills asked Sievier for a letter promising to cease the attacks, which letter was to be addressed not to Joel but to Mills. Sievier gave him the letter together with the photograph of Joel on which the moustache had been pencilled and which he thought a huge joke. Mills assured Sievier that the letter was being given in the same manner and on the same terms as had been done in Solly's case and to help him in furthering himself in Jack's favour.

Once he had secured the letter Mills, satisfied that he had preserved the friendship of two important people and knowing nothing of the pit he had dug for himself, returned with it to Joel. Joel said that he wanted a sentence added and sent Mills back with it to Sievier. By this time Joel was now being actively advised not only by his solicitor, Mr. Abrahams, but also by Charles Gill and Scotland Yard.

As soon as Mills had left, a sort of secret room was hurriedly rigged up in Joel's house by partitioning off an alcove. A panel was cut from the partition and a slit made in the red-plush covering so that anyone concealed could see and hear all that passed in the outer room. Then none other than Chief Inspector Edward Drew, formerly of Bow Street and now of Scotland Yard, was concealed behind the partition. On Mills' return he was shown into the room with the secret panel. He read over Sievier's letter while Drew listened in hiding. Joel took a copy of the letter, handed the original back to Mills who sealed it and put it in his pocket along with the photograph of Joel which he had also shown to him. Joel then gave Mills a cheque for £5000. Finally, Mills saw Sievier and gave him his own cheque for £3400 being the balance after the advance of £1000 had been deducted and also after Mills had also put into his pocket a further £600 which he said Sievier owed him. Joel knew nothing of these intermediate transactions nor that Mills had convinced Sievier the money was a loan arranged by him, nor did Sievier know anything about the letter which he had addressed to and given to Mills being read over to Joel and a copy handed to him. Nor, in fairness to Mills, did he know anything of Inspector Drew lurking in hiding.

Whether, in addition to Drew, Gill was also concealed behind the partition has never been disclosed. It seems certain, however, that Gill was in the house and that the concealment of Drew was carried out under his supervision and instructions. When Mills had gone Joel opened a bottle of champagne and it is said that he, Drew and Gill shared it. Mills afterwards declared that he was told Gill said as he lifted his glass: 'The archangel Gabriel cannot save Sievier now.'

Drew, of course, had his own reasons for disliking Sievier for he had come in for some attention from Sievier's pen and also from his superiors after his intervention in Sievier v. Duke. The manner of his execution of the warrant was calculated to bring Sievier into as much public disrepute as possible.

Just before the Atlanta Stakes was due to be run Sievier was laughing with a party of lady friends when Drew strode up to him and stood threateningly before him. Sievier ignored him for a moment or two and then, since he showed no signs of going away, said to him in cutting and insulting tones: 'I don't think I remember you.'

'I am Chief Inspector Drew of Scotland Yard and I hold a warrant for your arrest,' came the answer that rang all around the paddock.

Naturally everyone stopped to stare. They had even more cause for astonishment a moment later. Drew called up two constables who marched Sievier between them over to the iron railings. There he was pinned and Drew informed him that there he would remain until transport could be arranged for his return to London. Manacled to one of the constables like a captive beast on display he was kept in full view of the public throughout a long and blazing racing afternoon.

Drew then went off in search of Mills. When he found him, according to Mills, he jumped on to the rails at the members' enclosure and said 'I have just arrested Mr. Sievier for blackmail and want to talk to you quietly. You can give up your racing business for this afternoon as I shall want all your attention. You have a letter at home in your possession that I want and you must give it to me.'

Mills was dumbfounded for it must be remembered that throughout the negotiations no hint had been dropped to him that any prosecution was contemplated or pending.

He thought things over and then said to Drew. 'I have business here but I shall be willing, after the fourth race, to go home and to give you the letter.'

Drew returned to where Sievier was held captive on the rails of the paddock. He informed him that no transport was available to bring him to London and he would have to wait until suitable arrangements could be made. Sievier protested that his own car was in the car park and could be used. Drew ignored this and then publicly searched Sievier, finding in one of his pockets a post-dated cheque in favour of Mills which Sievier had intended to use as the first instalment in repaying what he all along maintained was a loan from Mills. This piece of evidence cannot have been an entirely reassuring find for Drew. Then Drew went off again in search of Mills to see about collecting the letter, taking him to Bow Street and obtaining a statement from him. During his absence Sievier's comments on his treatment, as might have been expected, became loud and strong and on his return Drew, whose behaviour along with that of his subordinates was now attracting considerable and unpopular public attention, capitulated. Sievier's car was sent for and he was escorted to London by two senior police officers in his own motor car driven by his own chauffeur.

On their arrival at Bow Street the charge was formally taken against Sievier and he was detained in custody for the week-end. The warrant was granted on the application of Mr. Abrahams, Joel's solicitor. Just at that moment Joel was certainly enjoying his pound of flesh.

The next day, Sunday, Sievier was visited, he says, in custody, by 'a nobleman known the world over for his sportsmanship'. He came to enquire if anything could be done for Sievier in the predicament in which he found himself and also by command of 'an exalted personage' with whom he was having luncheon and who wanted to know just what had happened. If this incident took place and it may well have done for Sievier's stories as to fact were usually accurate enough though he took care to twist the facts when he required them, no doubt the 'exalted personage' received a vivid and colourful account indeed of the facts as Sievier saw them.

The prosecution had, of course, first to bring Sievier before a magistrate to prove, or attempt to prove, that they could make out a strong enough case for him to be sent forward for a full trial before judge and jury. Whether by accident or design the magistrate in this instance was the same Mr. Marsham who had had Sievier before him on the perjury charge and who had recently fined him for sending indecent articles through the post. The case for the Crown was conducted by Charles Gill who had as his junior Archibald Bodkin who had been in charge of the perjury prosecution. Sievier's defence here was entrusted to Montague Shearman K.C. and R. D. Muir, two able and experienced police court operators.

At the end of the first day's hearing Muir applied for bail, pointing out that Sievier had a paper to carry on and that his mother, who was eighty-two years old, was very ill and that he might at any moment be called to her bedside.

Since one of the objects of the prosecution was to crush the *Winning Post* Sievier's convenience as an editor was scarcely likely to appeal to them.

Once the application was made Drew was instantly on his feet. 'I certainly oppose bail,' he said.

'On what ground? Do you say he won't turn up?' Muir asked.

'I certainly believe he won't,' Drew said.

'There is no ground for saying that,' Muir told the court. 'He has an estate in the country. I hope, sir, that you won't allow your discretion to be controlled by a police officer.'

But that was just what Marsham was determined to do. He refused bail and Sievier was removed to Brixton prison. There he remained for the first seven days of the sixteen the prosecution saw fit to drag out the preliminary hearing. He was permitted to see two visitors each day for five minutes in the presence of a warder which hardly gave him unrestricted opportunity to consult with his counsel or prepare his defence. Sellicks was left in sole charge of the *Winning Post* whose offices meanwhile were ransacked by Inspector Drew in pursuance of a search warrant he had obtained. Drew, despite Sellicks' protests, took away anything which he thought might assist the prosecution, including the photograph of Joel which had been returned by Mills to Sievier and which was in the safe.

Eventually, after tremendous protests by Shearman, Sievier was allowed to remain in custody at Bow Street and given temporary use of the doctor's emergency room. Here at least he could see solicitor and counsel in comparative peace and privacy.

As a matter of fact, and the prosecution must have known this, Sievier was the last man to have attempted to abscond his bail. Apart from the fact that it would have put him on a par with his arch-enemy Joel whom he was holding up to scandal, ridicule and disrepute for doing just that, the actor in him revelled in the sensation he was causing and was about to cause; nor would fear make him run, for his courage was never in question. When, just after he had started the *Winning Post*, some incautious scribe had rashly referred to 'Mr. Sievier's unwillingness to face the music' over something he had written, Sievier published a documented and damning refutation of the charge ending up with the proud boast, 'The amalgamated bands of Europe could not play the music Mr. Sievier would not face.' Even those who hated him were forced at one time or another to admit that this was true.

When on July 15th the prosecution closed their case Marsham fixed bail at two independent securities of £5000. If he and the prosecution hoped Sievier could not find men to stand for him in these sums they were immediately disappointed for the recognisances were forthcoming straightaway. The two sureties were Charles Blacklock, the eccentric millionaire who was one of the publishers of Bradshaw's Guide who kept a rat-fighting pit in his dining-room, and Major Henry Jasper Selwyn, a close friend of Sievier, who testified to owning forty houses at Peckham—all unencumbered—which produced £6000 a year.

The trial was fixed for the next sessions at the Old Bailey commencing the following week so Sievier had precious little time in which to gather all the evidence he wanted and to finish preparing his defence.

Shearman had conducted the case before the magistrate with great competence and Sievier always remained grateful to him for it, maintaining that it was he who had constructed a solid and indestructible foundation upon which another more brilliant man was to build. Nevertheless it was felt by both Sievier and his solicitors that a rather bigger

1	Lord Glanely.	8	Mr. Maynick Good.	15	Mr. Alec Taylor.	22	Lord D'Abernon.
2	R.S. Sievier.	9	S. Donoghue.	16	Mr. John Osborne.	23	Mr. C.T. Garland.
3	Lord Durham.	10	Mr. Sam Darling.	17	Mr. Walter Raphael.	24	Mr. A. P. Cunliffe.
4	Admiral Meux.	11	Mr. Solly Joel.	18	Mr. Henry Chaplin.	25	Sir R. B. Jardine.
5	Lord Villiers (Jersey)	12	Mr. P. P. Gilpin.	19	Maj.-Gen. Brabazon.	26	Sir Wm. Cooke.
6	Lord Lonsdale.	13	Capt. C. Boyd Rochfort.	20	Sir Walter Gilbey.	27	Sir R. Hermon Hodge.
7	Mr. Sidney Galtrey.	14	Lord Sefton.	21	Major M. Wayland.	28	Mr. James de Rothschild.

29   Mr. Fred Parker.   30   Hon. George Lambton.   31   Lord Derby.

9. Some Scalps from Newmarket

10. 'Old man' Wootton and his cronies after *Sievier v. Wootton*

gun than Shearman would be required before a judge and jury at the Old Bailey. Sievier asked for Avory who had so successfully demolished the Treasury witnesses in the perjury trial. Wontners rang Ashley, Avory's clerk, to tell him they wanted a retainer and, after enquiring the fee, told Ashley that it would be sent around immediately to Avory's chambers.

But, unknown to Wontners and Sievier, during the course of the trial Gill had been sending up distress signals. He, also, wanted a leader, and a good one and was insisting that he got one. The choice here, too, fell upon Avory. As a result of this two men arrived at almost the same time and were shown into Ashley both of them bearing retainers and cheques. Ashley solved the matter on Avory's behalf by refusing to accept either party's instructions and each side had to look again.

In Sievier's case Messrs. Wontner's decided to approach Rufus Isaacs, K.C. It was an unusual choice, for Isaacs seldom left the magnificent and lucrative practice he had built up in the civil and commercial courts to step down into the arena and take a defending brief in a criminal charge, however sensational the case or socially prominent the accused man might be. To the astonishment of many he accepted the brief marking a fee of a thousand guineas with refreshers of a hundred guineas a day. The surprise this decision caused was increased for those with long memories who recalled that Isaacs had been in Lawson Walton's chambers at the time of the Duke case and had actually held a watching brief for Major Sellar during it so that he must have been well aware of all the sultry stories concerning Sievier's past.

No one has ever really fathomed what went on behind the urbane exterior that Rufus Isaacs presented to the world. Bland, smiling, agreeable, unruffled, he made friends easily and widely but there were few who could call themselves his intimates. Strange and strong currents ran deep within him. Ambition certainly was one, a lust for power for its own sake appears to have been another; financial greed, too, seems to have played a part in his make up and, along with a genuine kindliness, perhaps an Old Testament feeling for the justness of vengeance and ultimate retribution was there as well.

For now a strange story began to go the rounds. As a young man Isaacs had been on the Stock Exchange. He encountered financial difficulties, failed to meet them and was hammered. Isaacs turned from the city to the bar. It was said then and has been repeated since that J. B. Joel had been responsible for the failure of Rufus Isaacs and his subsequent hammering. From an examination of dates it appears unlikely that this is literally true for at the time of Isaacs' failure J. B. Joel was a very young man and had scarcely the financial power to bring about his fall. It is a fact however that Harry Isaacs, an uncle of Rufus, continued in the city, eventually becoming Lord Mayor of London. He and Jack Joel were enemies and, in the words of one who knew them both, were constantly at each other's throats. The Isaacs and the Joels, as is the way with many Jewish families, had strong tribal bonds. Isaacs, though this is conjecture, probably felt a firm loyalty to his uncle and may even have been embroiled in some encounter between the two. At all events there can be no question but that his treatment of Joel throughout the hearing, especially in his cross-examination and final speech, do show a personal involvement unusual with him and inconsistent with his normal cold, detached approach. But, whatever manner he decided to adopt in his handling of a case, his was one of the clearest brains ever to be deployed at the English bar, he could grasp the essential point to put before the court on behalf of his client, display it in a few sentences and never divagate from it however complicated the facts or involved the testimony before him. Simplicity, suavity and pure intellectual ability allied to power concealed behind a persuasive manner were his weapons. He was one of the greatest advocates of that golden era of the English bar and Sievier was fortunate indeed to secure his services.

In the meantime Gill, too, had got the leader he wanted, none other than the redoubtable Sir Edward Carson, K.C., M.P., the destroyer of Oscar Wilde, the relentless cross-examiner who could matchlessly blend both strength and guile, 'Coercion' Carson of his early days in Ireland, the most powerful, successful and effective advocate to reach the English bar since the days of Sir Charles Russell. Carson was that anomaly not so rare as the writers of fiction a generation or so back cared to believe, the brave bully. He was ruthless and over-bearing in the conduct of his cases when he felt the occasion warranted it and often appeared to gain verdicts by a display of sheer elemental force. Though always and forever identified with Ulster and its struggle against the Crown he was, like Gill, a southern Irishman though, again like Gill, his character was at variance with those traits usually identified with the Irish. Unlike Gill he was a chivalrous opponent but he was dour, he hated losing and he totally lacked a sense of humour. As with every other man there was a private being behind the impressive public façade he presented to the world. Of tremendous height he had the face and features of a prize-fighter and the hands of an artist. These contradictions may go in some way towards explaining the dichotomy of the man. For, with all his forcefulness, brutality and apparent staying power, he had a delicate constitution and a nervous stomach or thought he had for he was something of a hypochondriac. He was a very great advocate, perhaps the greatest of them all. He had more finesse than Russell, more consistency than F. E. Smith, more human sympathy than Isaacs and more sheer genius in cross-examination than the whole lot of them rolled up together. He may well have owed this latter quality to his artist's vision which enabled him to penetrate into the very heart of a witness when the elemental in him gave him the ruthlessness necessary to strip that heart and every other treasured secret bare before a court.

Carson and Gill were old companions in arms. Gill liked nothing better than to be led by him. Together they made a formidable pair.

This was to be indeed a clash of Titans. When to the already sensational matter of the case itself was added the fact that it was to be fought out between the two leaders of the bar and that there was known to be personal enmity between Gill and Sievier, Isaacs and Joel, it was no wonder public interest and excitement grew daily more intense.

Then, to crown the whole thing and finally to put the stamp of important on the proceedings, the Lord Chief Justice, Lord Alverstone, signified his intention of coming down to the Old Bailey and hearing the case himself.

22

Rex v. Sievier

❧❧❧❧❧❧

On the day the trial opened all the approaches to the court were crammed with a crowd struggling to get in. Sievier, turned out immaculately as usual by his valet in top-hat and morning coat, drove in his carriage to the Old Bailey. The crowd was such that it had been arranged he should make his entrance by a side door so as to avoid delays and demonstrations. A policeman on duty not recognizing him refused to allow him beyond the doorway and enquired who he was and what was his business. Sievier's reply has passed into history. 'Just as you like, of course,' he said. 'But you can't damn well get on without me. I'm the bloody prisoner!'

The Lord Chief Justice took his seat at 10.35 a.m. and Sievier surrendered to his bail. The charges of 'feloniously, with menaces attempting to obtain from Jack Barnato Joel the sum of £5000 with intent to steal the same and for indirectly proposing to Jack Barnato Joel to abstain from publishing certain matters with a view to extort money,' was read over to him. He pleaded 'Not guilty' in a firm voice to the charges.

Isaacs immediately applied that all the prosecution witnesses, save only the one actually giving evidence, be excluded from the court. The object of this was obvious. Mills, Bendon and Joel, if not accomplices were very near to being so, and were they to hear each other's evidence might well adapt their own to fall in with it. Once excluded they could not know just what had been testified to or denied.

For Isaacs had already determined on his strategy. As usual with him he had brought the case down to one bare essential. Joel had tried to trap Sievier, the rich man had used his wealth to ensnare the poor one and wreak his vengeance upon him. The initiative had all along come from Joel and he had caught Sievier in the web his malice and riches had spun. That was Isaacs' case and every question he asked was directed to proving it.

Carson expressed surprise at the application but Carson's fairness as a prosecutor was never in doubt. He did not make any objection and Joel with the others left the court.

Then, rising to his great height, serried ranks of counsel about him on the benches in a court-room crowded to the last inch and with people still pressing for entrance from the corridors, Carson began slowly and impressively to open the case for the Crown. The most sensational of all Sievier's many *causes célèbres* had begun.

For now everything was at stake—his newly won reinstatement on the Turf, the paper of which he was so proud and which he had built from nothing, his popularity, his living, and, most of all, his liberty. Were he to be convicted he would face a sentence of at least eight years and probably more. He was forty-eight years of age and such a spell in the prisons of the time had broken hardier spirits even than his.

Yet he was probably the coolest man in the court. His nerve on this, as on other occasions, never failed him. He stood in the dock giving every appearance of enjoying his position in the centre of the stage, smiling at his friends and nodding to acquaintances.

Carson's opening, delivered fairly but with all the weight his powerful oratory could give it and stressing the importance of the case not only to those concerned but to the public at large, lasted an hour and forty minutes in the course of which he read out the letter Sievier had written, the letter upon which much of the case for the prosecution rested. It ran as follows:

Dear Charlie,—Many thanks for the money, which I will repay as agreed. I ought not to be pressed for ready but I have not had a winning week for some time. With respect to our conversation about J. B. Joel, and your request that I might leave his name out of the paper, you may take it from me that I have now done with that subject except in the ordinary way of referring to his horses when they are running. I have said all that can be said. I am glad you did not ask me to leave him alone earlier. If it is any pleasure to him to know it I have completed my remarks regarding him, and if you wish show him this letter.

At the request of Mills the following sentence was added during the time the secret room was being rigged up for the concealment of Inspector Drew: 'And I will not, as you say, molest him again.'

This letter, even with the additional sentence, was nothing like as incriminating as the prosecution could have wished. It was addressed to Mills, not Joel, it also contained an undertaking to repay and it referred to the request to leave Joel alone as coming from Mills and Mills only. This was vitally important for Sievier since his explanation of the whole affair was that he was dealing with Mills and no one else and that he understood the arrangement to be identical with that come to in the case of Solly which Mills had handled and in which no money had passed.

Bendon, the man who had started it all back in April, was the first witness called by the Crown. Isaacs' cross-examination of him, smooth, polished and exact, went a long way towards establishing those facts and a great deal more with them.

'Were there at one time attacks on Mr. Solly Joel in the *Winning Post*?' he asked.

'Yes.'

'And were you anxious to stop them?'

'Yes.'

'Did you succeed in doing so?'

'Yes.'

'Did you go to Mills for this purpose?'

'Yes. I knew Mills had a great deal of influence with Sievier.'

'After Mills had seen Sievier did the attacks stop?'

'Yes.'

'And was there any question of money in that transaction?'

'No. None whatsoever.'

Already out of the mouth of a prosecution witness Isaacs had made three important gains. He had established that Mills and Sievier were friends and that Mills had great influence with Sievier and that the transaction with Solly was an innocent one. Sievier's case in that regard had been confirmed and corroborated and by a witness called by the Crown.

Isaacs had a soft, mellow, persuasive voice. It was seldom raised. He appeared at times almost to bewitch the witness into giving the answers he wanted. Now, with Bendon, he was at his friendliest and most charming, in which attitude he was, those who knew him maintained, often most dangerous to an opponent's case. It was no part of his tactics to impute blame to Bendon or to suggest that he had been in any way involved in Joel's machinations. The quiet, innocent-sounding questions continued: 'When you saw Joel in April had any suggestion of a threat been made by Sievier?'

'No. None at all.'

'And did you tell Joel that Sievier was a villainous scoundrel and that you were afraid of him?'

'Certainly not. That is an absolute fabrication. I have never been afraid of any man in my life.'

Here was another great gain. The first prosecution witness was flatly contradicting what Joel had sworn to in the magistrate's court and was, in effect, calling him a liar.

But now Isaacs was approaching the very core of his cross-examination, the area of greatest danger and that in which, too, the greatest successes might be made. He did not burke the issue but began it by asking flatly the famous question on which the whole of the defence hung. It appears now to have been putting a lot of his case at risk but Isaacs had the police court evidence before him in which Bendon had made his distaste for the entire affair very clear and he may too have had other sources of knowledge as to what the answer was likely to be. Still in the same flowing, conversational tones he asked Bendon:

'Had you any notion while these negotiations were going on that a trap was being laid for Mr. Sievier?' He paused there for a second and then repeated quietly and impressively in a silent court 'Trap is my word.'

'When I spoke to Mr. Joel at his house.'

The answer was oblique and hedging but it gave enough encouragement to Isaacs to press on. 'You can explain as much as you like afterwards,' he said. 'I only want you to answer my question. Had you any notion?'

'I suspected something but I should like to tell you when.'

'When?'

'At the interview at his house, the second interview.'

'That's the interview you had at Grosvenor Square. You thought then, did you, that Mr. Joel was laying a trap for Mr. Sievier?'

'I did.'

So there it was. Another piece in the confirmation of the prisoner's story had slipped into place. Isaacs went on to consolidate his gains and to advance his case even further. 'And did you tell Mills that?' he asked.

'I told him exactly word for word what had taken place at the interview with Joel.'

But Isaacs knew that more had passed between these two and he wanted to have it from Bendon's reluctant lips. It had to be done step by step lest an incautious question should bring the wrong answer. 'What I want to know,' was his next question, 'did you convey to Mills?'

'I tried to.'

'You tried to convey to him what?'

'To be very careful.'

Here Alverstone intervened. 'I must have what you said,' he told the witness ' "Tried to convey" will not do. If you are going to use this, Mr. Isaacs, you must get it more distinctly.'

This was just what Isaacs wanted and Bendon, seeing no way out, then told the court: 'I will tell you the exact words. I told him the conversation I had had with Mr. Joel: that I did not like it, that I thought it was a very dirty business and I would have nothing to do with it. He said "You are quite right. I will see to it." I then said, "Be very careful Charlie, you are not dealing with Solly." '

Here indeed was a bonus for the defence elicited by Isaacs' careful and skilful questions. The whole sordid plan was out into the open now and at the very outset of the case. Isaacs went on to put the finishing touches to the picture he had painted. He asked Bendon, 'The "dirty business" that you refer to was the laying of the trap, was it not?'

'Principally.'

'But the result of it was, at any rate, that Mills then went into the business, so far as you were concerned, warned of what was going to happen?'

'In the words I have told you.'

'Did you think Mr. Solly Joel was more to be trusted?'

'Well, we knew him better.'

The next witness for the Crown was the vital one, the man who had carried through all the negotiations, Charles Anthony Mills, who gave his occupation as a professional backer of horses.

No one knew just what Mills had been up to during those few days late in June when he had been coming and going between Joel and Sievier and, by the time he went into the box, it seems that he scarcely knew himself. All it appears he did know is that, like many another man who has tried to serve two masters, he had failed both and was likely to come badly out of the adventure whatever the verdict. In his examination-in-chief he gave his version of the events which confirmed that Sievier had made no move after the April conversation and that in June, eight weeks later, the initiative had come entirely from Joel. But it was clear that he was turning further and further against Sievier for he swore that he had rung up Joel in Sievier's presence and said: 'Sievier is here and he wants £5000. He will not take a shilling less. You had better think it over. He says that if you do not consent he will put some very hot stuff in the paper including the warrant issued for your arrest and that he has two murderers between which he will put you.'

It was obvious that this witness required firmer handling in cross-examination than the friendly methods which had paid so well with Bendon. Primarily Mills was concerned to protect himself but he now also appeared anxious to do Sievier, his erstwhile friend, all the harm he could. In attempting this he had in his evidence-in-chief contradicted certain things he had said in the police court.

Isaacs, still suave, but with more hostility showing, set about destroying his credibility. He did so superbly, building bit by bit the essentials of his case at the same time.

'You wanted to stand in well with Joel?' he asked.

'Yes, as with anyone else I do business with. I had no idea I was doing anything discreditable.'

'Did Mr. Bendon say anything about the trap that was being laid for Sievier?'

'He said it was a dirty business.'

'Mr. Bendon just handed the matter over to you as one honourable man might to another?'

'He did tell me to be careful but he did not mention Solly.'

So now Mills was contradicting Bendon. The prosecution witnesses could scarcely be said to be unanimous in their testimony and the policy of keeping them out of court was paying handsome dividends to the defence.

'Do you consider you had a great deal of influence over Sievier?' Isaacs went on.

'Yes, we were very good friends.'

'Sievier kept Mr. Solly Joel's name out of the paper to oblige you?'

'Yes.'

'And did you say at the police court that Sievier might have told you that if you wished he would keep Mr. J. B. Joel's name out of the paper —that he would do it to oblige you?'

'Yes, I did.'

'And did you also say that you told Sievier you could get him a decent bit of money out of it and that Sievier said it was not a matter of money?'

'I did but I do not now believe that Sievier did say that.'

'You have thought it over since the police court proceedings. Have you talked to Mr. Solly Joel about it?'

'Yes, in front of other people.'

'Have you heard of the incident at Windsor races where there had been hot blood between Sievier and Joel as to the bidding for a horse?'

'Yes.'

'Mr. Sievier was very angry about it and said that he would publish an attack in the paper?'

'Yes.'

'Did you say to Sievier, "He wants a letter to say you will not put him in the paper again" and did he say, "I have already promised that?"'

'He may have done so.'

'Did you say "Write a letter to say so. It will show Joel the influence I have over you"?'

'I am certain I did not.'

'At the police court did you say "Possibly I did say so"?'

'I am now quite certain I did not.'

'Your evidence has become stronger against Sievier since?'

'There may be a doubt about it. I am not sure I did not say it.'

'Do you remember mentioning Mr. Leopold de Rothschild to Mr. Sievier?'

'Yes.'

'Did you say that Mr. Joel told you that Mr. de Rothschild had said that this matter must stop?'

'Yes.'

'Mr. Rothschild is a man much respected in racing and other circles and what he said would have great influence with Mr. Sievier?'

'Yes.'

'And did it have?'

'Yes.'

'The cheque for £1000 was lent by you to Sievier in the belief that Mr. Joel would keep his word and if he did not do so you would only have a claim for it against Sievier?'

'I was willing to take the risk. I told Sievier it was on account of the £5000.'

'You have never looked on this transaction as blackmailing, have you?'

'No.'

'Will you pledge your oath that Mr. Sievier said he was going to publish the woodcut between two murderers?'

'I understood him to say so but I may have been mistaken.'

'Did you say to Sievier you wanted the additional words put in the letter and did he say "well if it pleases you I will"?'

'Yes.'

'Let us come to the time when you took the letter to Mr. Joel. You did not know that a policeman was concealed in the room?'

'I had not the slightest suspicion.'

'Did you say to Joel, "It is a dirty business. Sievier is a villainous scoundrel"?'

'No, I did not. It was Mr. Joel who said "Sievier is a venomous scoundrel to the last".'

'It is suggested that you used these words. That's a lie, is it?'

'It is a lie.'

So now Mills, too, was contradicting Joel.

Mills left the box about as confused and discredited as a vital witness of fact in an important case could well be.

Then the moment came for which everyone had been waiting. Jack Barnato Joel was called to the box. In answer to Carson he gave his evidence-in-chief convincingly enough but he had to admit that it was he who had sent for Mills in June and told him to approach Sievier.

By this time the story of the personal enmity between Joel and Isaacs was common knowledge. As Isaacs rose to cross-examine there was silence in the court like that which falls in a theatre before the rising of the curtain. The comparison is exact, for drama is what those present had come to see. They were not to be disappointed. For now, for once, Isaacs threw away the velvet glove and applied the iron hand. Gone, for perhaps the only time in his career, was the icy detachment that was the hallmark of his advocacy. With Joel before him in the witness-box he became the impassioned defender displaying a force and vehemence towards the witness that observers had never seen in him before. And he wasted no time in getting to grips.

'You knew that Sievier had been losing money throughout June?'

'I knew he was broke, yes.'

'Did you think it a favourable moment to dangle money before his eyes and a good opportunity of getting evidence on which to prosecute him?'

'I had no idea of it. I first thought that if I could get evidence I would prosecute when the threat was made to publish my picture between two murderers.'

'At the police court you said that throughout the days of June 22nd to 27th you intended to pay the money provided you got what you wanted and that what you wanted was evidence on which to base a prosecution?'

'There is a slight mistake there.'

'You said you wanted to prosecute, not to give hush money?'

'Yes. There was never sufficient material on which to prosecute.'

'Well, I'm glad to hear you say that. I rather agree.'

'Until I had the letter there was not sufficient evidence.'

'At the first interview with Mills did you ask him to see what Sievier would take?'

'I did not use those words. I asked him to see what he could do.'

'Did you expect that Sievier would want money?'

'Yes.'

'Did you then hope to get evidence against him, so as to prosecute him?'

'Yes, if the opportunity occurred. He had been persecuting me for four years.'

'Did you know that Mills was a great friend of Sievier and possessing great influence over him?'

'Yes.'

'You were using Mills. Do you consider that was a dishonourable thing to do?'

'It was an unfortunate thing.'

For the first time in the case Isaacs' voice rose. 'What!' he exclaimed on receiving this answer. Then he looked sternly at the witness. In stronger, more menacing tones he repeated: 'Was it not a dishonourable thing?'

Joel seemed almost to shrink from him in the box.

'It was an unfortunate thing,' he repeated, and, then, as if to try to explain away his conduct to the jury, 'I had to do it. I had been perse-cuted in the most terrible way, and any other man would have done the same. Sievier would not have trusted anybody but Mills.' The answer only made his actions appear worse. Now Isaacs really had him on the run.

'It was a trap?'

'He had threatened to publish my picture.'

'Where was the Inspector concealed?'

'In the wall, behind the curtain. There was a dummy door. Mills was perfectly innocent in the matter.'

'You read the documents aloud. To whom?'

'To Mills.'

'Why? What was Mills to think you read it to him for?'

'He had brought it. I can't help what he thought. I read it so that Drew could hear.'

'Are you quite clear that Mills said it was a blackmailing business and that Sievier was a villainous scoundrel?'

'Quite'.

'Do you know that Mills says it is a lie?'

'I am sorry, he has made a mistake.'

'And when Bendon denies that he ever said that Sievier is a scoundrel and he was afraid of him he is telling a lie too?'

'Bendon did say that and to many people. He is scared of him.'

'Mills says that you told him Mr. Leopold de Rothschild had said that these attacks must stop.'

'I have no recollection of mentioning Mr. Leopold Rothschild's name.'

'So Mills is lying here, too?'

'He is mistaken.'

Joel's stature and credibility were diminishing with every answer. Isaacs spared him nothing. The Murray incident was put to him.

'Did you give Murray money?'

'Yes.'

'Was it given to injure Sievier?'

'Certainly not.'

'Do you know that Mr. Sievier charged you with giving Murray £200 for that purpose? Did you read the article of December 17th 1904 in the *Winning Post*?'

'I could not say.' This was a singularly disingenuous reply since Joel's entire complaint had been that Sievier had been making life hell for him in the *Winning Post* with his scurrilous attacks.

Isaacs handed him a copy of the paper.

'Yes, I did,' Joel continued when he had glanced at it. 'It was sent to my wife anonymously.'

'Did you in fact pay him £200?'

'Yes. Murray blackmailed me. I paid it on three separate occasions. Murray afterwards admitted to my solicitor that it was a conspiracy with Sievier.'

'In that event why did you bring no action against Mr. Sievier? Did not Mr. Sievier challenge you to bring an action for libel as to this Murray incident?'

'It was a general challenge.' It was no answer. It was an excuse and Joel's excuses were becoming almost pathetic.

Isaacs then turned to the incident in South Africa. 'Now, with reference to the South African episode there is no doubt that your bail was estreated?'

'No.'

'How much was it?'

'I don't know.'

'Do you tell the jury that you don't know whether it was £1 or £5000?'

'Yes, or ten millions. I never enquired.'

'Do you know that it was £4000?'

'I heard so at the police court.'

'Have you been in South Africa since?'

'No.'

'Did you promise Mills anything for his trouble?'

'No. It is an infamous suggestion.'

'You get him to get his friend into trouble without giving him anything. Have you bet with him?'

'No. My brother puts money on for me, and I don't care who he puts it with.'

'Has Mills ever complained to you of your conduct?'

'No. I expect he will never speak to me again.'

'It was a dirty business?'

'It was a very dirty business on my part to put him, an innocent man, into this affair.'

Certainly, if Isaacs had wanted revenge, he had got it. And more was to come before the case was out.

The three main prosecution witnesses had now been heard. All had been to some extent discredited, but more important, they had contradicted each other on one or more material facts and sometimes themselves as well.

After they had gone Inspector Drew told of his hiding place and agreed that Sievier's first words on his arrest were: 'Don't catch hold of me. I absolutely deny the charge.' He also had to explain that the two men whom Mills had described as murderers were in fact a bank manager and a grocer's assistant charged with embezzlement. The defence made further gains with the witnesses called from bookmakers and moneylenders to prove Sievier's insolvency. One and all of them testified in cross-examination that Sievier always met his obligations and that they would be glad to do business with him again. One bookmaker, indeed, told the court that in the last account he had rendered Sievier there had been a mistake of £75 in Sievier's favour and that he had pointed it out and insisted upon paying up. But it was from the representative of the National Provincial Bank that the most useful evidence in Sievier's favour came. He told Gill about Sievier's indebtedness to the Bank at the time but, on Isaacs asking him what Sievier's reputation with them was, he said: 'Mr. Sievier always keeps his engagements and we trust him implicitly.' He was also able to say in answer to Isaacs that Sievier had immediately cashed Mills' cheque for £1000 before the remainder of the money came in, thus refuting the prosecution's suggestion that all the money came directly from Joel and, as it were, was tendered together in exchange for the letter. So, when the Crown closed its case, Sievier and his advisors had good reason to be pleased with the way things had gone. They had advanced a long way towards establishing their own case out of the mouths of the prosecution's witnesses. But Sievier, of course, had still to go into the box to face what appeared certain to be a terrible cross-examination from Carson.

Isaacs himself may well have had his misgivings about what Sievier would say in evidence for no one ever knew what Sievier would do or say next and Isaacs' case was now down to one net point—the trap—and very finely balanced upon it. The next morning he called his unpredictable client and watched him being sworn.

As usual Sievier was completely self-possessed. He gave his answers in his examination-in-chief clearly and firmly and with all the emphasis of his actor's training. Nor did he divagate from the case Isaacs had presented. He had all along insisted, he said, that he wanted no money from Joel and had told Mills that if he couldn't get it for him he'd have to try Mr. Bass. Here the Lord Chief intervened to ask if Mr. Bass was a money-lender. No, Sievier, assured him, he was a brewer. He was, of course, the same Mr. Bass who had bought Sceptre. Sievier was able, too, to produce the receipt for the block of Joel's picture made in 1905 and he denied explicitly that he had ever told Mills that he was going to publish it between two murderers. Joel's picture had appeared in the *Police Gazette* he said, and agreed he had told Mills this, 'amongst a fearful set of people who might have been murderers.' He also said that he had told Mills that the description of Joel which had appeared in the *Police Gazette* had been 'the best he had ever seen in a few words' which brought laughter in court and did little to comfort Joel. By and large his examination-in-chief did not go too badly at all. But then, when it was finished, he had to face Carson.

Carson's very presence towards a witness was menacing and overbearing, the great height, the heavy lowering features and the immense out-thrust jaw appearing to demand subjection. But no man then or thereafter ever succeeded in over-bearing Sievier. Once a witness lost his primal fear of Carson the advocate was to some extent disarmed, and Sievier never feared any man. Carson appears to have realized this and the thundering attack expected by many failed to materilize. It is one measure of Carson's greatness that he could adapt his methods to the occasion and the man. Now he seems to have divined that the best way to deal with Sievier was to play upon his vanity, to lead him on to his own destruction and to confound him and his case from his own lips.

He very nearly succeeded. He began with Bendon and immediately inflicted great damage on the case Isaacs had so carefully built. Isaacs had never suggested that Bendon was a rogue, in fact it had been part of his case that Bendon had come out of the matter the best of the lot. Sievier was, however, still boiling with resentment against everyone who had given evidence against him and was determined to give that resentment expression.

'Mr. Bendon has grossly perjured himself?' Carson suggested to him. 'Undoubtedly.'

'He was the man who you had selected to get you £2000 on April 29th?' 'Yes.'

'You never had any dispute with him?' 'None.'

'And Mills said Bendon is prejudiced against Mr. Joel?' 'I heard his evidence on that point.'

'Can you give any reason why he should commit perjury with a view to injuring you?' 'I don't think Bendon is in a conspiracy but is mistaken.'

'Is he a respectable man or an awful scoundrel?'

Now Sievier appeared to see the dangers into which he was heading and began to mend his position. 'He is neither the one nor the other so far as I know. I would give him a good character.'

'Can you give any reason then why he should have invented the story that you asked him to get the money from Mr. Joel and said you would withhold his name from the paper if it was given?'

'No. I know I never said it.'

'He must be an awful liar?'

'Either he is or I am.' Which candid admission caused laughter to run around the court.

During this cross-examination one person, at least, thought that Sievier was not being handled with sufficient roughness. He did not like the sympathy which the prisoner appeared to be eliciting with his presence and ready answers and he feared for the outcome of the case. This was Charles Gill. He plucked at Carson's gown time and again muttering to his leader: 'You are not being severe enough, Ned.' He was to repeat this with variations as the cross-examination proceeded.

11a. Sievier at tea in the garden of Tilton Lodge

11b. Sievier in old age. Taken on the racecourse
shortly before he died. The last picture

After Bendon, Carson passed to Mills. His task all along was to lessen the impact of Isaacs' case of the trap and to show that, trap or not, Sievier knew very well what he was doing and had used Mills when Mills thought he was using him. But Isaacs, as has been seen, had left several options open with Mills. He had hinted, if no more, that Mills was not as innocent as he seemed in the matter and had been gradually building up an enmity to Sievier which had coloured his evidence.

Sievier for his part did believe that Mills had been in the plot against him. He never spoke to Mills again after this case and in the future was to do everything he could to injure him and to hold him up to ridicule so that his answers probably do reflect his true feelings in the matter though they did his case great harm.

'Mr. Mills is a friend of yours?' Carson said.

'He was.'

'And do you suggest he, too, is committing perjury?'

'I certainly suggest it.'

'Had you ever had a dispute with Mr. Mills?'

'No.'

'Why do you suggest he kept back Mr. Joel's name?'

'Probably he thought he could get the money from Joel and he knew I would not take it from him.'

'Why do you suggest Mills said you would not take less than £5000?'

'He either did it on his own initiative or on instructions from Joel. I knew nothing of it.'

'Joel and Mills were conspirators against you?'

'Yes, manufacturing evidence against me.'

This was indeed a most damaging suggestion for it had never been introduced into the case before nor suggested to Mills in cross-examination. Carson, at his quietest and most persuasive, was going a long way to winning back all the ground his own witnesses had lost and towards convicting Sievier out of his own mouth. Once he had the advantage he was quick to exploit it. But, despite Gill's urging, he retained the conversational method which was serving him so well in trapping Sievier into admissions.

'That has not been suggested before?' he said quietly.

In reply he received another answer damaging to the witness and helpful to his case.

'No, but I suggest it now.' If he did, why hadn't he told Isaacs about it?

'Why, now, are you making these suggestions that have never been made before?'

'My suggestion is that either he did this at the instigation of Joel or on his own initiative to settle matters between us and that having done it he sticks to it.' It was the best answer he could have made in the circumstances. He may well have seen the perilous seas he was approaching.

'So your opinion of Mills is very low?'

'He is either a blackguard or a coward. A blackguard if he did it at Joel's instigation, or a coward not to admit it if he did it on his own initiative.'

'He was doing a bit of blackmailing on his own account?'

'Yes.'

'Mills was pressing money on you and you were trying to resist it?'

'Oh! dear no. Oh! Lord no!'

There was more laughter here but some of the sympathy had gone from it.

'When Mills met you, did he say that Joel wanted a little more in the letter before he paid the money?'

'No.'

'Did he show you the cheque?'

'No.'

'Another lie?'

'Yes.'

'It is a mere coincidence that the letter and the cheque came together?'

'No, I think it was a piece of manœuvring. It was a slap-jammer stroke on the trap.'

In his answers to the last few questions Sievier had gone some way towards restoring his position and Carson's biographer says that, in the end, counsel had failed to shake him. Be that as it may he had certainly given Carson a great deal of material upon which to base his final speech and this was material Carson was unlikely to overlook.

When the question of the counsel's addresses to the jury came up Carson pointed out that since Isaacs had put in certain documents he had therefore lost his right to be the last to address the jury. A legal argument followed and, after it, Carson said that he thought in all fairness he should waive his objection and allow Isaacs the right to the last address.

'Thank you very much, Sir Edward,' remarked Sievier from the dock, bowing towards the barrister as he did so.

'I want no thanks from you,' growled Carson back at him. Perhaps he, too, thought that he had not shaken the prisoner and was wondering, with Gill, if other tactics might have paid better. At all events there was no lack of severity in his final speech to the jury. He went immediately to the contradictions in Sievier's cross-examination.

'We are now asked to believe,' he said, 'that this prosecution is the outcome of a conspiracy between Mr. Mills, the old friend of twenty years, the man Mr. Isaacs said had had a dirty trick played on him by Joel, and Mr. Bendon, the man described as having a prejudice against Mr. Joel. Mr. Sievier has been defended by one of the ablest counsel at the bar, whose powers of cross-examination we must all admire, and he has not suggested such a case by a single question. The whole case of the last two days has been abandoned at the eleventh hour. . . . Are you going to lay it down that the prosecution must fail because the evidence has been obtained in an unfortunate way? If you do, this day will be a day of *Magna Charta* for blackmailers.' He finished his address by saying, and it is significant that he thought it necessary to say it: 'Do not let any popularity of the prisoner and the cheers of the people outside or inside the court prevent you from doing your duty. Mr. Sievier may or may not be popular and Mr. Joel unpopular. You must act without any reference to that and do your duty.'

Isaacs in his reply met the challenge head on and turned it round on the prosecution.

'It was unfair of my friend', he said, 'to wring from the prisoner an answer to the effect that Mr. Mills and Mr. Joel had conspired against him. Prejudice! There has been enough prejudice introduced against Mr. Sievier in the matter. What was it that brought Mills as a witness of truth into this court? The accused when in the box was forced to say that Mills was either a blackguard or a coward. Sir Edward Carson in his opening said that Mills' conduct was open to criticism. The truth is that Mills' whole fortune depends on the Joels. He wants their valuable racing tips and that is why he has coloured his evidence against Sievier. . . . Sievier's bank manager has given him a testimonial of which any man might be proud and this is the man who is held up before you as a blackmailer. . . . As to Inspector Drew being concealed in the room . . . in this case a trap was laid to induce a man to commit acts which could be made to look like a crime.' Isaacs' voice rose and everyone in court knew against whom the coming passage was directly aimed. 'It was a dirty, disgusting, disgraceful transaction from which every man's mind will recoil with horror. I can hardly restrain my feelings when discussing it. The proposal in the case came from Joel not from the man in the dock. When it is considered what this case means, one trembles at the power of money in the hands of an unscrupulous person who does not hesitate to descend to dirty tricks. Can you imagine a man with the power of money behind him knowing that another man who he hated was hard up and very broke. Imagine him getting hold of that man's best friend and trusted confidant, setting him to work to make him take gold, forcing him to take it and then arresting him, prosecuting him, bringing him to the Old Bailey and trying to send him to durance vile for goodness knows how many years. I am not going to appeal for sympathy for Sievier or for mercy. Sievier is not on his trial for the articles he had published in the *Winning Post*. Some minds and those not the most delicate may disapprove of them but Sievier is ready to answer for them to Joel elsewhere and has already issued a challenge to him to bring them before another tribunal. Remembering the dirty trick that has been played and remembering all the evidence in the case I submit that I am entitled to ask you to acquit Sievier of this foul charge.'

At the end of this address Joel was seen to be sitting with his head in his hands. Isaacs was repaying with interest the injury there.

Lord Alverstone, the Lord Chief Justice, was not regarded by the galaxy of brilliant minds that then practised before him as being one of the best lawyers or cleverest men to have occupied that high office. Carson despised him and said so openly, on one occasion at least to his face, and his summing up has been branded by Carson's biographer as colourless. It is sometimes overlooked, however, that a clear mind and a cool head may be better attributes in a judge than brains, and that a colourless summing up if fair and adequate may do much to restore level thinking to minds bemused by powerful forensic oratory. In effect Alverstone put the issues fairly and clearly before the jury. They were only out for an hour and twelve minutes, a short time indeed for a case of this magnitude.

When they returned the foreman in answer to the Clerk of Arraigns said: 'We find the prisoner Not Guilty.'

In anticipation of the verdict every approach to the Old Bailey was crammed with people. The court itself was packed to suffocation. Immediately it was heard, cheering broke out inside the court which the officials were powerless to stop. It was taken up and continued down the passages and into the streets outside. Hats were thrown in the air, the crowd milled round the entrance to the court waiting to greet Sievier in person. They swarmed everywhere giving the most violent demonstrations of delight. In the court itself J. B. Booth, a member of the *Pink 'Un* staff and a chronicler of those times, saw men, 'Total strangers, shaking one another by the hand and patting one another's backs in an ecstasy of merriment.'

It was suggested to Sievier that in order to avoid exaggerating the demonstration which was beginning to take on almost the dimensions of a riot he should leave by a side door. He agreed to do this. His brougham was brought round. The driver could not resist giving vent to his feelings by shouting 'I've got him here.' Then he was borne away through the crowds while he beamed, took off his hat and waved to them on his way back to Hobart Place and celebration.

Someone wired the verdict to the clerk of the course at Goodwood who passed it on and as it became known a wave of cheering broke out there, too. This was taken up from the cheaper rings until it spread to all the enclosures where men took off their hats and cheered themselves hoarse over and over again. Lord Rosebery, who was there, says he never has seen anything like it on an English racecourse. The King, who was present, too, asked the reason for the extraordinary demonstration. On being told that it was because Bob Sievier had been declared 'Not Guilty', he expressed the view (or Sievier says he was told he did) that there could have been no other verdict.

It was Sievier's greatest triumph. It set the seal on his popularity. He was at the very peak of his career.

23

Warlingham and Wootton

꘏꘏꘏꘏꘏꘏

Now the great days really began. Power and fame and money were all at his command, for the *Winning Post* went from strength to strength after the Joel case. Ironically enough Joel, having had a winner of his hissed and booed on the racecourse shortly after the case, won the St. Leger with Your Majesty and finished the season leading owner for the first time. Having routed him and held him up to the public odium he felt he deserved, Sievier appeared largely to lose interest in Joel, contenting himself with the occasional contemptuous reference to him and 'his groom' Morton.

More than ever now he was a man about whom legends gathered and, of course, he took care to foster them. He threw a roast duck out of a window at the Savoy and threatened to throw the chef, whom he summoned to his table, after it if the next one was not cooked to his liking. Being temporarily short of money at Monte Carlo he was said to have extracted the pellets from the cartridges of a well-known pigeon-shot and then laid heavily against his killing his bird. The story, which widely went the rounds, was sometimes ascribed to his early days in Australia. It was not one likely to please him for he hated anything that reflected on his sportsmanship but it may just be true all the same for a famous personality who knew him well has truly remarked of him that he was a man who when he had money did everything right and when he had not did everything wrong.

But mostly those days he had money enough even for his demanding needs. He was all over the Continent in places where the best and the worst people were to be seen, Monte Carlo, Pau, Baden Baden, Biarritz, Deauville. Wherever he went he was recognized, flattered and courted by both men and women. His liaisons became even more open and numerous. He flaunted them and loved the notoriety they brought. One evening at Deauville he asked a pretty girl to leave the roulette table and join him in the baccarat room. 'I'm sorry,' she said. 'I only play one game.'

'That's a pity,' he answered in tones that resounded round the gilded halls, 'For I play lots of 'em!'

In England his bases were still Hobart Place and Hillmorton but, never able to remain long in one place at a time, there, too, he moved about and during the hunting season was to be seen out at one time or another with almost every pack in the country.

Out hunting he made another friend, Lord Howard de Walden, and the friendship thus formed proved a beneficial and lasting one.

The children were largely left to look after themselves. Gogo, who was pretty and precocious, was promoted to playing hostess at the week-end parties at Hillmorton during the all-too-frequent intervals when she had been asked to leave one school and was waiting to go to another. Her adolescence, in her own way, was as tempestuous as her father's, much of whose formidable temperament she inherited. The expulsions and escapades became so many and so flagrant that eventually a cousin asked and was given permission to try to find a suitable school for the girl where she might have a reasonable chance to steady down.

The choice fell on an establishment in Brighton and the cousin brought Gogo there to be interviewed by the headmistress. At first all went well. Gogo, warned to behave and demurely dressed, sat silent and apparently submissive while her elders discussed her curriculum. At the close of the interview the headmistress turned to her and said: 'Now dear, I'm sure we shall get on very well, but tell me, just why did you leave your last school?'

Gogo looked her straight in the eye exactly as her father did when about to say something really outrageous. 'I left because I was rude to the headmistress,' she said. 'She was a frosty-faced old bitch—just like you!'

Gogo finished her schooling with the horses and grooms at Hillmorton where, superbly mounted by her father's money, few could catch her across a country. Robbie, too, inherited his father's eye for horseflesh and some, at any rate, of his ability in horse-management. But contrary strains were at work in his character; he was artistic and musical and, ultimately to his own disaster, had little of Sievier's mental toughness and resilience.

With all his other activities Sievier was still writing and was still very actively an editor. The *Winning Post*, despite the fact that Sellicks frequently stood in for him during his absences abroad, never lost its touch or the verve that was Sievier's own and which stamped it as unique in sporting journalism. It went everywhere, and when King Edward VII died in 1910 he devoted a whole issue with every column edged in black to a fulsome eulogy of the late monarch. This was printed on vellum and a few copies were specially bound in tooled leather. One of these was sent by him to the new King as a tribute to his late father and was graciously accepted. Soon afterwards came a request from Queen Alexandra for a copy and a third was presented to the Prince of Wales. The letters of acknowledgment and thanks were some of his proudest possessions.

In 1909 he published a volume of travel essays and re-printed articles called *East is East and West is West* and in the same year started a magazine called *Sievier's Monthly*. This was similar in form to such monthlies as *The Strand* and *The Windsor* then at the height of their fame and popularity; in content it was sporting and slightly salacious, and in reality it was a vehicle to carry a racing serial written by Sievier and called *Warned Off*. This was modestly advertised in the *Winning Post* by its author as 'the most picturesque racing novel ever written.' Later it, like the autobiography, was published in book form and, also like its predecessor, enjoyed considerable critical attention and good sales, going into several impressions.

Warned Off is an undisguised racing *roman à clef*. Like the autobiography, it appears to have been written with the object of paying off certain scores still owing after a *cause célèbre*—in this case the Joel prosecution. The villains are 'Charlie Miles', a well-known backer of horses whom it does not take a great deal of imagination to identify as Charles Mills, and a Colonel Cornwallis who combines the worst characteristics of Joel and Dudley. Cornwallis manages to slip some lead from the weight-cloth of the hero, Frank Cuthbert, when he is about to saddle his mare, Deceit, for the National. Deceit wins but Cuthbert cannot draw the weight. There is an enquiry and Colonel Cornwallis' horse which finished second is given the race. Cuthbert is reported to the stewards of the National Hunt Committee and, largely through the perjured evidence of Miles as to betting transactions, is warned off without being given the opportunity of cross-examining Miles or of being heard in his own defence. Disgraced and ostracised he goes abroad, adopts another name and sinks into the Edwardian sub-world of semi-swells, half-sirs, and those who live by cheating, sexually and financially. Finally, through a series of well-managed if fortuitous events, evidence of the frame-up comes to light and Cornwallis is forced to sue for libel if he is to remain in society. There is a rousing, accurate and excellently staged court scene in which the leading counsel are 'Sir Edward Sharpson K.C.' and 'Mr. Rufus Reading, K.C.' Virtue is ultimately triumphant and Cuthbert comes back to his social position and his girl.

Warned Off is desperately dated now but it is far from unreadable even if the virtuous characters, in the convention of the day, are much too good to be true. But Sievier knew racing and he knew the world of which he wrote. It is in the scenes set amongst the *filles de joie*, the mistresses, the 'Lulus and the Lalas' in the *cabinets particuliers*, the shady-smart hotels of Paris and the gambling salons that he shows his real power. When Frank Cuthbert goes to the bad he comes alive and so do his surroundings and his associates. These episodes set the book far apart from the conventional racing novel. In the context of his times Sievier pushed the concealed sexuality of the age as nearly into the open as was then possible and in doing so exposed its total artificiality. Superficial and hurriedly written as it all is, it does show what he might have done with himself as a writer had he bothered.

But there were all sorts of other things to claim his attention. For one he had just then got hold of what appeared to be another cracking good horse. This was Warlingham by Horatio Bottomley's Wargrave who had figured in the trial against Sceptre, and out of Sunny South. He bought Warlingham cheap out of a two-year-old seller at Newbury when no one else wanted him. The colt was bred to stay and, although he looked dreadful at the time, there was something about him which caught Sievier's eye.

'I'll win the Cesarewitch with that fellow,' he said half-jokingly to Ted Robson who was standing beside him as they watched Warlingham being led away.

'I'm afraid not, Bob,' Robson said to him. 'I think you've bought a doped horse.'

At first it looked as if Robson had been right. When they brought him home Warlingham was very sick. His hair fell out in great patches and his skin erupted in sores. Sievier sent him for treatment to the well-known Epsom veterinary surgeon, John Coleman. Failing to diagnose the illness and not finding any satisfactory treatment, Coleman advised Sievier to put him down. This he refused to do. He told Coleman to send him back and after a long period of rest and careful diet Warlingham gradually began to recover. He was given plenty of time and then put into training with Tom Goodgames at Westbury. Goodgames had been with Sievier at Shrewton, he now had a licence and trained all Sievier's horses under the somewhat erratic supervision of their owner.

Sievier made no secret that the colt's objective was the Cesarewitch and that he thought he would win it. Shortly before the race Warlingham was beaten at Windsor by Irish Marine, another Cesarewitch fancy, but Sievier maintained that his horse had had the worst of the weights and his confidence was undiminished.

No one paid much heed to him and on the day of the race Warlingham stood at 33—1 at which price Sievier backed the colt to win him some staggering sums. Since all of the other leading jockeys were engaged for more fancied mounts, Clout, a French jockey who had been suspended the previous Sunday at Longchamps, was brought over to ride him. The two that shared honours in the betting were Balscadden at 11—2 and Captain Forester's Tootles at 6—1.

On the morning of the race Todd, the Newmarket plater, was sent for to put racing plates on Warlingham. When he arrived he found the colt had the worst feet he ever saw on a horse. So bad were they that when he examined them he told Goodgames that he didn't think he could plate them at all and that if he did he would take no responsibility if anything went wrong. Goodgames told him that the colt was running for a fortune and must carry the plates. Then he brusquely re-instructed Todd to get on with the job. Todd set to work and the dead feet came away, in his own words, 'like dead bark from a tree.' Working very slowly and with intense concentration, he began to put the plates on what was left. When he had finished it was, he says, the best and neatest job he ever did in his life.

In the race Warlingham made hacks of them all. Clout, who had to put up 2lb overweight, made his move at the Bushes, settled Tootles in a few strides and cruised home unhurried and unpressed to win by the easiest of three lengths.

It was Sievier's biggest win since Sceptre and he saw that everyone knew about it. Champagne flowed in the bars, Old Kate, the racecard seller got £25, every barmaid and attendant a fiver and anyone on the touch as much as Sievier felt like handing out. In all he got rid of close on £1000 in ready cash. But Todd, who had been on duty all the afternoon, missed the benefit. Next morning he met Sievier out walking in Newmarket in an old sweater and flannels. When he congratulated him Sievier barked back: 'What you really mean is how much am I going to give you for plating Warlingham?' As Todd stood silent, for this was just what he did mean, Sievier put his hand in his pocket and came out with one solitary sovereign. 'It's all I've got on me,' he said as he handed it over. 'You'll have to wait.' But he didn't forget and when

Todd reminded him of the incident later on he produced five ten-pound notes and gave them to him.

No one knew just how much Sievier won over that race. Todd's guess was £66,000 but Sievier himself admitted to a figure of about £28,000. At all events it enabled him to buy Fitzroy House in Newmarket and to set himself up there in some splendour. Once he was installed the fun began to be fast and furious. It was just like the old days in Toddington Park, only more so. Champagne was always on tap; he was more of a figure now in the great world than in the Toddington days and his parties were thronged with the rich and famous. It was all done on credit of course but sooner or later the tradesmen's bills did seem to get paid. One Newmarket butcher told a friend that Siever's account with him for meat alone ran to £1500. And during those hectic years he never quite touched rockbottom, however much he spent, or, if he did, someone was always ready to rescue him. It has appeared in print that, being pushed on one occasion, he wired Bend Or Westminster for a loan of £1000. 'A thousand no good to you am sending five,' came back the reply.

Now, too, there was another arch-enemy to take the place of Joel and to occupy his attention.

Richard Wootton had started life training in Australia. Subsequently he had transferred to South Africa and, about a year before the Joel case, had come to England to set up a training establishment at Tread-well House, Epsom. He was a tough, uncompromising man who had learnt his craft the hard way and knew it inside out. He wanted to win races and to make money by winning them. To do this he had to bet, for his training fees were moderate even by the standard of those days, his charge being £2 10s. 0d. per week for each horse. Bet he did and most successfully did he plunder the ring. Winner after winner mostly in sellers and handicaps—he never won a Classic—was credited to his name. No one ever knew just how great a fortune he did amass but by 1913 he admitted that, apart from his current earnings which he put at £5000 a year, he had remitted between £30,000 and £50,000 to an Australian account and that £31,000 was invested in the name of his son, Frank.

The betting operations of the stable were carried on by an associate called 'Deaf' Wilkinson who had come with him from Australia. But his greatest asset was the possession of two sons, Frank and Stanley, both outstanding jockeys. Frank may indeed have been one of the greatest jockeys ever to grace the English Turf. Tall and with a graceful style he possessed every quality of a rider—dash, courage, judgment of pace, hands and horsemanship. At the age of sixteen he headed the list of winning jockeys and stayed there, despite rivalry from the brilliant American, Danny Maher, for four consecutive years. Trouble with his weight told on him in the end and he looked at times like a walking ghost, someone who knew him has said, but he was a wonder while he lasted. Like Archer, whom in many ways he resembled, he was perhaps too keen to win and his methods did not always appeal to the authorities. He suffered several suspensions for unfair riding and was more often in the stewards' room than most jockeys. But it was desire to win, not hesitation in the hope of losing that brought him there.

Wootton himself, who came to be known to the racing world as 'Old Man Wootton,' apart from his ability as a trainer of racehorses was an exceptional teacher of the art of jockeyship. Soon he had a veritable school for apprentices at Treadwell House. Most of these were at least as skilled as many of their seniors and if another trainer wanted one so as to profit by the 5lb apprentice's claim Wootton in return demanded to know just what was going on. If a coup was being planned or a big bet in prospect Wootton made sure he was told about it or else no apprentice of his went to that stable again. With him racing was a business not a sport, an attitude almost universal now but unusual in those days.

Outspoken, demanding, given to harbouring a grudge, not everyone liked Wootton and Sievier hated him. At first they had been on friendly enough terms but this soon ended, Sievier says because he could not stand Wootton's methods on the racecourse and because on one occasion Wootton refused to raise his hat to a Royal winner saying, 'How could I, I had a tenner on the second?' Wootton, on the other hand said that the split came because he ceased to give Sievier stable information.

For whatever reason, attacks on Wootton began in the *Winning Post* and went on, becoming more vitriolic as they did so. Never a man to take things lying down, Wootton in 1913 launched an action for libel against the paper. He does not, however, appear to have chosen the best ground upon which to give battle.

Wootton's first complaint was about an article mentioning a 'trainer's ring,' allegations about which are as old as racing itself. Wootton was not named in the article which was so loosely and cleverly worded that it could have referred to almost everyone or anyone. However, the real sting of the libel was contained—or so it was alleged—in a 'spoof' competition and its solution which Sievier had published in the *Winning*

Post. It is worthwhile giving this competition in full because it is a prize example of Sievieriana:

'A RACING PROBLEM
The Home Sweepstakes of 300 sovs.
Five Furlongs STRAIGHT
With novel penalties and various allowances.

Horse	Trainer	Jockey
Cigar	Dick Dawson	Stanley Wootton
Bobbin II	Dick Wootton	Frank Wootton
Nankeen	Barling	W. Huxley
Junior	de Mestre	E. Huxley
Sister of Mercy	Escott	Escott
Gunwood	Victor Wild	Morton Smyth
Nedda	Wootton	McKenna

Which would be favourite?
and
Which would win?

A valuable prize—namely, a portrait of George Washington in silver frame—will be given to students of the book who solve this problem by choosing the right horse or horses in answer to the double question put to them. Should it be conjectured that the public favourite might win, then only one horse would have to be named: but, if otherwise, then two—namely, the favourite and the winner. It might be pointed out that McKenna is a rising apprentice.

It is proposed to ask

DANNY MAHER

To act as Judge.

Answers can be written on any kind of paper, but the trainers and jockeys who happen to have been selected are barred from competing, so that the public may have a chance. The competition will remain open until

THE FIFTH OF NOVEMBER'

The point of this problem was that all of the jockeys named were employees or apprentices of Wootton's except Escott who was in some way connected with the stable, and that Danny Maher rode for Wootton when he could.

The next issue of the paper carried the following paragraph:

'A RACING PROBLEM
The Home Sweepstakes of 300 sovs.
Five Furlongs STRAIGHT

We reluctantly admit that the above competition proved a failure, only ONE individual attempting to SOLVE the PROBLEM. He is an inmate of COLNEY HATCH.

As prize-winner we have sent him the original drawing of the following GUY:'

There was a picture of the GUY which bore a striking resemblance to 'Old Man Wootton'. Finally Sievier published a cartoon of a number board with the names of Wootton's sons and apprentices on it and a figure of Ali Baba in Eastern dress looking up at it saying 'Well, it's a good job I lived when I did!'

When, during the opening of the plaintiff's case, Mr. Justice Darling asked, 'Did anyone take this seriously?' he was echoing the opinion of many people. Wootton, however, was determined to bring Sievier into court and he briefed F. E. Smith and Eldon Bankes to assist him prove his case. Wontners were again acting for Sievier for whom they had engaged a fashionable leader to appear. At the very last moment, on the eve of the case, the leader sent back his brief. Wontner and Sievier determined to try to get Marshall Hall and together they went round to his chambers and interviewed Bowker, Marshall Hall's clerk. Writing many years later Bowker said that he could still remember the pungency and fluency of Sievier's language about the leader who had left them in the lurch. A fee was agreed and a conference hurriedly arranged to take place late on Sunday evening, the case being due to open on the following morning. Marshall Hall knew nothing about racing and he had to get up his brief in a hurry. At the conference he suggested that Sievier should appear on his own behalf as editor of the *Winning Post* while he held the brief for the company. Never averse to appearing on the centre of the stage and delighted to have the opportunity of cross-examining Wootton, Sievier willingly fell in with this suggestion. During the consultation Bowker had a farthing lying on the desk in front of him and was idly playing with it as they discussed the tactics to be employed the next day. The sight of the coin appears to have given Sievier an idea. As he was leaving he asked for a loan of it and took it away with him. The case began on July 15th 1913 before Mr. Justice Darling.

Another of Hardinge Giffard's 'favourite son' appointments much criticized at the time Darling was, in fact, a better judge than he allowed himself to appear. Castigated at first as a 'judicial lightweight' he had, by sensible, reasoned decisions and firmness when required, disarmed most of the criticisms made against him. But he had grave faults. He was far too much the court jester; his loathing of emotion made him slip too easily into what looked like unbecoming levity and although it is usual for a judge to allow a personal litigant a considerable degree of latitude where rules of pleading and questioning are concerned he exceeded all reasonable grounds in giving this dispensation. Later on, in the Pemberton Billing case, this was to place him in the centre of an unenviable controversy.

In this case from his very first question to F. E. Smith, 'Was this taken seriously?' he appears to have decided, probably correctly, that it was one which should never have been brought. Once his mind was made up on that point he concentrated on the aspects of it which interested and amused him and gave him scope for judicial wit. A hunting man himself he was fascinated by the details of jockeyship and the technicalities of racing and riding races. He and Sievier got on famously from the first and he gave Sievier to all intents and purposes the freedom of the court. This was a state of affairs Sievier knew well how to exploit. He loved courtroom battles and here he was in his very element for Darling allowed him to turn the court into a theatre in which he was the star player.

On one occasion F. E. Smith was examining in the well of the court a witness who was more than a little deaf. When he had finished it was indicated to the witness that he should turn round and face Sievier for his cross-examination. Having heard the instructions but having very little idea of what was going on, the witness did turn round. Finding himself face to face with Sievier, whom he recognized, he solemnly shook hands with him! Sievier prolonged the tableau while the whole court rocked with laughter which Darling did little to check.

All this infuriated Smith whose temper was never very far from hand. Flamboyant, brilliant and erratic, he was fresh from Ulster where he had been making inflammatory speeches against the Constitution in opposition to the Irish Home Rule Bill and where he was soon to earn the nickname of 'Galloper' Smith that stayed with him all his life.

Throughout the trial F.E. was at his most vituperative, slanging everyone in opposition to him with fine impartiality and on occasions only narrowly escaping collision with the Judge. When F.E. was vituperative he was very vitriolic indeed and on this occasion he had every excuse, for the whole case was in confusion from the start largely owing to Darling's laxness.

From the beginning Sievier and Wootton fought a wordy battle which had little if anything to do with the issues involved and at times descended to a mere swopping of insults. Sievier was rude to everyone called against him save only Wootton's sons whom he made clear he exculpated entirely from any blame for his father's schemes. Marshall Hall, who was far below his best and who had in any event to master a brief on a subject about which he was totally ignorant in much too short a time, rashly at one moment plunged into a technical racing cross-examination of one of Wootton's witnesses. This ended up leaving everyone in court including the witness and the jury far more at sea than when it had started and led Sievier to say that he totally dissociated himself from the questions put by his colleague.

Only Eldon Bankes preserved his dignity and his coolness but in the general air of farce which invested everything he, too, was moved to make a quiet joke. Because of his easy-going manner this has largely escaped notice from posterity but it must be one of the neatest legal witticisms ever made. When examining Frank Wootton he was told by the jockey that he had first ridden in public at the age of nine. 'You took silk even earlier than I thought,' was Bankes' quiet comment.

Over all this Darling presided like some impish circus-master who plainly thought that it was a tremendous and entertaining social comedy and took no pains to conceal his opinion.

A bevy of distinguished racing personalities was called on either side, no one quite knew why except, as Sievier himself said afterwards, just to cancel each other out. For Wootton there were the Hon. George Lambton, his brother Francis and Lord Derby. For Sievier Lord Durham, Lord Lonsdale and Sir William Bass. Darling allowed their evidence to be taken out of turn, interrupting others sometimes in the middle of a cross-examination, for each and every one of them pleaded urgent business on the racecourse necessitating their arrival at the law courts at unusual times and on unappointed days.

Just what Sievier's defence was it is quite impossible to glean from his conduct of the case. He was a really dreadful advocate, being irrelevant, verbose, intemperate and inconsequential all by turn. Obviously he considered himself another Bottomley but Bottomley had had legal training and had studied law and the technique of advocacy. Sievier had done neither. If he called Bottomley 'the fly mug' on the racecourse

Bottomley could have returned that remark with interest about Sievier's performances in the courts. But if his object was to irritate Wootton and F. E. Smith he succeeded admirably.

Wootton admitted in his examination-in-chief that he had had no formal education, but what he lacked in this respect he more than made up in shrewdness and the aggressiveness of his answers. Here are some of the passages at arms between him and Sievier whose main object, apart from attacking the witness, was to find out why 'Deaf' Wilkinson had conveniently taken off for a cruise round the world just when the case was coming on, and taken his betting records with him.

SIEVIER: How long have you known Mr. T. J. Wilkinson?

WOOTTON: He has been my friend for twenty years. He wouldn't stand you, though.

SIEVIER: Do you mean he wouldn't stand me a drink?

WOOTTON: He is a sensible man.

SIEVIER: He must be because he is now in Australia. Have you made any attempt to bring him here?

WOOTTON: No. He left in March on a voyage round the world as you very well know.

SIEVIER: Do you know an owner and trainer called Jack Fielder and is he a blackguard?

WOOTTON: No, he is an ordinary sort of man.

SIEVIER: Not such a blackguard as I am?

WOOTTON: Well, I won't contradict you.

SIEVIER: You are the only trainer in England who does not keep a trial book?

WOOTTON: Yes, but you must remember that I have won more races than any trainer in England.

SIEVIER: I see you have been to night school since yesterday.

This was an obvious reference to Wootton's lack of education, and here Darling interrupted the slanging match. 'You must not be rude to the witness, Mr. Sievier,' he said.

Sievier bowed ironically to Wootton. 'I do apologize to you, Mr. Wootton,' he said. 'I can't do more than apologize. I can't withdraw from the case.' He may have apologized but it made no difference to his approach to his cross-examination. 'Do you know a Mr. Skoyen?' he asked.

'You ought to know him anyhow,' Wootton answered. 'Do you owe him anything?'

'Now, Mr. Wootton,' Darling chided him in turn. 'You must not ask Mr. Sievier questions.'

'But he is so rude to me,' Wootton protested.

'And if you are rude to him he will be ruder still,' Darling told him, while F. E. Smith fulminated on the sidelines.

Sievier went back to Wilkinson. 'Has he been present at all the races every season since you have been in England?' he asked.

'Yes.'

'And this year he is travelling because he is hard of hearing? As far as this case is concerned he is deaf and dumb?'

'We couldn't get you up to scratch. You waited till he had gone away.'

'Where are your betting books?'

'I have none. I don't stand alone in that. There are not three other trainers in England who have such things. Where are yours? Oh! I beg your pardon, my Lord.'

'How many times in 1907 was Frank up for foul riding?'

'I cannot say. He has been head of the list more often than any jockey since Archer.'

'How long has he been head of the list of jockeys punished for their riding?'

'I cannot say.'

'If he had not been a jockey,' commented Darling, 'he would have been tried in the children's court.'

All this had very little to do with the libel. 'I'll give you a wrinkle, Mr. Sievier,' Darling said to him. 'The only thing that matters in a law case is getting a verdict and you are not likely to get the jury to give you one if you bore them.'

Sievier then did get on to a point which had some relevance. He accused Wootton of having Frank pull a horse called Stick Up in the Cambridgeshire, saying that Otto Madden had had to shout to him to get on. 'Is that not a fact?' he asked.

'You know my opinion of you,' was the reply from Wootton, now really furious.

'Perhaps. I still want an answer to my question.'

'It's a downright concoction and a cowardly—'

'A damned lie and what else? That's one sort of an answer I suppose.' There was loud laughter all over the court at this. Sievier was having some success projecting himself to the jury as a cheerful opportunist and making Wootton appear bad-tempered, domineering and unreasonable. 'And did Madden on one occasion at Newmarket report Frank for foul riding?' he went on.

'Madden would be quite capable of doing that,' was Wootton's reply.

242

This sort of abuse and counter-abuse went on for the best part of three days. F. E. Smith was not slow to join in. When Darling remarked 'I shall never get to the bottom of the wickedness of this world', 'I'm sure Mr. Sievier will help your lordship,' was Smith's answer to him. Sievier was not prepared to let this go. His reply has not been reported probably because it was unprintable but it moved Smith to protest. 'That was a grossly improper remark,' he said.

'Never mind, Mr. Smith, by next week Mr. Sievier will be more forensic,' said the judge, smiling. No wonder F.E. was in a bad temper.

It was only when the jockeys were called that some sort of reality was injected into the case.

Otto Madden swore that in the Cambridgeshire of 1907 he rode side by side with Stick Up for about four furlongs. He thought Wootton ought to be making more use of his horse and said to him: 'Why the hell don't you let him go?'

Danny Maher, in an aphorism Darling might have envied, defined fouling and pulling as the one being robbery with violence the other robbery without. William Smyth, then one of Wootton's apprentices, swore that he never had instructions to stop a horse and that the only time he was in the stable was when he lost a race in the stewards' room through forgetting to weigh in. He was about to leave the box before being re-examined by F. E. Smith when Darling stopped him. 'Wait,' he said, 'Mr. Smith has not weighed in yet.' Marshall Hall always maintained this was the best example of judicial wit he had ever heard in a law court. The offence, however, had been no joke for the unfortunate Smyth since, as well as losing the race, he told the court that when he reached home he had received a good thrashing from Wootton for his forgetfulness.

The only damaging witness of fact that Sievier could produce was a boy called Taylor who swore that Wootton had instructed him to lose a hurdle race by 'going too wide at the turn if I found him running too strong for me.' It was on Taylor that the full fury of F. E. Smith's wrath fell. Here is the cross-examination or most of it:

'When you get drink in you are you wild?'

'Yes, I suppose so.'

'When you were with Mr. Duller were you once told to bring a horse called Pessimist home?'

'Yes.'

'Was it your duty to groom him and leave him properly for the night?'

'Yes.'

'Was he found next morning with a saddle and bridle on ?'

'He might have been. I never went to see.'

'Would you have done that if you had been sober ?'

'No.'

'You were drunk ?'

'Yes.'

Here Darling interposed. 'There is a maxim,' he said, 'That drunken people tell the truth.'

'That is when they are drunk,' F.E. said brusquely, brushing the judge aside. Then, to the witness:

'Are you sober now ?'

'Yes.'

'Who took your statement for this case ?'

'Mr. Sievier and a lady in Henrietta Street.'

'Were you told that you would get £100 and more if you gave evidence ?'

'No.'

'Have you been drunk often during the last three weeks ?'

'Yes, pretty often.'

'Have you rarely gone to bed sober in the last three weeks ?'

'Very rarely.'

'Do you get your living by touting ?'

'Yes.'

When this witness left the box he should have been thoroughly discredited but in fact his frank admissions had preserved what little dignity was left to him and if he openly told the truth about his own bad character might he not also have done the same about another's ? That, it appears, was what many in the court thought.

In his opening address to the jury Sievier had held up Bowker's farthing to them and told them that this was basically a case about money and that money talked. Money, he kept stressing to them, was what Wootton wanted in racing and what he wanted now. The correct amount of damages, if any, was represented, Sievier suggested, by the coin in his hand. This theme he continued in his closing address. Why wasn't Wilkinson here? he demanded. He was the man who oiled the machinery with liquid gold. Money talked. Once again the farthing was held up before the jury. 'They were out for the gold which came from Australia in nuggets and returned as sovereigns. Take the case of the horse "Excelsior" that "strange device". He ran unplaced, unbacked. Sixteen days later, the machinery oiled, free from rust, he ran with £200 on him each way and Wootton admitted winning £3000. But other bets bringing the winnings up to £5000 had now been discovered. He went to Folkestone and had a bit of seaweed for breakfast and won at 7—1. That kind of pulling, for that was what running a horse first time out unfit was, in effect gave them a double pull—lighter weight and longer prices. And that was the basis on which this man's fortune had been piled up.'

All this in a way had very little relevance to the libel and, punctuated by furious interruptions from Smith of which he took absolutely no notice at all, Sievier grew more and more outrageous as he went along, holding the farthing up all the time. It was, however, effective in its own way for the general public are always suspicious of the morals of the Turf and here their worst suspicions were being confirmed out of the mouth of a Turf notability. Satan, as Sievier himself told them, was rebuking sin.

In reply F.E. unleashed an onslaught on Sievier and his one good witness, Taylor. 'He has been warned off the Turf himself,' he said of Sievier, 'this cleanser of the Augean stables, this vindicator of the morality of the Turf. If this is the new standard of morality of the Turf then all I can say is "God help the Turf".' Of Taylor he had this to say: 'What was his character? Dismissed by Wootton for drunkenness, a man who admitted himself that he had not been sober for five years and who had gained his living by skulking in ditches and watching trials in order to sell information. How strong would be the resistance of a man like that to the offer of money to buy his evidence?' It was a tremendous piece of sustained invective but it may not in the end have done his client's case much good.

In his summing up Darling showed that, despite all the assaults on his attention throughout the eight long July days that the case dragged its course, he had not lost his grasp upon its essentials. He told the jury that it was a matter of suspicion that neither the records nor Wilkinson were produced and, on the question of Taylor's evidence, he pretty clearly indicated that he had been impressed by it and was not swayed or shaken by F. E. Smith's onslaught on the boy. 'It does not necessarily follow that because he is a drunkard he has been bought and is lying. If you believe him it proves something so discreditable to Wootton that you may give weight to it when considering the question of damages.'

They did. They awarded Wootton one farthing, the very coin which Sievier had in his hand throughout his speeches, and which Bowker afterwards complained he never got back!

Another attempt to muzzle or suppress the *Winning Post* and ruin its editor had failed. It was not, however, an unqualified victory for the costs were awarded against the paper and amounted to £6000 though the gains accruing from the publicity and advertisement may to some extent have offset these. Sievier at any rate was delighted. Always ready to enlarge upon his successes and to depreciate his failures he looked upon it as total defeat of yet another adversary and was further convinced that it was brought about entirely by his own advocacy. In this, in a way, he may just have been right. It was undoubtedly the high watermark of his career as an advocate. Unfortunately for him it engendered a conviction that he could beat the barristers at their own game which was to bring him nothing but troubles some of which were even now rumbling beneath the surface and were about to burst forth.

24

Blackmail?

On the face of it everything looked as prosperous as it could possibly be. The Hoxton Conservative Association had adopted him as their Parliamentary candidate and he threw himself into constituency matters with characteristic energy. On the platform he was as ebullient as ever. When a heckler shouted at him, 'Are you in favour of giving votes to women?' he bowed in the direction of the questioner and said, 'I would never refuse anything to a lady.' His old associate T. H. Dey was at the same time a candidate for the Hoxton County Council. Throughout their careers Sievier and Dey had had a stormy relationship, being at times close friends and at others deadly enemies. At the time of their respective adoptions as candidates they were in a period of friendship and Sievier was in fact godfather to one of Dey's daughters. Much of the acrimony between the two men appears to have centred around Sievier's cousin, Edward Sievier, and Dey's association with him in business. Edward Sievier was a defaulter. Sievier said that the public mixed up the two names, and, since he was much better known, he was blamed for Edward's sins and, moreover, that Dey exploited this. When Edward died in penury in 1911 it was Bob who paid for the funeral and agreed to give his widow a pension of five pounds a week for her lifetime. He may have resented this and thought that Dey, the business associate of Edward, should have contributed. At all events the friendly relations then existing began to deteriorate. Dey, who was a fairly tough customer himself, was, a little later, asked to resign his candidature for the Hoxton County Council owing to an attack upon him in a local paper, or so he alleged. He blamed Sievier—wrongly—for this and then, quite deliberately, sent out a circular to all the electors of Hoxton stating that Bob Sievier was a welsher and a blackmailer.

Sievier has often been accused, verbally and in print after his death, of blackmail and especially of using the page *Celebrities in Glasshouses* as a blackmailing column. Before dealing with Dey's allegation—which had nothing to do with the *Glasshouses* Column—it is worthwhile looking at this accusation in some detail, for it was never brought home to him.

The *modus operandi* attributed to Sievier has been variously described. One version says that he sent to the victim a proof of the forthcoming article which contained a damning exposure. The messenger who brought the article was instructed to tell the recipient to call to see Sievier. On doing so he learnt the price of suppression. Another says he sent *two* proofs one containing the exposure and another omitting it. The victim was then asked to choose which he would like published— at a price. Neither of these suggestions was ever proved nor was any action taken concerning the *Celebrities* column. It may be said of course that those who are blackmailed do not care to court the publicity of a prosecution but one would have thought that if the offence was as frequent as has been alleged someone would have been found with the courage to come forward. Moreover, the last or almost the last survivor of those who appeared in that column says that he, at any rate, never received any advance notice of his appearance and certainly not a threatening one.

There is, however, an authenticated story which has been thought to lend some weight to the accusations. It may or may not. It is for the reader to judge.

Ralph Rowland, 'The Jabberwock,' one of the *Winning Post*'s two cartoonists, had a flaming row with Sievier over a proposed caricature of some public figure who was then one of the editor's bitter enemies. Rowland, who was quick-tempered and excitable, said that what Sievier wanted went too far. Hot words followed. Rowland tore the drawing up, threw the pieces in Sievier's face and walked out of the room and his employment.

Subsequently Rowland fell a victim to tuberculosis. As was the way of the Bohemians of the time he had nothing saved and when he was in the Middlesex Hospital J. B. Booth went to see him. 'You'll never guess who's been here,' Rowland told him. 'Bob Sievier,' he went on and then said, 'Look what he left behind him.'

Booth crossed to the bedside table and found crumpled into a ball beside a glass of water and other invalid requirements five ten-pound notes. 'And I know Bob's been having a damned bad time,' Rowland told Booth. 'I never thought I'd see him again. When we had that row I called him a damned blackmailer and a bloody thief!'

That anecdote may well illustrate the best and the worst of Bob Sievier.

Dey's accusations however, as has been said, were not concerned with the *Celebrities* column. In 1907 Sievier and Dey had had a blood row concerning Edward Sievier's defaulting and Dey's alleged use of the name Sievier & Co. which brought, Sievier said, himself and the *Winning Post* into disrepute. As a result he had launched against Dey the most bitter and vitriolic series of attacks in the paper, which attacks were damaging to Dey's business and reputation. He would not stop them until finally, so Dey said, he was bought off by him for the sum of £1000 of which £300 was paid for advertising and £700 'in a bag of golden sovereigns' went straight into Sievier's pocket. This was the act of blackmail of which now, six years later, he accused Sievier.

Immediately the Hoxton circular was brought to his notice Sievier applied for a writ of criminal libel against Dey. This was duly granted and the case was heard, the jury finding for Sievier on the lesser charge, thus exonerating him from the accusation of welshing. But they held that Dey had justified his charge against Sievier of blackmailing.

Sievier refused to lie down under this. In the *Winning Post* he gave the decision such publicity and launched such a series of scurrilous attacks against Dey that the authorities had no option but to institute against him a criminal prosecution for blackmail.

In December 1913 he faced this charge. He elected to defend himself before the magistrate and he made an appalling hash of it, his cross-examination of Dey being a mixture of abuse and poor jokes. He did, however, establish that Dey had been mixed up in the promotion of what appeared to have been a very shady sweepstake, for Dey and his nominees had, or so it seemed, won all the prizes. Possibly because of this and the further disclosures that might be sprung upon him when Sievier was returned for trial, Dey was singularly reluctant to go on with the case. There was one adjournment on medical grounds and when, eventually, in January 1914, it came on at the Old Bailey, Dey was still unwell. He was the first witness to be called and Sievier attacked him violently about the sweepstake.

After the luncheon adjournment Mr. McCall, who appeared for the prosecution, stated that they did not wish to proceed. He said that Sievier had agreed to withdraw the allegations about the sweepstake and so Dey would withdraw his about blackmail and both would agree not to attack the other again. When the judge put this to Sievier his reply was: 'I agree to that course, my Lord, but while I have the opportunity I wish to say that I came here quite prepared with my answer to this charge. I will say no more but I was prepared to go on.'

The Judge then directed the jury to return a formal verdict of 'Not Guilty.'

Sievier considered this a great triumph for his advocacy which in its own way it may have been. He also maintained that by securing a verdict of 'Not Guilty' he had been cleared of all charges of blackmail. Most laymen will agree with him, especially since the incidents were six years old and the charges almost certainly maliciously made. But when lawyers came to scrutinize them later on they were not so sure.

Afterwards, through the intervention of Charles Clark, the two men became friends once more and remained so for the rest of their careers.

To Sievier, as to many others, the world, just then, must have seemed set fair on its course for the coming year. But in August 1914 war was declared and the roof fell in.

25

War, Waterbed and Royal Bucks

❦❦❦❦❦❦

'I had a paper which had gone to pulp and horses which had gone to catsmeat,' was how Sievier described his situation after the outbreak of war.

It was the end of an era. Bohemia and Society as he and his like knew them were blown away for all time with the first shell that burst over Mons. But, indestructible as ever, he took good care it was not the end of him. He kept the *Winning Post* going and this alone was something of a feat. His competitors, the *Pink 'Un* and *Town Topics* which the staff of the *Pink 'Un* had started when Corlett sold the paper over their heads to de Wend Fenton, were early casualties. Racing was, of course, restricted and many grandstands and tracks taken over by the military so he had to use all his invention and ingenuity to fill the paper.

Since at fifty-four Sievier was far too old for active service he threw all his energies into the recruiting drive, addressing meetings here, there and everywhere. Soon Bobbie had joined up and was in action. In addition, as the war went on, he was able to announce with pride that no one could accuse him of not doing his bit since he had no less than seventeen illegitimate sons serving in the armed forces of the Crown! As these young men went to France one after the other their pictures in the uniform of their chosen corps were put up in the study of Fitzroy House to be displayed proudly by their putative father to visitors and callers. Reticence was one quality which could never be attributed to Bob Sievier.

The war, too, brought one unexpected bonus. The privilege of having a special licence to train on Newmarket Heath is jealously guarded by the Jockey Club. Although he had lived at Fitzroy House for two years Sievier had not yet received one. Since so many trainers had left for the front or were engaged in war work the stewards decided to issue further licences to train on the Heath. Sievier was given one of these and this enabled him to carry on and moreover to take in horses for outside owners. Two of these were the Marchioness of Queensberry and Lieutenant-Colonel Sir Henry Busby Bird, the Mayor of Shoreditch, a pompous individual with a sweeping moustache and a grand manner. Sievier despised Bird and laughed at him but he did him well just the same, as will be seen.

The feud with Wootton and the attacks on him continued. It helped to fill the *Winning Post*, amused Sievier and attracted readers. Wootton, still smarting under his failure in the law courts, brooded over them and plotted revenge. Sievier certainly took care to pick powerful enemies, highly likely to retaliate. It all added spice to the game.

For Wootton was every bit as vindictive as he was. Meyrick Good, the racing reporter, has told how on one occasion when he was doing the starting prices for the *Sporting Life* he returned the price of Wootton's horse Excelsior at a figure shorter than Wootton thought correct. Excelsior, who was, it will be remembered, one of the horses that had figured in Wootton *v.* Sievier was clearly the subject of an s.p. job. Wootton went to Good. After accusing him in strong language of having made a mistake he ordered him peremptorily to alter the price. Good refused whereupon Wootton brought him to a bookmaker who appeared to confirm what Wootton had said and that Good's price was wrong. Fortunately for Good a well-known professional backer who was standing by overheard what was going on since Wootton, like Sievier, was not inclined to moderate his voice during these rows. He told the bookmaker in plain terms that he was lying. Loud and furious words then flew around which ended in Good still refusing to give way and Wootton stamping off in a tremendous rage after accusing Good and the professional backer of being in collusion to defeat him. Wootton continued to bear a grudge against Good for this incident and did everything he could by way of intrigue and influence to have Good removed from the staff of *Sporting Life*. Later the quarrel was patched up through the intervention of a third party and Wootton then proposed to Good that they should start a racing paper which the trainer would finance. Good was to have the position of chief writer but the main object of the paper was to reply to Sievier's attacks and if possible to put him and the *Winning Post* out of business. Good replied with caution that it would be well first to make sure that a competent editor could be engaged and in the end he heard no more of the project. But Wootton went on plotting revenge.

When, as the war progressed, racing and the size of the paper were further curtailed, Sievier turned more and more to politics. But he was not a political animal and much of what he wrote was merely silly though it was all pungently expressed. But when he dealt with racing he was still as percipient as ever. He was quick to spot promising jockeys and to write them up and even quicker to pounce on sharp practice by those who were established. He had won the battle for compulsory number cloths a few years before; now he was campaigning for overnight declarations. He was having some success with his training too.

In 1918 Sievier bought for Bird from F. H. Bennett a big raking chestnut called Waterbed. By Featherbed out of Coolbawn, Waterbed had won three high class hurdle races on the trot including The Champion Hurdle Cup at Gatwick. Sievier sent him chasing and in January 1919 he won the Victory Steeplechase at Manchester with him. Since Waterbed carried 12st. 4lb and was giving the second a stone it was an impressive performance. Bird was delighted and they began to think hopefully of the Grand National.

Their National hopes were dashed, however, when Waterbed went wrong, and immediately after this something much worse for Sievier happened.

Wootton had now determined on the counter-stroke which he reckoned would bring him his revenge and ruin Sievier. Just as Duke had done he expended a considerable amount of money upon investigations into Sievier's past. With the result of these before them he and his lawyers drafted a pamphlet which it was proposed should be printed and published under the title INCIDENTS IN THE PUBLIC LIFE OF ROBERT STANDISH SIEVIER.

The text of this pamphlet was, under the guidance of counsel, very carefully and cleverly worded. It followed closely the statement in mitigation filed in the Duke case, adding to it a précis of the worst parts of Grantham's summing up, and an exact statement of the result of the Joel case and the criminal libel prosecution of Dey. It also said, and here was its real sting: 'He has from time to time been publicly stated to be a swindler, a card-sharper and a thief, and a man with whom no decent person would associate.'

Wootton made no secret of the fact that in preparing this pamphlet and publishing it his object was to get Sievier's trainer's licence withdrawn and to have him warned off the Turf. In February 1918 he had 20,000 copies of it printed and commenced the sale and distribution of them to racegoers on Grand National day. The circulation of the pamphlet by Wootton continued at race meetings and elsewhere but the authorities were neither impressed by it nor best pleased by his methods of distribution. When advertisements for it appeared nailed to trees at Newmarket the stewards ordered them to be taken down. Wootton went on selling it in shops and other outlets open to him but it did not really have the *succès de scandale* he must have hoped for. Many people recognized it for what it was; to others it was a stale repetition of very ancient history. Sievier would have been far wiser to ignore it, but wisdom was not a word that figured at all in his vocabulary especially when he was confronted with a challenge. Besides, it was five years now since he had had a rousing and spectacular set-to in court. And, as has been said, he dearly loved the battle and the breeze of courtroom encounters, the theatricality of the trappings, the clash of wits and wills and the opportunity to hold the centre of the stage. In May of that year he issued proceedings for libel. His statement of claim was served in June, but the case did not come on for hearing until almost another two years had elapsed. In the meantime much was to happen, for yet another good horse had come his way.

This was Lady Queensberry's Royal Bucks, a six-year-old by Buckwheat out of a mare called Teofani. Once Sievier started to work Royal Bucks he knew he stood a good chance of picking up the big Spring handicaps with him. When the Lincoln handicap was published and he saw that Royal Bucks was in with only 7st. 5lb he was sure of it. Straightaway he started to back Royal Bucks for the treble—The Lincoln, The City and Suburban and The Jubilee Handicap. It was just like the old days—a good old-fashioned gamble with anything and everything he could find piled on day after day not only for the treble but for the individual races too. When he had finished he stood to win a quarter of a million if the treble came up. Nor did he conceal his intentions.

But by now people were rather talking of Bob Sievier in the past tense. A new generation, new people and new money had come into racing. The weight of Joel money had told too, and the Joel name was by now carrying everything before it. Solly was less successful than Jack but his horse, Rivershore, was expected to win that Lincoln with a lightweight, Arion, the chief danger. Royal Bucks was allowed to start at 100—7. George Hulme rode him and brought him home two untroubled lengths in front of Rivershore.

'That makes up for Sceptre, Bob,' someone shouted to him in the unsaddling enclosure. It didn't of course. Nothing made up for Sceptre, but victory was sweet and its sweetness increased by the fact that he had defeated a Joel. So were the spoils.

Royal Bucks had 10lb more to carry at Epsom and no one but Sievier really believed he could do it. He went on doubling up as he had always done, and engaged the immortal Steve Donoghue to ride him.

Steve's Derby successes had so far been gained in substitute races at Newmarket and he was not then the Epsom specialist he was to become. It was thought that the extra weight and the stiff Epsom finish would find out Royal Bucks. He was largely ignored in the betting and Sievier had the market to himself. It was not through his own reticence about his horse's chances that this happened, for he made no secret of his confidence.

A destroyer named H.M.S. *Sceptre* had been commissioned into the Harwich Flotilla a year or so before. At the time of her commissioning Sievier had presented the wardroom with some sporting prints, at the same time sending his apologies for not making a larger gift. Now he remembered the ship and resolved to make good what a temporary lack of funds had prevented him giving before. He sent the captain a wire *City and Suburban. Royal Bucks. Help yourself. Sievier.* It was a typically thoughtful gesture and the wardroom followed his tip.

Royal Bucks started at sixes. He and Steve were never headed and came cruising home to win by a length-and-a-half. H.M.S. *Sceptre*'s wardroom duly toasted Sievier. It looked as if that quarter-of-a-million were within his grasp. The ring, who had ignored the old lion to their peril, now frantically tried to hedge.

By this time everyone wanted to get in on the act and Royal Bucks was backed as a certainty for the Jubilee. He started at 13—8 on and there were many who were glad to get it. Sievier himself knew, however, that the horse was lucky to start at all for he had been under treatment for cracked heels. Arion, who had been fancied in the Lincoln and who had been second in the City and Suburban, was quietly expected to beat him here even without the handicap of cracked heels. A promising lightweight called Tommy Weston, then at the beginning of a great career, was given the ride. He was nervous about it because two other lightweight jockeys had been tried on Arion who was a difficult ride especially round bends. They had failed to manage him, and had been blamed in some quarters for his defeats. Weston did not want the same thing to happen to him. In the event all went well for him and badly for Sievier. He handled Arion perfectly and, taking the lead some way out, was never headed. Royal Bucks, running sore, was down the field. Sievier had not won half a million but his individual bets were considerable and despite doubling up he was in profit after the race.

But someone was making trouble for him again with the authorities. He was, it is true, being more than usually vitriolic in the *Winning Post* about the standard of stewarding at recent meetings and other articles criticizing in unmeasured terms the administration of racing after the cessation of hostilities had appeared from his pen. It is also true that many of his criticisms were well-founded but they were most intemperately phrased.

Late that season a caller came to Fitzroy House and told him unofficially that the Jockey Club had decided that no one writing for the press should be allowed to hold a licence to train. He took very little notice of this and shortly afterwards was astonished to receive a terse note from Weatherby's telling him that his permission to train at Newmarket had been withdrawn. He wrote to Lord Lonsdale protesting against this decision and received the following reply:

> *Barley Thorpe, Oakham*
> *December 27th, 1919*

My Dear Sievier,—Thank you for your letter of 24th inst., re training at Newmarket.

I think you will remember that when you came to Newmarket, at the same time as some others, racing being confined practically to Newmarket, the licence was granted conditionally, and it was clearly understood it would not be permanent and that others who had trained at Newmarket for a considerable time prior to the war should have priority of claim of training on the Heath to those who came during the war.

There is not ground enough for all the horses to train at Newmarket, and, therefore, those who came into residence there for the duration of the war are naturally those to whom fresh licences cannot be given, which is obviously a question of justice.

It has nothing to do with any question as regards running or training of horses, or of the way in which they have been run or conducted.

I have told you on more than one occasion that I have never heard anyone knowledgeable on Turf matters express an opinion that your horses were not run most correctly, properly, and to the best interests of themselves and the public. Therefore, do not let anything to do with the latter get into your mind as any reason that the licence should not be granted.

> Believe me, yours truly,
> (signed) LONSDALE

Durham wrote in much the same vein. But he lost his licence just the same.

The horses were then sent to Walter Griggs though they remained under the control of Sievier as their racing manager and he continued to live at Fitzroy House.

By now the forthcoming case of Sievier v. Wootton should have been claiming all of his attention if he were to have any chance of success, but it was not. He was negotiating for the purchase of a villa at Cap d'Ail and, once it was bought, was off there to enjoy the sun and the tables. There too he held court in his own way. Nor did he forget his old friends. 'Charlie' Shrewsbury, who was dying and in pain, spent the last winter of his life there with him as his guest.

All sorts of things were occupying his mind and least of all did he allow the law case to worry him. When he heard that the Lord Chief Justice, Lord Reading, the former Rufus Isaacs, was going to hear the case he was reinforced in the belief that he could not lose. Quite openly he went around saying that since Rufus Isaacs had defended him in the Joel case he would not give a verdict against him now. It was an example of his extraordinary naïvety once he was off the Turf and it was to cost him dear.

26

Sievier v. Wootton

᪥᪥᪥᪥᪥

Although it occupied the attention of the courts for six days the ultimate result of the last of Sievier's libel actions to both plaintiff and defendant and especially to Sievier has been much exaggerated, notably by Patrick Hastings who was briefed with Carson for the defence and whose first great chance it was to display his talents before the public in a *cause célèbre*. He has left behind him two highly-coloured and vainglorious accounts of his own performance in it, one of them entitled, quite inaccurately, 'The End of Robert Sievier.' This is all the more unfortunate in that subsequent biographers have followed his account.

Hastings was, in fact, a bit of a buccaneer himself. As a young barrister he had bluffed his way into Gill's chambers shortly after the Duke case and he may well have heard there from his master a considerable amount of prejudiced information about Robert Standish Sievier. In court he was a gambler, prone to take tremendous risks which made him at times a dangerous counsel to employ. Arrogant and bullying, in that style he was a fine performer. He was the last of the great barnstorming advocates and, although a very good one, he did not achieve the total command of the courts or the universal admiration of the profession as did Carson, and F. E. Smith or, in an older generation, Clark or Russell.

Hastings' chance did not come until the third day of the hearing. During the first two days Sievier faced Carson at his most belligerent and penetrating. If Carson had been something less than sufficiently severe to Sievier in the Joel case he more than made up for it now. He was relentless, probing without mercy into Sievier's answers, bent on destroying him as he had destroyed Wilde. With all his tremendous force and skill he plied question upon question, forcing Sievier, however he might turn and twist and use his active wits for evasion, back on to the unpleasant facts.

Whether or not Reading had heard of Sievier's boast about the foregone result of the case, and that this influenced him in favour of the defence, will never be known but there is no doubt that he was dead against Sievier from the start.

Apart from the fact of his having acted for Sievier in the Joel affair, one of the matters on which he was now being called to account, which raises certain issues concerning the propriety of his taking the case at all, whether Reading as a man was best qualified to adjudicate in matters of honour, must remain in some doubt.

He had, as has been said, been hammered on the stock exchange, but to gain admission to it at all he had falsely and knowingly misrepresented his age in his application. During his parliamentary career he had been involved in the Marconi Scandal from which it can at least be said that he had not emerged with his personal reputation unscathed. His conduct then and subsequent elevation to the position of Lord Chief Justice had moved Rudyard Kipling to write *Gehazi*, one of the most vitriolic hate-poems in the language.

Not only did this poem unabashedly point to Reading but it was understood by the public to do so. It was also clearly defamatory but Reading took no action against it or its author, in which he was wiser perhaps than Sievier. At the time of the hearing of the case he had been back on the Bench for ten months after tasting the wider spheres of influence and power as British Ambassador to the United States during the war. Shortly he was about to embark on the extraordinary series of political manœuvres and intrigues which were ultimately to bring him to India as Viceroy. At this time, as a judge, he was bored, frustrated and as near to open irritation in court as he ever allowed himself to come.

Sievier, believing that the Judge would favour him, proceeded to act with unparalleled recklessness. The decision to appear on his own behalf may have followed his belief in the favour of the court but it was an error of the first magnitude. Here, if ever, the services of an advocate not only skilled in questioning but in the niceties of pleading were essential to success. He told the jury that he appeared in person because he had discovered that most counsel know nothing of the technicalities of racing. This was—and is—true but this case had nothing to do with racing. He made another terrible mistake in his pleadings, too, when he or his solicitors omitted to plead that the expressions used in the pamphlet concerning his warning off implied that he had committed misconduct on the Turf. Had this been done he might have been able to set up his blameless conduct on the Turf against the other offences alleged and he called Lord Lonsdale and Lord Crewe to help him do it.

The moment they opened their mouths on the subject, however, Carson was on his feet objecting. A long technical legal argument ensued in which Sievier, naturally enough, was hopelessly at sea and as a result Reading held with Carson and excluded their evidence.

The case, then, was about Sievier's past just as the Duke case had been. It was significant—and in Sievier's favour—that only three allegedly discreditable incidents were pleaded since the hearing of that case sixteen years before and nothing at all since the Dey case in 1913. It was open to him to point out that virtually he was being accused twice over and that the statement about the Joel case was an exact repetition of what had actually happened and therefore needed no justification. But Sievier did none of those things. He never really got to grips with the kernel of the case or adopted any coherent line at all. Instead he plunged into a hurly burly of self-defence, innuendo, abuse and irrelevancy which tried Reading's patience almost to breaking-point and which must have exasperated the jury. Worse still, he had not taken the trouble to check his facts, to re-read his answers in the Duke case or to do any home work at all. Constantly he gave different answers or explanations from those he had given in the earlier trial. Thus, time after time, he was tripped up in inaccuracies or what must have seemed to the jury plain lies. For instance he told the court that he had not gone on with the libel action against the *Hawk* because he had at that time been on a long visit to Australia. When Carson questioned him further about this he had to admit he was not sure of his dates and finally to concede, when it was shown to him in black and white, that he had not been in Australia at all at the time.

He retained, it is hardly necessary to say, as always, his bounce and his brashness. He stood up to Carson's fiercest onslaughts without flinching, though in the witness box bravery is no substitute for fact. Here are some of their interchanges:

CARSON: Do you now know that Wootton has been before the stewards and that they are satisfied about the running of The Gun'ah?

SIEVIER: I do not know that they are satisfied.

CARSON: Did you enquire?

SIEVIER: I did not enquire.

CARSON: Why did you not bring some of these stewards here instead of those ornamental Peers who were here yesterday and proved nothing?

SIEVIER: If the Marquess of Crewe and Lord Lonsdale are ornamental Peers so are most of the Jockey Club.

CARSON: I meant ornamental Peers as regards this case because they came her to prove nothing.

SIEVIER: They came to prove something and you objected.

At another point he protested that Carson was firing questions at him so fast that he did not know where he was. Reading thereupon snapped at him: 'You are in the witness box. Sir Edward Carson is cross-examining you. I am presiding over the trial. If you want to know what is being done Sir Edward Carson is reading the pamphlet of which you complain and putting you questions upon it.'

When Carson, who persisted in calling him 'Mr. Seevier', put in a letter of his he asked him: 'You know that is a very abusive letter?'

'Yes, but a very truthful one,' was the answer.

'A very Seevier sort of letter?'

'I think it is a very de-Sievier sort of letter.'

There was laughter in court after this and he did score over Carson when he was being examined about his remarks concerning the jury in the Duke case and the obscure—or worse—places he said that they had hailed from.

'A man might be a very honourable man living in Tottenham Court Road?' Carson asked him.

'He might, or even in an attic.'

'And a man might be a very dishonourable man having a suite of rooms at the Metropole Hotel, Brighton?'

'Most decidedly, or even in Belfast.'

This was a palpable hit. But points scored like this meant nothing in one of Carson's cross-examinations. It was the culminating, crushing effect which told in the end.

'In 1892,' Carson went on, 'you were made bankrupt in May and then you went down in July and took a suite of rooms at the Metropole Hotel, Brighton?'

'Quite.'

'Had you a suite also at a hotel in London?'

'I think I was living at the Hotel Windsor but I did not have a suite there.'

'With the ease of a bankrupt?'

'With the comfort of a bankrupt. I had no debts.'

'I suppose the bankruptcy court did not make you an allowance?' Carson enquired with heavy sarcasm.

'No. I suppose they considered I was the richest bankrupt in the world.'

But persiflage, as Wilde had found out years earlier, availed little against Carson. All the discreditable instances in the Duke case were dragged out into the daylight once again and made to look even worse under his skilful and probing questions. The Horn incident especially was laid bare once more.

And then, at the end of the second day, Carson was called to Ulster and Hastings, young, ambitious and thirsting to show what he could do, took over the case. All the groundwork had been already done. By this time Hastings could scarcely have lost the case though he might have failed to have sewn it up as tightly as he did. Contrary to his usual custom which was, he says, never to prepare a cross-examination at all, he sat up all night getting up this case which he was determined would make his name, and preparing his line of attack.

With both massive and damaging material at his disposal he went for Sievier from the start. He has recorded how, when he had finished with the Horn case, 'even the carnation in his' (Sievier's) 'buttonhole appeared to droop, and the sweat began to glisten on his face.' Hastings was there and one must accept what he says but one would be more ready to do so were not his own account of his own case riddled with inaccuracies. Sievier was not accustomed to flinch before any man, and even Reading in his summing up was moved to comment that he had at no time shirked the issues in the case.

In his accounts Hastings devotes most of his space to the manner in which he handled Sievier and Charles Mills whom he called to give evidence about the Joel case. He states that Sievier said to him concerning that case: 'I have been acquitted at the Central Criminal Court. You have called me a blackmailer and that you can never prove.'

'I told him,' Hastings continues, 'That we were going to try.' He goes on to say that Sievier challenged him to put Mills into the box.

All that can be said about these interchanges quoted by Hastings is that if they took place at all they do not appear in the transcript of evidence. In fact Hastings' cross-examination of Mills on the Joel case was surprisingly cautious and mild. 'In the past,' Hastings says, 'undoubtedly he' (Mills) 'had proved to be Sievier's greatest asset at his trial. No one had ever questioned his integrity and he was undoubtedly Sievier's friend.'

So far from this being an accurate statement of the facts it was of course the case that Mills' integrity had been questioned by Isaacs, Sievier himself and Alverstone in the trial. And as to him still being Sievier's friend, the truth was that Sievier had never spoken to him since that day save to insult him in public and he had constantly held him up in print to hatred, ridicule and contempt.

Just at that time Mills had hitched his fortunes to those of the eccentric financier Jimmy White and was shortly to be dragged down when White crashed. Unquestionably he was a frightened man and a reluctant witness but his apparent unwillingness to say anything that might damage Sievier would appear to have sprung not from friendship but from fear.

Mills' evidence-in-chief put Wootton's case no further at all despite all that Hastings could do by way of attempting to persuade him into admissions. These efforts of Hastings led Sievier to protest: 'My Lord, counsel is cross-examining his own witness.'

'It is going near it,' Reading said. 'But there comes a point at which it is my discretion to allow it. The point is as fine as a needle at present.'

At the end of Mills' examination by Hastings it was clear that counsel's gamble had not come off. Sievier had enough sense to see that he had been at least as much helped as harmed by Mills' testimony and that he should leave the matter there and not cross-examine. 'My Lord,' he said. 'Unless there is anything serious in Your Lordship's mind which I cannot see, I do not wish to cross-examine this witness.'

There the matter should have rested but Reading's tortuous mind would not allow it to do so. 'The difficulty of it is this,' he told Sievier. 'I have a shrewd notion and I think you have of what Mr. Hastings is going to say when he addresses the Jury on these facts. The Jury will be asked to draw the inference that although they do not and cannot challenge the acquittal for a moment, it was very near it. . . . The moral obloquy of it remains the same. And that is why I put it to you in plain terms so that there should be no misunderstanding.'

This was said in the presence of the jury so Sievier was now, whether by accident or design, placed firmly on the horns of a horrible dilemma. Were he to refuse to cross-examine, this course would almost certainly be construed as an admission of guilt. If he did cross-examine, he risked re-examination and all its consequences. As always he chose the rasher course and faced the fence in front of him. 'Then I will ask a few questions,' he said.

He has been much criticised for this, notably by Lord Birkett who blames him for the 'terrible mistake' of cross-examining, but Birkett appears to have been following Hastings' account, which makes no mention of the Judge's intervention. Given the position in which he was placed by Reading, one which might well have taxed the ingenuity of a

Carson or F. E. Smith, it is hard to see how he could have done otherwise.

The 'one or two questions' brought from Mills confirmation of the story that had been told in the Joel case.

Hastings then rose to cross-examine and here is what he says happened:

" 'Had Sievier shown you any photographs to be incorporated with the proposed article on Joel?'

'He had.'

'Who did the photographs represent?'

'Two well-known criminals.'

'Where were they to be placed?'

'One on each side of a picture of Joel himself.'

'What for?'

"Mr. Mills began to be confused. 'I do not know.'

'How could publication be prevented?'

'If Mr. Joel paid £5000.'

'Did Mr. Joel hand you £5000?'

'Yes.'

'What did you do with the money?'

'I handed it to Mr. Sievier.'

'And was publication stopped.'

'It was.' "

Birkett cites this as a model of re-examination. There must be some doubt, however, if it took place at all in that form for here is the re-examination as given in the transcript:

HASTINGS: Did Mr. Sievier, before the money passed show you some documents?

MILLS: He did.

HASTINGS: What were the documents he showed to you before the money passed?

MILLS: The documents of two men in South Africa.

HASTINGS: Had the men been alleged to have committed crimes in South Africa?

MILLS: Murder, I believe.

HASTINGS: You told me it was in relation to Mr. Joel. In what way? What had two pictures of murderers in South Africa to do with Mr. Joel?

MILLS: I do not know.

HASTINGS: Tell us quite simply what Mr. Sievier said he was going to do with them if the £5000 was not paid?

MILLS: I know no more than he said that if the £5000 was not paid
             the two pictures would be in the next issue of the *Winning
             Post*.
HASTINGS: How was that connected with Mr. Joel?
MILLS: Mr. Joel was to ornament them in the centre.
HASTINGS: That is what Mr. Sievier told you and showed you?
MILLS: Yes.
HASTINGS: Was that for the purpose of you conveying the information
             to Mr. Joel?'
MILLS: I suppose so.
HASTINGS: Did you do what Mr. Sievier wanted?
MILLS: Yes.
HASTINGS: After that did you get the cheque for £5000?

Here Reading felt it time to intervene, as indeed it was. 'You are
going rather far in leading now,' he said.

'I will not go any further. I will stop there.' Hastings said.

It will be seen that in fact no question as to publication being stopped
was ever asked in this re-examination. Had it been, Sievier could, of
course, have called re-butting evidence as to the real reason for stopping
publication if, that is to say, he understood the rules concerning rebuttal which is unlikely.

In his speech to the jury Hastings attempted to use Mills' evidence
to show that Sievier had in fact committed blackmail on that occasion
but when he did so he was pretty smartly pulled up by the Lord Chief
Justice. 'What you have just said,' Reading told him, 'is saying he was
guilty of the offence. He has the verdict of the jury that he was innocent
of it. In the two observations you have made you went a little further. I
do not think that is right. A man once acquitted is acquitted for all
time.'

When Reading summed up in a manner wholly hostile to Sievier
he dealt with the Joel case with considerable circumspection; it was the
incident with Horn and Williams long ago in Monte Carlo which once
again was used with deadly effect against Sievier. 'We are dealing here,'
Reading told the Jury, 'with actual cheating, with dishonest transactions,
and so we are outside all debatable realms of morality or ethics.'

Whether Sievier ever had a good explanation for the £700 cheque
given to 'Tricky' Williams it is certain he never gave it. In the course of a
rambling and ineffectual speech to the jury in this case he never dealt
with it at all.

After Reading's summing up no one in court had much doubt as to what the result would be. The jury were only out for 45 minutes before returning with a verdict for Wootton.

Hastings says that Wootton was carried by the public shoulder-high into the Strand. He goes on 'The glory of Robert Sievier had departed, and he left the precincts of the court by the back door, never again to be allowed on an English racecourse.'

This sentence contains the most mischievous of all Hastings' inaccuracies. It is in fact a flat untruth. No action whatsoever was taken by the stewards against Sievier and he was free to and did return to Fitzroy House and his career on the Turf. It was fortunate indeed for Hastings that he made this untrue statement some years after Sievier's death for here was a libel which affected his honour in racing. Had he been alive it must be considered certain that he could and would have issued proceedings against Hastings and that heavy damages would have followed. Whatever could be said about his private life, in racing he was blameless and it is greatly to be regretted that subsequent writers have followed Hastings' account and repeated the calumny.

Most racing people, and certainly Sievier's friends, cared little about the re-hash of ancient allegations and the stirring up of years-old mud that might have been far better left undisturbed.

Wootton, though he had the personal satisfaction of victory, did not succeed in his avowed intention of getting Sievier warned off and the *Winning Post* silenced. A year or so later he retired from racing altogether and returned to Australia.

In fact Sievier had at that very time under his care and management a colt who he believed might well bring to him some of his greatest triumphs on the English Turf and whom he was now actively preparing for his two-year-old career. This was Monarch and his first race was to be only a month later at Newmarket under Sievier's watchful eye. So much for the statement that he was never again to be allowed on an English racecourse.

27

Monarch

꠷꠷꠷꠷꠷

Monarch was by Tracery out of Teofani and therefore a half-brother to Royal Bucks. Sievier had bought him as a foal from Mr. Edward Kennedy of Straffan, County Kildare, a breeder for whom he always had the utmost admiration. He had reared him and passed him on to Sir Henry Bird who refused £6000 for him as a yearling. Sievier was sure he had classic potential and he was further convinced of this when Monarch began his outstandingly successful two-year-old career. At the Newmarket First Spring Meeting he was ridden by Joe Childs who had a tremendous touch with two-year-olds coupled with the most delicate hands. Monarch needed these things. He had Galopin blood on both sides of his pedigree and where that was there was usually temperament too. He won his first race at Newmarket without being extended. Once more ridden by Childs he won again at the Second Spring Meeting. Childs was on him, too, in his next race when he was beaten into third place in the Coventry Stakes at Ascot. In this defeat he was, however, far from disgraced. He was in a lather of sweat before the race having been upset, so Sievier says, by passing motor-cars—the drivers of which received a salvo from his pen in the next issue of the *Winning Post*—when coming from the stables to the course. Also he tripped when crossing the tan and was almost on his knees. At the time he was half a length in front, and looked all over a winner.

His next appearance was in the July Stakes at the First July Meeting and this he won. In the Chesterfield Stakes at the Second July Meeting he was beaten into second place but once more there were valid reasons for his defeat. Some difficulty had arisen about training the colt at Newmarket. Sievier, with typical hyperbole, says that 'Monarch was driven off Newmarket Heath.' He had had to be taken hurriedly to Royston for his winding-up gallop which upset him and they discovered after the race that he was suffering from sore shins. He was then put by until the autumn, with the Middle Park Plate as his objective.

Monarch was a shy feeder and very often would not eat up. They were worried about keeping condition on him. Sievier and Hogg, the head lad, tried all sorts of things and eventually discovered that a diet of fresh dandelion leaves whetted his appetite. Mr. William Clark of Swaffam Prior used to supply a number of trainers, including Sievier, with forage. Sievier went to him and contracted for a constant supply of these leaves as well as his other needs.

He was always erratic in his payments but Clark, in common with most people in the town and countryside, liked him and he let the bill run. It was invariably paid in the end and Clark knew that while the people who could afford it were frequently kept waiting those who could not were paid promptly enough and he knew, too, of the countless instances of Sievier's kindness and bounty to the poor and sick in the town.

During this time, however, Sievier left for London and was away for a long time. Fitzroy House appeared to be all but closed up and rumours began to fly about that he had gone for good. When the bill for forage amounted to about £500 Clark, hearing the rumour, began to be worried. He ascertained Sievier's London address and resolved to make the journey to find out what he was up to and if he intended to return to Newmarket. His son-in-law had just bought a small car and they arranged to drive together to London.

The address they had been given was at Eccleston Place. The housekeeper, whom they knew well, opened the door and asked them in. Sievier was in his bath, she said, but would not be long. They were shown into a study, a decanter was put before them and they were told to help themselves. In a short time they heard a roar from upstairs: 'Is that you, Clark?'

They went out and saw Sievier leaning over the banisters clad only in a minute bath towel. Clark's son-in-law remembers the tableau vividly with Sievier leaning over the banisters and themselves below looking up at him. His body, he says, was covered with fine black hair. Even then he gave the impression of immense power and vitality. 'I know what you want,' he called, 'I shan't be long. Help yourselves.'

As he entered the downstairs room a minute or two later, still clad only in the towel, he said immediately: 'I know what you are looking for. Come along with me, Clark.' Together they went into another room. Soon Clark returned with a cheque for £250 and a promise of the balance in a few days. More refreshment was provided with a lavish hand and Sievier told them he had no intention of leaving Newmarket but would be back there within a week. Both promises were kept. Clark received the balance of his money and Sievier returned to Fitzroy House to supervise Monarch's preparation for the Middle Park Plate. Clark continued to supply him with forage until he left Newmarket when he was to say of him that there were many who missed him, especially the poor.

Monarch's first race in the autumn was the Newmarket First October Meeting when, ridden again by Childs, he won the Boscawen Stakes handsomely. Then the final touches were put on him to get him ready for the big race.

There was an exceptionally good field for the Middle Park that year. It included Humorist the next year's Derby winner and Polemarch who was to win the 1921 St. Leger. Bullock had the ride in place of Childs who was claimed elsewhere. Sievier and Griggs instructed Bullock to get Monarch smartly away and come for home as hard as he could. They both knew the colt had brilliant speed and they wanted him to make the best use of it. He obeyed his orders exactly for he was out of the gate like a shot and was never headed. Carslake on Humorist made every effort to get at him but could not quite succeed. Looking all over a champion, Monarch came storming home by a neck without really appearing to be pressed. Polemarch was third.

On that splendid note Monarch ended his two-year-old career. Out of seven starts he had won five times, been second once and third once. He was never unplaced and had won stakes to the value of £8172. When the Free Handicap was published he shared the top of it with a colt called Leighton. Sievier, it seemed, had indeed got hold of something to shout about.

He did not shout very much. Though he was still not to be trifled with, he was mellowing. He could even write in the *Winning Post*: 'After Monarch we wish J. B. Joel luck with the son of Polymelus—Jest, for his horses run in the interests of the public.' That was a bit of a change!

Apart from writing the racing articles he was taking less and less interest in the *Winning Post*. Before, if a space-filler was needed, he could dash off a witty and probably salacious sketch or short story at a moment's notice. Now either his interest or his invention had flagged and, in place of his own writing, pieces culled from such near-pornography as *The Memoirs of Harriet Wilson* began to appear. Without his hand on the tiller and his flair to inspire it the paper commenced to flag. In places, too, he became oddly prim as when he rebuked Maugham for bringing 'the morals of the farmyard' into one of his plays.

The fact was that the paper, like himself, was out of touch and out of sympathy with the times. Edwardian smut was no longer fashionable. Hints and innuendo did not satisfy the post-war generation. They were all for outspokenness. They despised their elders and said so openly and with emphasis. Sievier was one of them and his paper one of their voices.

But he still held high revel at Fitzroy House. And when he wanted to he could still exercise his former fascination for both men and women. Everywhere he went it was 'Hallo, Bob,' and 'What's doing, Bob?' He was on christian names terms with high and low, he had a word for everyone, especially the poor and unfortunate. They often found the word accompanied by a pound note or, in good times, a fiver.

About this time a young and well-connected girl was coming out and was staying with friends at Portland Place. During the course of a reception at which Sievier's friends Lord Waring and Gordon Selfridge were present one or the other of them introduced her to him. He took a tremendous fancy to her and despite the difference in their ages (which would not have bothered him anyway) he bombarded her with invitations. His hired Daimler swept them to Skindles and the Carlton, then the most fashionable rendezvous in Town, and many other places where money could buy the best. She was fascinated and repelled at the same time, and held spellbound by his anecdotes. He was a wonderful storyteller. He knew everything about everybody. Alone or in small groups of friends all the brashness went and something of the inner, gentler man buried deep inside him peeped out. His speaking voice, his expressive eyes, his sympathetic chuckle all made him a far different man from the rough-tongued racegoer the public—and his enemies— knew.

Then came for her the invitation to spend the week-end at Fitzroy House with Sir Henry and Lady Bird as chaperons. When she arrived, she found herself greeted, as Clark had been in London, by her host clad only in an exiguous bath towel. He had been suffering from eczema, he explained and clothes hurt his skin. Not in the least embarrassed by the inadequate garb he showed her round the house. In the study, by way of making conversation, she admired the photographs of young men in uniform that proliferated on the mantelpiece and tables. 'All my sons,' he told her proudly, 'But only one is legitimate!'

In her room she found that there were no locks on the doors and that her host had the disturbing habit, still clad only in the towel, of entering without warning and walking in and out of the guests' bedrooms talking incessantly all the time.

When the house-party retired to dress for dinner an elderly house-maid came to her room. 'This is no place for you, miss,' she said. An argument ensued which the housemaid won and which ended in the young lady being packed off to London in the Daimler without even saying goodbye to her host. Next day a gold and tortoiseshell fitted dressing case arrived from Aspreys together with a letter from Sievier full of apology and speculation as to what had caused her hurried departure. Further pressing invitations followed.

Despite the parties, the champagne and caviar existence that he liked so much and that his splendid constitution still enabled him to live, he was managing to keep an eye on Monarch's progress. Bobbie was out of the Air Force where he had had a successful war and won an M.C., and was now helping with the horses.

But Monarch did not winter well and signs of temperament were becoming more and more apparent. It was decided not to run him in public before the Two Thousand Guineas. There, to the intense disappointment of Sievier and Bird, he fretted his race away. He was troublesome at the start and broke the tapes twice. Before the field had reached half-way he was done with, Craig-an-Eran winning from Lemonora and Humorist.

After that he was taken out of the Derby. As a three-year-old he could only win twice from ten starts. He was a sad and costly disappointment to them all. There were recriminations, too, and the horses left Griggs and went to Walter Earl.

Sievier, however, had great hopes that the colt would redeem himself in the big handicaps the following year and backed him at long odds to do so. These hopes were illusory. Bad luck pursued Monarch from the finish of his golden year as a two-year-old. In 1922 he was second in the Lincoln, beaten five lengths by Granely and followed that by being second again in the City and Suburban.

He was in the Victoria Cup and Sievier could not believe that he would be beaten again. He engaged Joe Childs to ride him and went for the last of his great old-fashioned gambles, backing Monarch with every penny he could raise.

Behind a somewhat forbidding exterior Joe Childs was a highly-strung and temperamental man. He did not much care about riding for betting owners and has said himself that he believes the fact of knowing such a huge sum was at stake may have interfered with his judgment. In fact he thinks he should have won the race. He always preferred to win his races from behind but in this instance both Earl and Sievier cautioned him not to wait too long. With this warning very much in his mind and the knowledge of the money involved bringing on an anxiety to make sure of winning, he thinks he may have timed his effort a fraction too soon. In fact he believed that he had his race won but just on the post The Yellow Dwarf, carrying a very light weight, flashed up to him, caught him and beat him a short head. Monarch was second again. To make matters worse he was beaten into second place once more in the Jubilee Handicap at Kempton a week later. In the Eclipse he was third, third again when well-backed in the Rivermead Handicap at Kempton and third once more in the Liverpool Autumn Cup.

Bird and Sievier were now both feeling the strain. More recriminations flew around and as a result Bird took all his horses away and sent them to Len Hammond at Lewes. Sievier contended that some of the horses were his and had only been allowed to run in Bird's name. Rows, ructions and threats of legal action followed. Everything was eventually settled by the payment to Sievier of a sum of money and the handing over to him of three brood mares including Teofani, the dam of Royal Bucks and Monarch. But Sievier, of course, did not forget. Bird had a bad time on the racecourse after this for whenever Sievier saw him he cursed him loudly and fluently.

The *Winning Post* was by this time going very badly indeed. In 1922 it ceased publication during the steeplechasing season. It shrank steadily in size and in 1924 died altogether. Sievier was by now once more broke or very near it. He gave up Fitzroy House and moved to Lanehurst near Hurstpierpoint. But he did not leave Newmarket without one last splendid gesture in the face of the great and the grand.

The Aga Khan, who just about that time was entering racing in a big way, had a filly called Charley's Mount in the Cesarewitch. She had been well backed early on and Sievier had picked her out as a likely candidate. Nine days before the race she ran very badly in heavy going at Nottingham when joint favourite. The ground at Newmarket was firm but no one seemed to want to back her and she drifted out to 100—1. Before the race Sievier was standing in the paddock when the Aga passed him. Sievier bade him good afternoon in a civil fashion but the Aga, then anxious to know only the right people and be known only by them, walked on, deliberately cutting him dead.

Infuriated, Sievier looked at his card and then went down to the ring and backed Charley's Mount with everything he had. The filly came home on a tight rein unbacked by owner, stable or anybody else, apparently, save Bob Sievier.

He did not forget the insult and was determined to have his revenge. Waiting for a moment when the Aga was chatting with some influential acquaintances he approached him. When still some distance away he stopped and roared out at the top of his voice, 'Hi, you!'

Everyone in the paddock turned round to see what was going on. Giving them plenty of time to hear his next remark, Sievier stared directly at the Aga. Then, sweeping off his hat and bowing low, he shouted, 'Thanks for the tip, your Highness. I've just won enough to buy you a bloody banjo!'

28

Downhill

꧁꧂

All the great days were over now. Lanehurst was the last good residence he was to have. It was a small Georgian house and there was a paddock where he could keep the brood mares. He continued, too, his hobby of breeding bull-terriers, fierce beautiful brutes whom he loved and who had, when roused, tempers nearly matching his own. He still went racing, of course, nothing could prevent him doing that. He had lost his press pass when the *Winning Post* folded but he still used the press stand and it would have been a brave man indeed who tried to turn him off. He kept his eye for a horse, too, and his skill in reading races and spotting jockeys. He was taken on for a bit as racing correspondent for the *People* and tipped Forsetti to win the 1925 Cambridgeshire at long odds. He recognised Hyperion's greatness and told all his friends to back him for the Derby, doing so himself, too, with everything he had.

But, basically, now it was downhill all the way. He was getting older, he hated the post-war world and he refused to change with it. Sometimes those very close to him seemed to sense in him regret for many of the things he had done, for talents squandered and gifts misused. In private he was gentle, slightly melancholy, looking backward, and utterly charming when he talked about people, places and things he had known and enjoyed. But the old demonic spirit could still flash out as when a young relative staying with him at Lanehurst came down to breakfast to find him studying the obituaries in *The Times*. 'Hooray,' he said looking up from the chopped raw steak on toast with which his digestion still enabled him to start the day. The young man enquired the reason for his pleasure, thinking that he had just brought up a long-priced winner. 'Old Henry Bird's in Hell,' came in a growl from his host, accompanied by a satisfied chuckle.

Then arrived what seemed to be another chance. Reginald Denny, the well-known Hollywood character-actor, fixed up a film deal for him. He was to go to Hollywood to work on the script of a racing film with Edgar Wallace and, if that was successful, to do further work on scripts. He had, however, hardly arrived in America when Wallace died and the whole thing fell through. The money he had been advanced was soon spent and he hated America. He sent a cable to ten of his friends asking for his fare home and something to go with it, ending with the words: *It is worse to be broke in New York than naked in Jerusalem.* This touch brought him in £1000, £500 of which, or so it is said, was contributed by Bend Or Westminster and £500 by Lord Howard de Walden. He had one gorgeous fling in New York and then sailed for home. He was over seventy years of age.

In 1932 there was an effort to revive the *Winning Post* and to put him in as editor. It failed and then he went bankrupt again, this time for £3500, a sum he would have regarded as paltry in his heyday.

Then, at last, his splendid physical health began to fail him. He was to all intents and purposes penniless and he took up quarters in a small, dark, ground-floor flat in Stanhope Gardens. A failing heart had brought on fluid in the chest and much of his time was spent in bed. The doctor who attended him found him 'short of breath but never of humour'. Seeing a picture of Sceptre on the wall the doctor asked him if he was still interested in racing. Immediately Sievier sat upright in bed. 'What, me?' he said. 'Still interested in racing? I'm interested in anything that's nefarious!' Finding that the doctor, too, liked his bet he took to sending him notes. *Dear Doctor—if of gold you would have more, put your siller on Greenore.* The doctor did and collected a nice little sum.

Charles Clark rescued him from Stanhope Gardens and set him up at Tilton Lodge, Ifield Wood, in Sussex. Here he surrounded himself with his treasures and his memories of the old days, pictures of his great horses, a painting of himself as a swash-buckling soldier in South Africa and a full-length portrait of Mrs. Master. His health took a turn for the better in the country air.

He made friends with his neighbours, the de Bounevailles and the daughter of the house sometimes went racing with him, revelling in the good company he gave her, the stories he told and his little attentions and kindnesses. He bought a pony and trap and became a film fan, haunting the local cinemas where he soon became almost as well known as on the racecourse.

As always he loved his bet even if now it was only a few shillings. When he picked Chumleigh to win the 1937 St. Leger and backed him it gave him almost as much pleasure as his huge coups of long ago. He tried his hand at writing again but the one novel he finished 'John

Ironside' was hopelessly stilted and dated and was never published. Occasional stories and articles did find a market and brought in something with which to gamble.

In 1938 he insisted on going to Doncaster for the St. Leger. He refused to bring a coat, the weather suddenly turned wet and cold. He returned home, drenched, ill and tired. A few weeks later he collapsed at Sandown. Rumour had it that he had died and the London dailies were constantly on the telephone. 'Tell them I'm dead,' he said. 'I'll write my obituary tomorrow.'

He survived to see Blue Peter win the Derby in 1939, but after the first day of Ascot that year he never went racing again. He was very quiet and gentle at this time; the public man and his image had vanished utterly. Now he was himself, alone with a few friends as perhaps he would always have liked to have been but which the warrior in him and his turbulent spirit had never allowed him to be.

He died quietly in his sleep on October 8th 1939 and was buried at St. Peter's Church, Crawley, in the presence of his close relatives and a few friends. A wreath in his racing colours was laid on his grave. Someone in the crowd, looking at the hearse which had carried him, was heard to murmur: 'Well, it's as it should be. The old man's last ride was in a Rolls Royce.'

He had done many things he ought not to have done but at least he had never preyed on the weak. It was the strong, the arrogant and the mighty whom he attacked, bitterly and at times without sense or reason. But he befriended the poor and never used the terrible force of his invective against those unable to hit back.

On the racecourse his horses were always run openly and straight. Throughout his long career as an owner, trainer and manager of racehorses, the running of a horse in his care was never questioned or queried by the stewards or any Turf authority. Of many a better man might worse be said.

Appendix

❧❧❧❧❧

PRICES PAID BY SIEVIER AT AUCTION WHEN YEARLINGS

	£
For Sceptre, by Persimmon—Ornament	10,500
For Duke of Westminster, by Orme—Gantlet	5,880
For Sandflake, by Trenton—Sandiway	5,775
For Consort, by Orme—Console	735
Total ...	£22,890

PRICES RECEIVED AND STAKES WON

	£
Duke of Westminster (bought by John Porter for Mr. George Faber)	22,050
Consort (bought by John Porter for Mr. George Faber) ...	2,100
Sandflake (bought by the International Horse Agency on behalf of Mr. W. Bass)	1,680
Sceptre (bought by Mr. Arthur Chetwynd on behalf of Mr. W. Bass)	25,000
Stakes won by Duke of Westminster	2,645
Stakes won by Sceptre	25,650
Total ...	£79,125

Bibliography

WILLIAM ALLISON. *Memories of Men and Horses.* Grant Richards Ltd. 1922.

F. W. ASHLEY. *My Sixty Years in the Law.* John Lane, The Bodley Head. 1936.

DUDLEY BARKER. *Lord Darling's Famous Cases.* Hutchinson & Co. Ltd. 1936.

THE EARL OF BIRKENHEAD. *The Life of F. E. Smith, First Earl of Birkenhead.* Eyre & Spottiswoode Ltd. 1959

LORD BIRKETT. *Six Great Advocates.* Penguin Books Ltd. 1961.

SIR CHARTRES BIRON. *Without Prejudice.* Faber & Faber Ltd. 1936.

ERNEST BLAND, Editor. *Flat Racing since 1900.* Andrew Dakers Ltd. 1950.

J. B. BOOTH. *'Master' and Men, Pink 'Un Yesterdays.* T. Werner Laurie Ltd. 1927.

J. B. BOOTH. *The Days We Knew.* T. Werner Laurie Ltd. 1943.

A. E. BOWKER. *Behind the Bar.* Staples Press Ltd. 1947.

SIR EDMUND CADOGAN. *Before the Deluge.* John Murrary Ltd. 1961.

CAPTAIN X. *Tales of the Turf.* Partridge Publications Ltd. N.d.

THE EARL OF CARDIGAN. *The Wardens of Savernake Forest.* Routledge & Kegan Paul. 1949.

SIR CLAUDE CHAMPION de CRESPIGNY. Bt. *Sporting Memoirs.* Laurence & Bullen. 1896.

SIR CLAUDE CHAMPION de CRESPIGNY, Bt. *Forty Years of a Sportsman's Life.* Mills & Boon Ltd. 1910.

SIR GEORGE CHETWYND, Bt. *Racing Reminiscences and Experiences of the Turf.* (2 vols.). Longmans, Green & Co. Ltd. 1891.

JOE CHILDS. *My Racing Reminiscences.* Hutchinson & Co. Ltd. 1952.

LOUIS COHEN. *Reminiscences of Kimberley.* Bennet & Co. 1911.

THEODORE A. COOK. *A History of the English Turf.* (5 vols.). Virtue & Co. 1901—1904.

HARDING COX. *Chasing and Racing.* John Lane, The Bodley Head Ltd. 1922.

SAM DARLING. *Reminiscences.* Mills and Boon Ltd. 1914.

THOMAS HENRY DEY. *Leaves from a Bookmaker's Book.* Hutchinson & Co. Ltd. N.D.

DICTIONARY OF NATIONAL BIOGRAPHY.

EX-C.M.R. *With The Cape Mounted Rifles.* Richard Bentley & Son. 1881.

SYDNEY GALTREY. *Memoirs of a Racing Journalist.* Hutchinson & Co. Ltd. 1934.

MEYRICK GOOD. *The Lure of the Turf.* Odhams Press Ltd. 1957.

MEYRICK GOOD. *Good Days.* Hutchinson & Co. Ltd. N.D.

SIR PATRICK HASTINGS. *Autobiography of Sir Patrick Hastings.* William Heinemann Ltd. 1948.

SIR PATRICK HASTINGS. *Cases in Court.* William Heinemann Ltd. 1949.

PATRICIA HASTINGS. *The Life of Patrick Hastings.* The Cresset Press. 1959.

JOSEPH HONE. *The Moores of Moore Hall.* Jonathan Cape Ltd. 1939.

H. MONTGOMERY HYDE. *Sir Patrick Hastings His Life and Cases.* William Heinemann Ltd. 1960.

H. MONTGOMERY HYDE. *Lord Reading.* William Heinemann Ltd. 1967.

ROBERT JACKSON. *The Chief.* George G. Harrap & Co. Ltd. 1959.

STANHOPE JOEL. *Ace of Diamonds.* The Story of Solomon Barnato Joel. Frederick Muller Ltd. 1958.

STANLEY JACKSON. *Rufus Isaacs First Marquess of Reading.* Cassell & Co. Ltd. 1936.

THE HON. GEORGE LAMBTON. *Men and Horses I have known.* Thornton Butterworth Ltd. 1924.

A. DICK LUCKMAN. *Sharps, Flats, Gamblers and Racehorses.* Grant Richards Ltd. 1914.

EDGAR LUSTGARTEN. *The Judges and The Judged.* Odhams Press Ltd. 1961.

EDWARD MARJORIBANKS, M.P. *The Life of Sir Edward Marshall Hall, K.C.* Victor Gollancz Ltd. 1929.

EDWARD MARJORIBANKS, M.P. and IAN COLVIN. *The Life of Lord Carson* (2 vols.). Victor Gollancz Ltd. 1932 & 1934.

RICHARD MARSH. *A Trainer to Two Kings.* Cassell & Co. Ltd. 1925.

EDWARD MOORHOUSE. *The Romance of The Derby* (2 vols.). The Biographical Press. 1908.

ROGER MORTIMER. *The Jockey Club.* Cassell & Co. Ltd. 1958.

ROGER MORTIMER. *The History of The Derby Stakes*. Cassell & Co. Ltd. 1962.

ROGER MORTIMER. *Twenty Great Horses*. Cassell & Co. Ltd. 1967.

VINCENT ORCHARD. *The Derby Stakes. 1900 to 1953*. Hutchinson & Co. Ltd. 1954.

VINCENT ORCHARD. *Tattersalls*. Hutchinson & Co. Ltd. 1953.

JOHN PORTER. *John Porter of Kingsclere*. Richards Press Ltd. 1919.

ARTHUR J. SARL. *Horses, Jockeys and Crooks*. Hutchinson & Co. Ltd. 1935.

ARTHUR J. SARL. *Gamblers of the Turf*. Hutchinson & Co. Ltd. N.D.

R. S. SIEVIER. *The Autobiography of Robert Standish Sievier*. The Winning Post Ltd. 1906.

R. S. SIEVIER. *Warned Off, a racing novel*. The Winning Post Ltd. N.D.

JULIAN SYMONS. *Horatio Bottomley*. The Cresset Press. 1955.

CHARLES ADOLPH VOIGHT. *Famous Gentlemen Riders at Home and Abroad*. Hutchinson & Co. Ltd. N.D.

DEREK WALKER-SMITH. *The Life of Lord Darling*. Cassell & Co. Ltd. 1938.

DEREK WALKER-SMITH. *Lord Reading & His Cases*. Cassell & Co. Ltd. 1953.

TOMMY WESTON. *My Racing Life*. Hutchinson & Co. Ltd. 1952.

DORNFORD YATES. *As Berry and I were saying*. Ward Lock & Co. Ltd. 1952.

NEWSPAPERS, PERIODICALS, Etc.

The Argus (Australia)
The Age (Australia)
The Bandolier
The Hawk
The Herald and Evening Journal (Australia)
The Illustrated Sporting and Dramatic News
The Field
The People
The Sporting Life
The Sportsman
The Sporting Times (*The Pink 'Un*)
The Sporting Judge (Australia)
The Sunday Sportsman
Sievier's Monthly
The Times
Victorian Law Reports, Vol. XIII
The Winning Post

Index

Russell, Sir Charles, 58–9, 210–11, 258

Sanders, Vic, 62, 66, 68
Sceptre (racehorse), 110–13, 115–18, 124, 126–44, 146–52, 165–6, 175
Selfridge, Gordon, 270
Sellar, Major David, 153–4, 158–9, 165, 209
Sellicks, F. J., 189, 198, 199, 208, 231
Selwyn, Major Henry Jasper, 208
Shearman, Montague, 207–9
Sherwood (trainer), 56, 62
Shrewsbury, Earl of, 169, 257
Sievier, Alicia Mary, 13
Sievier, Bob: birth of, 13; precociousness of, 15; sent to school in France, 15; his growing taste for sophisticated vice, 15–16; enlists in Frontier Armed and Mounted Police, 16; his fondness for the stage and histrionic streak in his character, 17; his gambling recklessness, 17; becomes sergeant in Queenstown Volunteers, 19; character of, 20; proposes to become actor, 20; arrested and charged with obstruction and bad language, 21; offered and accepts acting role in India, 22; his financial difficulties, 23; early association with racecourse, 24; his enthusiasm for racing, 27; lives at Week's Hotel, 23–7; moves to Brighton, 27; decides to become bookmaker, 28; goes to Monte Carlo and Naples, 29; books passage for Australia, 29; sets up as course bookmaker, 31; elected to Victorian Club, 32; his success in Australia, 33; marriage of, 33; separation from wife, 34; served with divorce petition, 34; elected to Boodles' Club, 35; books passage to England, 37; his quarrel with Lord Deerhurst, 38–46; awarded costs against Lord Deerhurst, 46; takes flat at Burlington Gardens, 47; has himself presented at Court, 47; revenge sought on by Lords Deerhurst and Dudley, 48; contemplates owning and running racehorses, 50; becomes bankrupt, 52; revisits Australia and Monte Carlo, 52; writes play Stone Broke, 53, 57; courtship of Lady Mabel Brudenell-Bruce, 56; quarrels with C. F. Gill, 60; drops libel proceedings against The Bat, 60; marriage to Lady Mabel Brudenell-Bruce, 61; sets up as off-course bookmaker, 62; daughter born, 66; son born, 67; transfers business to Bob Howett's son, 67; sells business to Charles Clark, 67; engages Charles Morton as trainer of his horses, 68; his involvement in sundry escapades, 75–6; purchases Toddington Park, 78; third child born, 78; parts from Lady Mabel, 80; lives at Toddington with Mrs. Eleanor Master, 80; discharged from bankruptcy, 81; purchases racehorses, 81; raises troop of South Bedfordshire Yeomanry, 84; disbandment of troop, 85; buys Toddington (racehorse), 89; concentrates on cricket, 93; buys Duke of Westminster (racehorse), 98; buys Sceptre (racehorse), 100; buys Lavengro (racehorse), 101; sells racehorses, 111; seeks loan from J. B. Joel, 114; sells racehorses to John Porter, 121–2; moves to Elston House, Shrewton, 126; accused of malpractice over Sceptre's defeat, 137–8; heads winning owners list, 144; racing failures and successes, 144–52; claims damages from Sir James Duke for slander, 155; awarded one farthing damages against Sir James Duke, 168; warned-off Newmarket Heath, 171; seeks backer, 178; charged with perjury, 179; discharged, 184; starts weekly racing paper, 184–5; moves to Hobart Place, 195; buys cottage at Taplow, 195; moves to Hillmorton Manor, 195; conducts campaigns through The Winning Post, 196–7; notice of warning-off withdrawn, 198; insensate vindictiveness of, 199; arrested on charge of extortion, 202, 205–6; his continuing libellous attacks on J. B. Joel, 203; charged at Bow Street, 206–7; found not